Praise for Kevin Davis and His Groundbreaking Work
DEFENDING THE DAMNED

"Kevin Davis brings the reader into Chicago's courtrooms and into the lives of the lawyers who handle the criminal justice system's toughest cases. *Defending the Damned* reads like a fast-paced novel but delivers with realism and compassion a compelling, insider's look into capital murder trials."

—Alafair Burke, author of *Close Case*

"In his remarkable narrative, Kevin Davis uncovers the true heroes of the court system. This is one of those rare books that will change your mind about lawyers."

—Gerry Spence, bestselling author of
How to Argue and Win Every Time

"Stunningly real and poetically unromantic, *Defending the Damned* delivers us into a world of accused monsters and the complex souls who have sworn to stand by them. Davis's subjects trust him—an astonishing result in a part of Chicago where trust disappears first—and he hears everything they say."

—Robert Kurson, bestselling author of *Shadow Divers*

"An intimate and gripping look at the members of the Murder Task Force. . . . The range of complexity makes this story especially engrossing."

—*Time Out Chicago*

This title is also available as an eBook.

DEFENDING THE DAMNED

INSIDE A DARK CORNER OF THE CRIMINAL JUSTICE SYSTEM

KEVIN DAVIS

ATRIA BOOKS

NEW YORK LONDON TORONTO SYDNEY

ATRIA BOOKS

A Division of Simon & Schuster, Inc.
1230 Avenue of the Americas
New York, NY 10020

First Atria Books trade paperback edition September 2008

ATRIA BOOKS and colophon are trademarks of Simon & Schuster, Inc.

For information about special discounts for bulk purchases,
please contact Simon & Schuster Special Sales at
1-800-456-6798 or business@simonandschuster.com.

Manufactured in the United States of America

10 9 8 7 6 5 4 3 2 1

The Library of Congress has cataloged the hardcover edition as follows:

Davis, Kevin.
    Defending the damned : inside Chicago's Cook County public defender's office
    / Kevin Davis.
        p. cm.
    Includes bibliographical references and index.
    1. Oliver, Aloysius—Trials, litigation, etc. 2. Trials (Murder)—Illinois—Cook
County. 3. Defense (Criminal procedure)—Illinois—Cook County. I. Title.

KF224.O45D38 2007
45.773'101—dc23   2006052606

ISBN-13: 978-0-7432-7093-9
ISBN-10:   0-7432-7093-2
ISBN-13: 978-0-7432-7094-6 (pbk)
ISBN-10:   0-7432-7094-0 (pbk)

To my wife, Martha. There *is* justice.

Contents

Author's Note

In the summer of 2002, while in the early stages of researching this book, I went to the Cook County courthouse in Chicago to watch a murder trial that left me rather shaken. A young woman got on the witness stand that morning and told a story so ghastly that it prompted people to walk out of the courtroom. I stayed to listen as the woman recounted how she and her boyfriend choked and beat her baby daughter to death while trying to stop her from crying. Then, in a matter-of-fact voice, the woman described the couple's elaborate and gruesome plan to dismember and dispose of the little body with the help of kitchen appliances, a frying pan, flour batter and hot oil. Her story sounded like some kind of sick joke.

I sat there appalled and deeply disturbed, trying to grasp that this woman was telling a real story about a real little girl who was butchered like a piece of meat because she simply cried, as children do. I wondered how her public defender felt about this, how she was able to handle such a sad and grotesque case. I wondered how this lawyer and her public defender colleagues were able to represent clients accused of such horrible crimes day after day, year after year, while keeping a safe emotional distance and preserving their sanity. What motivated them to come to work in such a dark place?

The woman's public defender, Marijane Placek, later told me she got cases like that all the time. It didn't bother her. She refused to let it penetrate the wall she had built around herself. This was her job. And like her colleagues in the Murder Task Force of the Cook County Public Defender's office, Placek worked with a singularity of purpose: to do the best she could for her client no matter how repulsive the crime—whether she liked her client or not.

I arrived as an outsider to Placek's world, a corner of the criminal justice system where she and her fellow public defenders on the Murder Task Force labored on behalf of some of the ugliest cases and most unlikable clients. Not all of their clients were accused of such hideous acts as dismembering their victims, but they all were charged with killing another human being, a hideous act in itself. Early on, I found that public defenders like Placek got tired when outsiders asked the same old question: "How can you defend those people?" It's known in the profession as the cocktail party question. To public defenders it feels more like a provocation, a statement loaded with judgment and preconception, implying that public defending is less than noble, that these lawyers must explain themselves whereas prosecutors do not. It suggests that public defenders represent already guilty clients unworthy of a vigorous defense, much less compassion.

Many public defenders have well-rehearsed answers to the cocktail party question, something along the lines that everybody deserves a defense, that it's fundamental to our adversarial system of justice, that the accused have constitutional rights that must be guarded and guaranteed. These are all good answers, all noble reasons. But my intention in writing this book was to avoid the cocktail question and seek a deeper understanding of their personal and professional motivations by observing these lawyers and letting their words and actions speak for themselves.

I was fortunate to have met a public defender named Shelton Green, who was the chief of the Cook County Public Defender's Murder Task Force. His supervised a team of lawyers who specialized in handling only homicide cases. I told Green I was interested in exploring the inner workings of his office with the intention of writing a book. He said that public defenders usually didn't talk with journalists because they knew their reputation with the public was unfavorable. But he decided to open the door. "People may not like us," Green said. "But I hope they understand us." To help foster that understanding, Green allowed me unfettered access to his unit. If lawyers wanted to talk, they could speak freely, unrestrained and uncensored. I visited the office on and off for five years, observing, listening and asking questions.

I hadn't intended to focus this book on the Murder Task Force at first, but I found its lawyers and cases irresistibly fascinating. They were veteran public defenders who had the benefit of years of experience, knew the system well and practiced law where the stakes were highest. As I watched some of these public defenders in court I knew, as well as they did, that many of their clients committed the crimes for which they were charged. But the lawyers always fought to win, and they savored every minute of the battle. Because I grew to like the public defenders I spent time with, I sometimes rooted for them. I felt a stake in their success, and thought victories over impossible odds would make for better stories in the book. But it didn't always feel right. I thought about the victims, and the victims' families, and I'd start to feel guilty for wanting the lawyers to get not-guilty verdicts, unless I truly believed in the innocence of the client. I liked the lawyers, but I hated the crimes.

I felt this struggle of allegiance most profoundly during the trial of Aloysius Oliver, who was charged with murdering a Chicago Police officer named Eric Lee, and whose case became a focal point of this book. Outside of the trial, I got to see what Oliver's public defenders did not. I saw the pain of the victim's family and friends, just as I so often had when I was a crime reporter visiting the loved ones of murder victims. I spent time with Officer Lee's widow and looked into her grief-worn eyes. I went to his parents' house and sat in their living room, looked at his baby pictures and graduation photos, and watched his parents cry and thought to myself what an awful thing if the man responsible was never brought to justice. That the Lees invited me into their home knowing that I was working on a book about public defenders was an act of graciousness and trust for which I will always be grateful. The Lees understood that as much as they hated Aloysius Oliver, he deserved a defense. They respected the law and the system in which his public defenders worked.

This book is not comprehensive, nor should anyone infer that the public defenders described in these pages are representative of the profession at large or the lawyers who make up the Murder Task Force. It's a sketch drawn from a small and select group of lawyers who were kind enough to give me their time and share their stories. These are people who are rarely celebrated except among themselves. They have the guts to labor in a difficult and unpopular profession, dedicated to something higher than themselves, unafraid to speak on behalf on those people society would rather cast away. Early on, one public defender told me that anyone who chooses this work has to be fearless and unconcerned whether people like them. It's not a job for those seeking approval. It's a job for those willing to rattle cages, make enemies and raise hell. By raising hell, these lawyers honor the law.

—Kevin Davis, June 2006

CHAPTER ONE

Killer Defense

"The odds," Assistant Public Defender Marijane Placek said as she gathered her files for a morning court hearing, "are completely stacked up against us."

It was just after nine on a brilliant blue Tuesday morning in late April 2003, unusually pleasant and warm for Chicago this early in spring. Outside the massive, gray stone Cook County courthouse at Twenty-sixth Street and California Avenue, a stream of government employees, cops, corrections officers, lawyers, social workers, investigators, jurors, witnesses, felons, petty crooks, drug addicts, gang-bangers—the guilty and the innocent—all converged for another day in the administration of justice. Buses disgorged clusters of people out front, and at the corner near the Popeyes Chicken & Biscuits. Waves of others marched across California Avenue from the five-story parking garage, some stopping at the stainless steel paneled lunch truck for coffee and pastries.

"Everybody saw him do it," Placek continued. She was telling me about her client Aloysius Oliver, a twenty-six-year-old unemployed ex-convict charged with fatally shooting an undercover Chicago police officer. "He did it in front of God, country, and four cops." Soon after his arrest, Oliver gave a videotaped confession. It seemed as if the state couldn't have asked for a better case. Placek couldn't ask for a more difficult one. But she knew that in every case, all was never as it seemed.

Placek was briefing me on the case in her eighth-floor office, a 9-by-12-foot windowless room designed in bureaucratic government drab, with carpeting the color of cherry cough medicine, dull off-white walls, beige metal furniture and stacks of cardboard boxes with words and phrases she scrawled in green ink that said "dope," "keep mouth shut" and "sick."

Atop her desk was an old twelve-inch black-and-white television set tuned to *Divorce Court*, and next to the antenna sat a round purple plastic mirror in which Placek, who was fifty-four years old, could see herself when she spoke on the phone. Her bobbed hair was dyed golden blond with streaked highlights. Her eyes were large and menacing, emboldened by dark mascara, her full lips colored bright red. Taped to the wall were movie posters from *The Road Warrior* and *The Usual Suspects*. Behind Placek on the floor was a wire shoe rack, jammed with flats and pumps, boots and tennis shoes; a pair for any occasion, available to match her outfits and moods. The snake-skin cowboy boots were reserved for when she wanted to look like a gunslinger, a nickname she earned in court from her readiness to do battle and shoot up the young state attorneys she liked to intimidate. That morning she decided on a pair of beige pumps to complement her black and brown herringbone outfit, which was comfortably draped over her large frame.

Placek was getting ready to argue a motion, along with cocounsel Ruth McBeth, in which they would try to get Oliver's confession thrown out, a confession she contended that never should have happened. "Why did he confess? Because the police beat the shit out of him." That was one of her theories, anyway. She knew of course that the police would contend that Oliver was injured while resisting arrest, and offered his confession voluntarily. "That's bullshit," Placek said, her tone sounding angry and a little too loud this early in the morning. "But we probably won't win the motion. Do you know how far you have to go to prove the police have lied?" She paused and waited for me to answer, then rolled her eyes and shook her head. "Pulheese!"

As she talked, Placek took a pair of scissors from her desk and cut out the crossword puzzles from the *Chicago Tribune* and *Chicago Sun-Times*. She would carry them with her to court, as she did every day, so she had something to do while waiting for her cases to be called. There was a lot of waiting in the courtrooms as a never-ending supply of criminal suspects and lawyers lined up to stand before judges to make motions, offer plea agreements and ask for continuances. She slipped the puzzles into her appointment book so the judge couldn't see them. Judges prohibited reading of newspapers while court was in session.

It was a newspaper headline that initially alerted Placek to the Oliver case, which became one of Chicago's most highly publicized killings during the summer of 2001. Oliver was charged with shooting Officer Eric Lee, who had tried to stop Oliver from beating a man in an alley behind Oliver's house. Lee was the fifth plainclothes Chicago Police officer slain in the line of duty in the past three years. The shooting rocked an already deflated department that felt it was losing control in a city where they were powerless over criminals who had no respect for the badge. The state's attorney vowed justice and declared that Oliver would pay for his crime with the ultimate penalty: death.

At his first court appearance, Oliver told the judge that he couldn't afford a lawyer, and the judge assigned his case to the Public Defender's Office. A few days later, Placek walked into the office of her supervisor, Shelton Green, and demanded to be put on the case. This was the kind of case she loved best—high-profile, seemingly impossible, full of land mines, epic battles and headlines. She smelled blood and savored the idea of taking on the cops and prosecutors. Green told Placek that Ruth McBeth, another lawyer in her unit, was already assigned to represent Oliver. Placek wanted in, and let Green know she was going to be on that case, too. It turned out that McBeth already planned to ask Placek to join her, knowing they'd make a perfect fit for this case. Their styles complemented each other—like good cop, bad cop. Placek was a roaring, in-your-face intimidator, a dominant figure who relished the spotlight, commanded the courtroom and drew attention to herself in fiery rhetoric and in florid clothing. McBeth, who was forty-two years old, was low key, more conservative in style and in dress, her wire rim glasses giving her a studious appearance. She tended to wear earthy, more muted colors than her counterpart, and had curly brown-gray hair that fell just below her shoulders. As a lawyer, McBeth was stealthy, steady and cool, preferring a quiet, straightforward approach to her cases, and avoided the media spotlight.

Placek knew the case was going to be tough. But for her, there was an inverse relationship between the difficulty of a case and how much she wanted to try it. That Oliver confessed didn't matter. It made no difference that there were plenty of witnesses. Placek was not intimidated that the State's Attorney's Office would surely put everything it had into prosecuting Oliver and assign their best lawyers to the case. Bring 'em on, she would say. The more hopeless, the more she liked it. "The challenge is why I want it," she explained. "It's going to be *fun*."

Fun. That seemed like an odd way to describe defending a cop killer. But that's what it was to Marijane Placek who spoke of cases as if they were chess games, horse races or jousting matches. Like most of her clients, Aloysius Oliver was poor, black and out of work. He was another of hundreds of accused murderers she had represented in her twenty-four years as a public defender. Placek was part of an elite, highly experienced team of lawyers assigned to the Murder Task Force of the Cook County Public Defender's Office, a group of lawyers that operated in the dark corners of the criminal justice system. They were the lawyers for the damned, paid by the people to represent the enemies of the people, working to thwart prosecution of those accused of some of the most vile, repulsive and cold-blooded killings in Chicago, and in doing so were to seek justice for those defendants who were innocent, and to ask for a measure of mercy for those who were not. Placek took on the Oliver case even though she already had an overbooked schedule of clients, including a woman charged with killing her baby and, with her boyfriend's help, dismembering it to conceal the crime, and a man accused of raping and killing a two-year-old girl. She would handle those, and a few other murder cases, simultaneously. More would pile up; it was virtually guaranteed. Just a few steps outside of Placek's office, tacked to a bulletin board, was a newspaper clipping with the headline, "City's Homicide Rate on Rise." Next to the headline, someone wrote in red ink, "We have job security" and drew a little smiley face.

Ten minutes before Placek had to leave for court, Assistant Public Defender Francis Wolfe walked in to her office, flopped down in a beige tweed stuffed chair and slowly exhaled.

Placek looked sympathetically at Wolfe. "Hi, honey. What you got going today?"

Wolfe, who was seventy-two, was the oldest public defender in Cook County. A former commodity trader, he decided to get a law degree while in his sixties. This was his first job as a lawyer. Placek immediately took a liking to him, became his mentor and brought him along to assist on several cases during his training. Now they were close friends. Wolfe had been paying his dues in a misdemeanor court and was recently assigned to a bigger courtroom at Twenty-sixth and California. He was wearing a tailored navy pinstripe suit and red bow tie, and looked like a white-haired Gregory Peck in his role as lawyer Atticus Finch in *To Kill a Mockingbird*.

"I've got a fraud and embezzlement case," Wolfe said. "The guy is guilty as hell. I don't know what I'm going to do." He sighed in frustration.

"You doing all right?" Placek asked with concern.

"I'm kind of stumbling around." Wolfe adjusted his hearing aid. "In misdemeanor court, they were kind of nice to me. But here, here they're so mean."

"This is the big time."

"Everyone is so egotistical," Wolfe complained.

"You got it," Placek said. "We have to be."

Placek was interrupted by a phone call. "He already *has* a costume," she barked into the receiver. "He's coming as the Great White Hope."

She was talking about her dog, Spartacus, who would be marching in a suburban pet parade in the coming weekend. "Yes, Spartacus is a boxer. Get it? No, he's not coming as Tyson. He'll be wearing a towel and gloves."

When she finished the call, Wolfe continued. "I've also got a marijuana case today," he told Placek. "She was caught with more than twenty grams. She claims she's self-medicating."

"Honey, dear," Placek shot back. "Ask her for her prescription." Wolfe laughed. "She doesn't have one."

"I think you're shit out of luck."

Ruth McBeth joined Placek and Wolfe in the office. As McBeth

sat down, Joseph Runnion, their law clerk, peeked in. Runnion was
scheduled to be a witness for the hearing that morning. He planned
to testify about his meeting with Oliver at the jail after Oliver was
released from the hospital, offering support for the argument that
Oliver was beaten at the police station before he confessed. "He
looked like he hadn't slept or eaten in days," Runnion told me when
I asked about Oliver's condition at the jail. "And he looked like he
had been worked over."

Placek and McBeth planned to argue this morning that Oliver's
confession was the result of physical and psychological coercion, and
obtained out of the bounds of his constitutional rights. McBeth
would deliver the opening statement, and Placek would make the
closing argument. Placek knew that getting the confession tossed
out was unlikely, but it was a motion she filed in case after case because sometimes a judge would find cause. "It takes a very, very
brave judge to throw out a murder confession," Placek explained.
But filing the motion had another purpose. By forcing the state to
respond to her claims, Placek would get a glimpse at her opponent's
case and witnesses, a strategic move before trial, which could be
months down the road. Whether the confession was admitted into
evidence probably wouldn't matter much anyway. "Some confessions you can live with, others you can't. This one I can live with,"
she said.

The reason she could live with it was because Oliver said something at the end of his confession that might save his life.

About 9:30 a.m. Placek and McBeth left the office to catch an elevator down to the main courthouse. They wheeled a television
monitor and videotape player, along with a cart containing the case
files, into the hallway outside the elevator bank. On the west side
of the hallway was a picture window overlooking the old Cook
County Jail and the newer Department of Corrections lockups
that made up a vast campus of brick and stone buildings surrounded by coiled razor wire fencing. Beyond the jail complex was
a view of Chicago's sprawling West Side and the impoverished and
crime-plagued neighborhoods from which many of Placek's clients

came. Along 26th Street were the mostly Mexican businesses, the *supermercados*, *carnicerías* and *fruterias*, clothing stores and shops that lead to an arch marking the Little Village neighborhood and gateway to the "*Magnifico* Mile," a nickname for the Mexican version of the city's opulent Magnificent Mile on North Michigan Avenue. Farther out were the smokestacks of the manufacturing plants and warehouses that helped drive Chicago's blue-collar economy.

As Placek stepped out of the elevator and walked through the halls of the courthouse, people couldn't help but look at her. She demanded attention, and her presence was as large as her self-described ego. She was heavy and walked with strained gait, slowed by her large frame and the deteriorating cartilage in her knees. She wheeled the case file cart past a bank of metal detectors where deputy sheriffs wearing latex gloves patted down visitors, barking orders, frisking for weapons and contraband, instructing them to take off their belts, hairpins, jewelry and shoes before entering. On the other side of the metal detectors, the men hiked up their drooping pants and looped their belts back on, their buckles clacking in a chorus. On a wall next to the snack shop, which reeked of cigarettes and the sweet smell of frying minidonuts, were computer printouts with the daily court calls. The printouts were tacked in fifteen rows and were three pages deep. Defendants gathered at the wall to look for their courtroom assignments. Placek and McBeth continued to another set of elevators and went up to the sixth floor.

The last time Placek came to court to appear on Oliver's behalf, the courtroom was filled with cops, some fifty or more. For Placek, it was like walking onto a stage before a hostile audience for which she could not wait to perform. That's how it was much of the time. If it were not a courtroom that demanded respect and decorum, she might have been booed by the police and victim's family as if she were a villain making her entrance onto a scene. Every time she walked into a charged room like that, she felt tension, a surge of energy ran through her body, and she primed herself for the fight. "You look out there and you just smell blood," she told me. During that early hearing, Placek recalled overhearing a cop whisper to Oliver, "We should have fucking killed you when we had the chance." That was the kind of thing that excited her.

But on this April morning, only a handful of cops was gathered in the hallway when Placek and McBeth emerged from the elevator. They wheeled their carts into courtroom 606, presided by Judge John J. Moran Jr. The lawyers took their seats at a long and well-worn oak table and laid out their case files and legal pads. Placek flipped open her appointment book and removed a crossword puzzle. The courtroom felt old and stately, with high ceilings, brass and metal latticework and leather-backed chairs for the lawyers. The wooden benches in the spectator gallery were worn smooth by the bottoms of thousands who sat in them and defiled by scratched graffiti of gang symbols, names and initials.

About a dozen people were in the courtroom on other business, mostly defendants waiting for a calendar call and the lawyers who were there to offer plea agreements, ask for continuances or file motions. Placek was surprised that only a few police officers were there. A middle-aged black couple walked in and sat in the front row to the right of the judge. They were the parents of Officer Eric Lee, the man Aloysius Oliver was accused of killing. A man in a blue suit walked up and introduced himself to the couple, saying he was the representative of the Fraternal Order of Police, and handed them his business card.

Placek worked on her crossword puzzle at the defense table. Francis Wolfe walked into the courtroom and took a seat beside Placek. He whispered something, and she whispered back much more loudly, revealing that even though she planned to put on a great argument to suppress the confession, she expected to lose. "This motion is going to be denied because it's the murder of a cop," she told him, her voice reaching beyond her intended audience into the first few rows where the public sat. "What we're trying to do is like playing a chess game. You're looking ten moves down the road."

More members of Officer Lee's family trickled in: his widow, Shawn, his partners, a few cops and the victim's advocate from the State's Attorney's Office. Other cops walked in, some in uniform, others in street clothes, some in uniform with Chicago Cubs or

White Sox baseball jerseys worn over their blue shirts—an indication that they were off duty, but members of the brethren. Assistant state attorneys David O'Connor and Joe Magats made their way toward the bench. They were well dressed in dark suits, white shirts and ties, and wore their hair short and neat. Their files were in organized piles, and they used three-ring binders to keep everything in order. They did, after all, represent law and order.

Finally, about noon, Moran was ready to hear the motion to throw out Oliver's confession and called for the bailiff to bring Oliver into the courtroom. The bailiff escorted Oliver to a chair and he sat next to McBeth. He looked small in his loose-fitting jail khakis with large black letters on his chest that said XL and DOC. His hair was cropped short and his face was thin with the beginnings of a mustache and beard. He appeared nervous and withdrawn, and sat silently as Placek nodded in his direction. She looked over to McBeth, who stood up to give the opening statement.

CHAPTER TWO

The Crime

ON THE NIGHT OF AUGUST 19, 2001, on the South Side of Chicago, Aloysius Oliver was sitting on his back porch with his fourteen-year-old girlfriend, Johanna Harris. Aloysius had been drinking beer most of the day, and Johanna was nudged close enough that she could smell the alcohol that lingered on his breath. As they sat and talked, Aloysius heard someone rustling around by the alley. It was just after 9:00 p.m., and the sky had darkened. Aloysius stood up to get a better look. He peered out to see a man urinating in his backyard. Aloysius told Johanna to get his brother, Andres, and cousin, Tommie Leach, who were in the house. Aloysius then went down from the porch to a back door outside the basement where there was an old couch. He fished around underneath it where he kept hidden a fully loaded .357 magnum revolver. He decided he was going to teach this ill-mannered man a lesson.

What Aloysius didn't know was that five undercover Chicago police officers were standing and talking at the south end of the alley several yards away. The officers were in the neighborhood for a drug sting operation, but their efforts weren't paying off that night. An informant had just told them a drug house they hoped to bust wasn't in operation, so now the officers were contemplating their next move. As undercover cops, they tried their best to blend into the neighborhood by dressing casually—wearing blue jeans, oversized sports jerseys and gym shoes. Still, most people who lived in this South Side neighborhood could easily make them out as cops if they saw them driving around in their unmarked cars, those large and wide Ford Crown Victorias with the "M" license plates. While working undercover drug stings like this one, the officers would usually conceal their badges and guns, and take them out when necessary or when they felt they didn't have to hide their identities. As a matter of routine, they wore bulletproof vests under their jerseys.

Among the officers working that night were Eric Lee and his partner Andre Green, who were friends on and off the job. Both had known each other more than ten years, having attended the police academy together in 1991. They had been partners on the force for about eight and a half years. Andre, thirty-nine, was a father of three; Eric, thirty-eight, had a six-year-old daughter. They were large men, tall and muscular, but with gentle dispositions, at least for cops who worked in one of the city's most dangerous areas. Their shift began that day at about 5:00 p.m. in the Seventh District of the Englewood community, one of the highest-crime areas of the city. This was a section of the South Side where unemployment was high, self-esteem was low and crack houses and litter-strewn lots marked nearly every block. Eric and Andre were part of a team of cops known as the Englewood Rangers or the 7th Cavalry. "Rangers are no strangers to danger" was their motto.

Not much happened during Eric and Andre's shift that night. They broke up a drunken disturbance and arrested some people for disorderly conduct and public drinking. Around 9:00 p.m., they were called to assist a group of tactical officers—also known as TAC officers—on a drug surveillance near 63rd and Carpenter Street, a block from Aloysius Oliver's home. As the officers stood in the alley down from Aloysius's house, Andre Green saw a man straggle along, unsteady on his feet. Andre tried to start a conversation with him, but the man mumbled, unable to make sense. The man continued to meander north in the alley and then stopped behind the Oliver house to take a leak, temporarily out of the officer's line of sight.

As the man relieved himself, Andre and Eric remained at the south end of the alley with three other officers: Broderick Jones, Corey Flagg and Vincent Barner. The officers discussed where to go next. As they chatted, Aloysius Oliver, gun in hand, walked down into his backyard. Aloysius's cousin, Tommie Leach, soon joined him out back, along with a friend, Damon Rogers. Aloysius grabbed the drunk man on the shoulder and asked what he was doing. The man, stinking of booze and barely coherent, tried to walk away. Aloysius started kicking and beating the man, knocking him to the ground. Aloysius recognized him as a local drug addict known as the "Hype," a nickname for junkies who used hypodermic needles. The Hype pleaded for Aloysius to stop, but Aloysius kept pummeling him as he lay cowering on the ground. All three men beat and kicked the defenseless man. The Hype curled up in a fetal position to try to protect himself.

According to the official police version, and from sworn statements later taken from the officers who were there, this is what happened next: The five officers down the alley heard the commotion and saw the scuffle. Andre Green and Eric Lee volunteered to go down and break up the fight. The two officers began jogging down the alley, with Officer Vincent Barner following behind them by a few steps. As they approached, the plainclothes officers identified themselves and would later say under oath that they had their police badges visible on chains around their necks or clipped to their clothing. None of the officers had a weapon drawn. As Andre stepped closer, he heard one of the assailants say they better break it up because the police were coming. "Man, fuck the police," Aloysius yelled. "This motherfucker is pissing in my yard."

Andre came up to the scuffle and tried to be the peacemaker. He told Aloysius and his friends to stop beating up the man, that his offense of pissing in the yard was no big deal and the crime did not fit the punishment. As they talked, Officer Barner, who was a few feet behind them, stepped in closer and saw that Aloysius had his hands in the pockets of his sweatshirt. "Take your hand out of your pocket," Barner ordered.

Then Barner saw something big and shiny in Aloysius's left hand and yelled, "He's got a gun!" The cops scattered for cover while unholstering their own weapons. Aloysius, Tommie Leach and Damon Rogers ran into the backyard. Tommie and Damon headed for a gangway on the north side of the house. But Aloysius stopped for some reason. He turned, raised his gun and fired two shots toward the officers in the alley. The first shot hit Officer Eric Lee in the right ear. Another hit the right side of his head, crashed through his

skull, traveled through his brain and came out the left side. Eric fell
to the ground.

Tommie and Damon fled down the gangway along the north side
of the house. Officer Barner ran down a gangway along the south
side in an attempt to parallel the fleeing men and catch them as they
emerged onto the street. Unable to see well, Barner fell down a cut-
out stairwell, got up and continued down the gangway but was
stopped by a closed gate. He saw Tommie on Carpenter Street.
Tommie was holding a blue steel semiautomatic pistol in his hand.
Tommie turned and pointed the gun at Officer Barner, who fired a
shot at Tommie first but missed. Tommie continued running and
disappeared into the darkness. Officer Barner turned around to go
back down the gangway and saw Aloysius at the other end. Barner
pointed his gun at Aloysius and yelled out that he was the police.

"You the police?" Aloysius yelled back and then pointed his gun at
Barner.

Barner screamed out for help, alerting his fellow officers of his location. He then crouched down, afraid Aloysius was going to shoot.
As he lowered his body, Barner trained his own gun on Aloysius. He
squeezed the trigger of his 9 mm semiautomatic, but the gun
jammed. Barner stood up and rushed toward Aloysius. He tackled
him and struggled to take away Aloysius's gun, dropping his own
weapon as they wrestled. Aloysius's gun went off during the fight,
and there was a moment when both men wondered whether they
had been hit, though neither took the bullet. Officer Broderick
Jones dashed down the gangway to help Officer Barner. Aloysius
shoved Jones into a chain-link fence, causing the officer to knock
part of the fence down. The two officers finally got Aloysius subdued and cuffed him.

Back in the alley, Eric Lee lay on the ground. His gun, which had
never been fired, was next to him. Andre Green ran over and saw
blood running from his partner's head. "Eric! Eric! Eric!" he said,
trying to get a response, holding Eric and trying to comfort him.
Andre hollered for help. He felt numbed and confused. Officer
Barner walked back out into the alley and, when seeing the mortally
wounded Eric, began to breathe rapidly, gasping for air and feeling

dizzy. As he looked up, Barner saw the homeless man, whose decision to urinate in Aloysius Oliver's backyard had triggered the fatal series of events. The man, whose real name the police later learned was Lamar Logan, had picked something up in the alley and was walking away. Barner collected himself and walked over to speak to Logan. But Logan continued to walk away, so Barner had to tackle and hold him down until backup officers arrived.

In minutes, squad cars and ambulances converged on the scene, lighting up the alley with their blue and white spinning lights, the beams bouncing off the garages and trees and windows of the homes where neighbors peeked out to see what was happening.

Andre Green was in a daze. He had a few cuts and scrapes from the struggle, and was picked up by paramedics and taken by ambulance to Christ Hospital and Medical Center, the same hospital where Eric Lee was taken. "I was like in a dream," Andre later told me in an interview. "I was really stunned." Andre was aware enough to know that Eric had been shot, and his feeling of helplessness and desperation grew when he saw scores of cops gathered in the emergency room and in the parking lot outside the hospital. "There was just a line of cops there, and I knew then that it had to be bad," Andre recalled. Around 10 p.m. he learned that Eric, his partner and friend, was dead.

Police drove Aloysius Oliver to Area One Violent Crimes headquarters about a mile away and placed him in an interrogation room. At about 11:30 p.m., Detective Thomas Kelly read Aloysius his rights and asked him what happened. Aloysius said he didn't know anything. All he knew was that he was under arrest for some reason. A police officer got shot? That was news to him. During the next five hours, Aloysius sat in the room, visited by officers now and then and having time to think about what happened. The police fed Aloysius a couple of sandwiches, gave him some cigarettes and soda and let him think some more. Detective Kelly came by to chat, and kept asking Aloysius if he was sure he didn't remember anything. Detective Kelly told Aloysius that he knew a little more about the incident after having spoken to some cooperative witnesses. About 4:45 a.m.,

Kelly persuaded Aloysius to confess, or at least to tell his version of what happened. Aloysius told Kelly that yes, he would voluntarily give up his right to have a lawyer present and would tell the cops what they wanted to know. They waited for someone from the State's Attorney's Office to tape the confession.

At 7:20 a.m. with a video camera set up at one end of a table and Aloysius sitting at the other end, he laid out his version of events to Detective Kelly and Darren O'Brien, an assistant state's attorney who was summoned to the station. The confession took about fifteen minutes. When it was over, rather than take Aloysius to jail, police officers took him to a local hospital to be treated for the injuries he received in his effort to flee police.

The official account of Eric Lee's death that night was pieced together by police investigators and prosecutors who interviewed officers and witnesses at the scene, at the police station and during a grand jury hearing. It all happened fast, the whole event unfolding in seconds, the seemingly harmless act of a man relieving himself in an alley escalated into the killing of a police officer. For the next three years, the events leading to the death of Officer Lee would be deconstructed and picked apart repeatedly—by the investigating officers, detectives, forensic scientists, the prosecuting attorneys and by Aloysius's defense team. There would be allegations of police misconduct, and claims that Aloysius didn't offer to confess but was beaten into admitting the crime. But some things seemed perfectly clear to the law enforcement community at the moment: a man shot a cop, several people saw him do it, and he wasn't going to get away with it. Many hoped that he would pay with his life. In Illinois murdering a police officer was punishable by death.

"Officer down" is the worst thing a cop can hear on the police radio. The phrase is a rallying call, a force that shakes every cop to the core, triggering a rush of adrenaline, anger, fear, sadness and a rage that brings every available cop to the scene, to the hospital, to the police station and to the fallen officers' families' homes. Cops tell you that they handle all murder cases equally. But everybody knows that the murder of a cop is different. It pushes detectives and street cops to their limits to catch the killer and follow through to make sure he's convicted and—many hope—sentenced to death. This was already a tense time for Chicago cops. Just two months earlier, Officer Brian Strouse, thirty-three, was shot to death while working undercover on a drug investigation in the city's Pilsen neighborhood, an area beleaguered with gang activity on the Southwest Side, a few miles from where Officer Lee was shot. A teenage gang member was arrested for shooting Strouse. He claimed he didn't know he shot at a cop.

When word got out on the radio that Eric Lee was down, dozens of cops converged on the scene of the shooting behind the Oliver residence on Carpenter Street. Fire trucks parked in the alley to power the spotlights that police needed to illuminate the crime scene. Detectives searched the area for evidence, hunched over in the alley and gangways looking for cartridges, bullet fragments, clothing, weapons, anything. It was chaotic, with television news trucks descending on the neighborhood, camera crews shooting footage, and reporters demanding information. The story led every television broadcast and covered the front pages of the Chicago papers. At a press conference the next day, a shaken and tearful Police Superintendent Terry Hillard spoke of the tragedy, publicly offering his condolences to the family of a valiant officer who died in the line of duty. These, unfortunately, were the risks that young officers faced on the job, Hillard explained. "They're going to get hurt, they're going to get harmed. This is just a fact of life," he said. "I wish I could stand up here and tell you that this is not going to happen again. But I'd be lying to you." Mayor Richard M. Daley, a former prosecutor and son of the late Richard J. Daley, issued a statement through his office about the death of Officer Lee. "He died as he lived, defending Chicago from the menace of guns, gangs and drugs."

If it was any consolation, police announced that they had their killer in custody and he would surely be brought to justice. The case appeared to be a slam dunk for prosecutors. They had a videotaped confession, eyewitness accounts and the murder weapon. Already a convicted felon who served time for drug and weapons charges,

Aloysius was, in the eyes of the police, the embodiment of evil, worst of all, a cop killer.

A day after his arrest, Aloysius was escorted by guards to a bond hearing in violence court on the first floor of the Cook County courthouse. This was where suspects arrested the previous night or early morning for violent crimes ended up for their first appearance. They were paraded into the room, one by one, to hear the charges against them. Or, if they were in another lockup elsewhere in the county, they would appear on a video monitor. Tony Eben, the public defender on duty to represent Aloysius that morning, attempted the nearly impossible by asking Judge Neil Linehan to set a reasonable bond. Eben argued that Aloysius was beaten and coerced into confessing. He said police officers hit Aloysius in the head and struck him in the back. "He was threatened and said he would be beaten if he didn't come forward," Eben argued. But Assistant State's Attorney LuAnn Rodi Snow dismissed the story, arguing that Aloysius's injuries were the result of toppling into a fence during a struggle with officers. The judge ordered Aloysius held without bond. Given the seriousness of the crime and Aloysius's previous criminal history, it was hardly a surprise. Judge Linehan did, however, allow the public defender's office to take photos of Aloysius's injuries before he was carted back to the jail. Documenting the injuries might later prove important in the defense argument that police beat a confession out of Aloysius.

Aloysius's mother, Lillian, watched the proceedings from the public gallery, which was separated from the courtroom by glass panels. After her son was led back to the jail, she rushed out of the room and left the courthouse, followed by a group of reporters who wanted to get a comment. On the courthouse steps, Lillian stopped to talk with the press. She was nervous, ashamed and in fear for her own life given the volatile nature of the case. She said that she wanted to send her condolences to Officer Lee's family. "I'm so sorry for having my son do it because nobody, nobody—not just their family—deserves to be killed," she said. Her son was assigned to the maximum-security section of the Cook County Jail where he would begin the long wait for his case to come to trial. The Lee family began preparations to bury their son and would feel the embrace of the law enforcement community and a public hungry for justice.

There was a full day of ceremonies honoring Officer Eric Lee on August 24, 2001. The funeral service was held at the Salem Baptist Church on the South Side of the city. Officers and mourners who could not fit into the sanctuary spilled out onto the streets and sidewalks of the neighborhood, and in a basement gymnasium next door. There were loudspeakers broadcasting the service for those who could not get inside. Police bagpipers played the haunting and funereal "Balmoral." Lee's casket was draped with the blue, white and red–starred Chicago flag. His funeral program contained twenty-one photographs documenting Lee's life—images of him as a baby, a boy sitting in Santa's lap at Christmas, at a birthday party, as a young man in his Marine uniform, a groom embracing his new bride, a proud father holding his newborn, a man hanging out with his buddies. An estimated one thousand mourners were there that day. The Reverend Jesse Jackson Jr. walked arm in arm with Lee's widow, Shawn, and their daughter, Erica. Mayor Daley was among the guest speakers and gave a moving tribute. "Officer Lee personified courage, not only for himself, but for the people of Englewood and the Seventh District. There are many who have a second chance at life because he defended their right to peace and hope." Lee's death became an opportunity for politicians and community leaders to promote their causes. The Reverend James Meeks, pastor of Lee's church, urged officers and their families to lobby for a ban on handgun sales. Reverend Jackson concurred, "If we left here today more determined to get guns off our streets, we will do more for his wife and daughter."

. The loss of Eric Lee left his wife and parents nearly inconsolable. It was too awful to fully grasp, and they would be forced to relive the story again and again as the case slogged through the court system. Amid the grief, Marijane Placek was getting charged up. She knew that representing an accused cop killer created a certain kind of isolation and required a suit of armor. It meant she would be facing angry, seething cops in the hallways and in the courtroom in the months to come. This invited name-calling and looks of disgust. Marijane was aware that representing such defendants helped fuel the perception that public defenders were bleeding-hearts yet heartless liberals. It forced them to stand alone in an already lonely place among a group of lawyers loathed by much of the public. Yet Marijane was impervious to the kinds of backlash and venom that drove more sensitive lawyers into retreat and self-doubt, prompting them to question the very nature of their work, to quit or to leave the profession altogether. "I want to win more than to be loved," Marijane said to me in her office not long after being assigned the case. "I love the challenge. This is what I live for."

CHAPTER THREE

Anarchist Under Contract

"I ALWAYS WANTED TO BE A LAWYER SINCE I WAS A LITTLE GIRL," Marijane Placek told me one afternoon while we were having lunch at a Mexican restaurant not far from the courthouse. "I always thought lawyers were gods."

If lawyers were gods, then Marijane saw herself as one of their goddesses—a larger-than-life character whose astute legal mind and courtroom bravura earned her a reputation as a fearsome opponent and sharp tactician with an unapologetic sense of grandiosity. She had a flair for the dramatic and the soul of a performer. "I have a big ego," she admitted between bites of a fiery red shrimp dish and sips from a salty frozen margarita, "and people find me intimidating."

When she made the rounds of the courthouse at Twenty-sixth and California, Marijane seemed to part the sea of people who crowded the hallways as she moved about, wheeling a metal cart with case files, law books, psychiatric manuals and a blue paperback called *Dirty Tricks Cops Use and Why*, a carefully displayed prop she used during the Oliver case to send a message that she was not afraid of the police, or anyone else. She had battled with her weight since childhood, but settled into a place where she was both self-confident and self-deprecating. Marijane sometimes referred to herself out loud, and for all to hear, as "morbidly obese" or "the fat girl," declarations that prompted those around her quickly to correct her or reply with a compliment. If they didn't, she would nudge them a little. "This is the moment where you're supposed to say, 'Oh, no, you're not. You look great!' " And sometimes it was hard to tell if she was joking or serious, which is why most people offered something nice to say, just in case.

Marijane took great care to look her best, and did so in a most unabashed fashion. Her wardrobe was legendary around the court-house and often prompted discussion and speculation among lawyers, judges and clerks. They wondered what she was going to wear each day—which wig, which gargantuan piece of costume jew-elry (brooches in the shapes of leopards and spiders, rings with stones the size of golfballs, a huge dragonfly with wings that flut-tered). Would she wear a hat today? The straw one with the pink ribbon or the Ferrari cap? What color scheme would she choose? And, of course, which shoes? On casual days she would sometimes put on a pair of red, white and blue–sequined tennis shoes, the likes of which had never been seen before in these halls of justice.

Staying stylish required work, and on her days off, Marijane shopped for bargains to keep her courthouse wardrobe fresh—at the Saks and Lord & Taylor outlet stores, and at flea markets where she could load up on her costume jewelry and knockoffs of expensive brands. "Honey, I need to get some more Rolexes," she said to a friend one day on the phone while planning a shopping trip. "It's cheaper to buy the new ones than to replace the batteries." A bed-room in her home served as one giant walk-in closet, a shrine to her bold and playful sense of style.

But all this shopping and attention to appearance was for reasons beyond vanity. Being well dressed in court before judges, juries and colleagues was as important to Marijane as her legal skills. "Look good, or they won't take you seriously," she explained. Marijane knew that as a large woman, she had to work a little harder in a legal system dominated by men, though many of her role models were men. She drew inspiration from the late film and television star Jackie Gleason, who, despite his girth, carried himself with the grace and poise of a dancer. "He's big. I'm big. I'll always be big. Look at Jackie Gleason. He wore tailored suits like I do, nicely cut. He had a certain grace. I loved him in *The Hustler*. You know that scene where he runs the table and sinks a shot and he just nods his head." And she nodded her head and said, "See, I've got it, baby!" She also identified with the late singer Sophie Tucker, whose stage persona emphasized Tucker's self-described "fat girl" image with style, humor and sexy outfits. Tucker's repertoire included songs such as "I Don't Want to

Be Thin" and "Nobody Loves a Fat Girl, But Oh How a Fat Girl Can Love," which Marijane memorized and sometimes sang to friends for no particular reason other than it was fun.

"I wasn't always this big," Marijane told me. "I used to look like Dyan Cannon, you know." She was referring to the slim blond actress, who among her many film and television roles, played a judge on the once-popular *Ally McBeal* show. And in photos on a bulletin board in Marijane's office, it appeared that her description was not far off. Slimmer, with cascading curly blond hair, Marijane was posed in pictures at parties and bar association events with friends, colleagues and judges, a gleaming smile and big blond hair. But when Marijane was in the midst of a trial, that smile was gone and she became transformed, single-minded and looking as if she were a lioness ready to pounce. She wouldn't eat breakfast or lunch while on trial and waited until court was recessed for the day to take her first meal. Her explanation was that it was important to stay hungry like a beast, to feel the base desire for food and sustenance, which helped prepare her for the kill. She would feast later. During a trial she didn't have time for small talk or phone calls and would get this look on her face that said "Get out of my way." When Marijane was on the attack in court, her facial expressions would suggest to lawyers, clients or anyone else who crossed her path that they better not mess with her. She would get this scowl with a stop-you-in-your-tracks stare, her mouth slightly turned down, her bottom teeth showing, an eyebrow raised. No one liked getting the *look*. Young, inexperienced lawyers were not sure what to make of her. Witnesses unlucky enough to be subject to her ferocious cross-examinations would leave the stand mentally and physically exhausted, either ready to strangle her or run away as far as they could. She could confuse and frustrate and cite statutes verbatim in front of the judge. It was a game and performance that she savored.

And then, back in her office later in the day, she would soften, especially when talking about her dogs: Spartacus, a boxer, and Caesar, a spitz, who were like children to her since she never had any of her own and remained single, though boasted of having had many men in her life. Sparty and Caesar were probably the best fed and best cared for dogs in the city, treated with such meals as premium-grade steaks, which Marijane bought from supermarkets or carried home in Styrofoam containers from leftover meals at one of her favorite Italian restaurants. She almost always ordered steak when she went out. Thick New York strips or rib eyes, very rare, bleeding onto the plate. That was the animal in her. She could identify with beasts sometimes better than with people.

Marijane, or MJ, as friends sometimes called her, was a complex and often elusive person whose life story was as intriguing as any court-room drama. Her stories of childhood during the late 1950s and early 1960s had a fabled quality. She told people that she was born in a taxicab and that her mother named her after her favorite caramel candy in the gold and brown wrapper. She grew up in the midst of one of Chicago's poorest neighborhoods on the city's South Side, where her father was head of security for Sears, Roebuck and Co. Their home was on Sears headquarters property, protected from the neighborhood around it. Her parents, both of Bohemian descent, were in their forties when she was born. When her mother had gone to the doctor thinking she was pregnant, he told her he doubted she was and suggested she had a tumor. He never ordered any tests and sent her home. She knew better and never went to that doctor again. "My mom was very petite, and she only gained about twenty pounds during her pregnancy," Marijane said. "My parents were on their way to a Christmas party in a taxi during a blizzard when it hap-pened. My father delivered me. I was just two ounces shy of five pounds."

Marijane adored her father, Ed, a big, strong man who stood over six feet tall. He hung around pool halls and with burly men who had blue-collar jobs. He was also a lover of art, literature and theater, passions he shared with his only child. As Marijane got older, her fa-ther became her best buddy, taking her by the hand along his trips through the neighborhood to see his pals and shoot a few games of pool, or to the racetrack where he bet on the horses, and to stables out in the suburbs where he set her up with riding lessons. While protective and doting, Marijane's father wanted her to understand the darker side of life as well, and took her to visit the criminal courts where she got a taste of the city's underbelly, watching as robbers, thieves and killers appeared before the judge. She learned about murder firsthand when she was just eleven years old. In what was supposed to be the sheltered safety of Catholic school, she saw a boy get stabbed to death. Marijane had been assigned to work as a junior patrol girl, guarding an entrance to the building at Our Lady of Sorrows Church and School. Students were gossiping about a black patrol boy who supposedly had tried to fondle a Hispanic girl in the coatroom. The story spread throughout the school and into the neighborhood. A group of Hispanic boys seeking vengeance confronted the black kid and beat him badly. The kid came back to school carrying a knife and stabbed the girl's brother near the doorway as Marijane watched. The police came, and it turned out that one of the officers knew Marijane's father. He took her aside and drove her home. "He told me, 'You saw nothing.' " She never had to give a statement or go to court.

Seeing a boy spill his life's blood at school didn't scare or traumatize Marijane as it might another child. "I know it may sound funny, but I wasn't hysterical or anything like that. I don't think I really knew what death was at the time. I lived in a very secure world where my dad could take care of everything. Now I realize I should have been traumatized. But at the time, I thought it was exciting. It was absolutely fascinating to me."

Her father taught Marijane other lessons that became valuable many years later. She told me a story about one night during which her family went to a funeral service for a friend of her father's. Afterward, there was a reception at the funeral home, which had a pool table in the basement. Marijane went down to watch her father play pool and get drunk on gin, which he kept pouring straight into a glass, one after another. By the end of the night, he was stumbling around and losing games, and it scared Marijane, who left the room. Later, riding in the car home, her father seemed to have sobered up instantly. He had a thick stack of cash in his pocket. He said he won big at the pool table after she left the room. He explained to his little girl that he had diluted his gin with water. He lost on purpose and later won when playing for the big money. It was all a hustle. "I had cried. He put up his finger and wiped a tear from my eye with it and told me 'Sometimes you have to lose to win.' " Telling the story years later made her teary-eyed.

Even though her father did not go to school beyond eighth grade, he never stopped educating himself or his daughter. He read to Marijane at night—the detective stories of Perry Mason, books on Greek and Roman mythology, poets famous and obscure. He frequently read a poem to her called "The Shooting of Dan McGrew" by Robert Service, a poet who wrote of gritty characters in the rough-and-tumble Yukon during the Gold Rush. The poem described a shooting inside a saloon over a lady named Lou—a scenario that would become familiar in her work as a public defender.

Beyond exposing her to such dark works, her father also introduced Marijane to the live theater and took her and her mother to see musicals. They flew to New York to see shows on Broadway. They went to London to see Shakespeare. It was his way of bringing culture to his little girl. Theater would later become a powerful influence for Marijane, who was drawn to the timeless tales of love and betrayal, of power and greed, the very human traits that would motivate many of the murderers, thieves and adulterers she would later represent as clients. She was moved by the lyrical language and majesty of the theater, inspired by the great orators of the stage, learning how to command an audience and demand attention. She was awed by the performances of Richard Burton in *Camelot* and Rex Harrison in *My Fair Lady*.

"Burton, when he was on the stage, was like a force of nature. When he was on the stage, you were just moved by his mere presence," Marijane recalled. She got her parents to buy her the original cast albums of the plays, and learned every line of every song of both male leads. She put the records on, stood back and recited the lines as if she were giving a speech in front of an audience. The sophisticated and powerful voices of those male characters inspired her to speak as they did, and she struggled to disguise her hard Chicago accent as she mimicked them. "The women were so powerless in both plays. It was Julie Andrews both times. I didn't want to speak like her. I could do her songs, but I didn't want to speak like her. I wanted to speak like Richard Burton and I wanted to speak like Rex Harrison. Their accents, in fact, are something that attracted me, and I thought that was the proper way to speak."

Diagnosed as dyslexic, a disorder that made interpreting letters and symbols difficult, Marijane had trouble reading and writing, though it didn't inhibit her intellectual capacity and logical mind. It just took more work. Her parents sent her to private Catholic high schools, hoping that the close attention and disciplined approach would help her through these challenges. She attended four different high schools, including a boarding school in the suburbs. Leaving home was especially difficult because her father was diagnosed with lung cancer, and the prognosis was not good. His illness progressed rapidly, and he died a short time after she went off to school. She was crushed. "The one person who was always my hero was my dad," she said. "And he never let me down." Still mourning the loss of her father in the months that followed, Marijane got distracted and fell behind in her history homework at Marywood Academy, the school she was attending at the time of his death. Her poor performance prompted a nun to berate Marijane in front of the class and declare that her father was burning in hell. Marijane shot back: "My daddy is not in hell." The nun replied: "Yes, he is because he spawned something like you."

From here the story sounded a bit embellished, though Marijane insisted it really happened. She said she made a fist and swung at the nun. "I decked her. I hit her in the face with a right. I thought I killed her. She was about half my size. I still remember her name. It was Sister Helen Rita. I can say this now because she's probably dead." According to Marijane, the attack got her kicked out of school and secured her reputation as a fighter who refused to be intimidated or talked down to by anyone. "It was in defense of my father, and it was the right thing to do." As she grew into her later teens, Marijane became even more self-confident and rebellious, and developed her offbeat fashion sense. She was hooked on the television show *The Avengers*, the stylish British spy series. She nagged her mother to buy her a leather suit like that worn by the sexy character Emma

Peel, played by Elizabeth Shepherd and later Diana Rigg. Her mom looked all over the city, but could find nothing like that for a girl. (Later, as an adult, Marijane assembled her own collection of leather suits in different colors.)

Marijane finished up high school at Immaculate Heart of Mary in Westchester, a suburb of Chicago, although school officials threatened to take away her honors after Marijane led a boycott of the cafeteria because students weren't allowed to go though the line again for second helpings. Marijane and her fellow rebels argued that good food was being wasted, so why not let the students come back for more? She went on to study the classics at Rosary College, a women's school at the time. At Rosary, Marijane debated the now disgraced White House lawyer G. Gordon Liddy on ethics in politics. They argued over whether breaking the law for the so-called greater good could be justified. Liddy argued that yes, it could, as in the Watergate break-in, and that such an act was not *malum in se*, or wrong in itself. Liddy said he did nothing morally wrong. Marijane said he did. "My position was you are a lawyer and were once an FBI agent. You took an oath to do that, and when you took the oath you swore to God that you would, in fact, not violate the laws of the United States. So the breaking of the oath was the *malum in se*. He had to give in on that." Afterward, Liddy gave her a signed photograph that said, "to a worthy opponent." The debate gave Marijane a delicious taste of what it felt like to use her oratory skills to make a persuasive argument. She continued to hone her fighting skills in other ways, competing as an equestrian rider and joining the fencing team at Rosary where she learned that the men were afraid to strike women with the same aggression and force as they would men.

With a developing sense of rebellion, Marijane decided to pursue a career that would allow her to challenge the authority she began to question. She went to DePaul University College of Law in Chicago where her interest in having a good time soon superceded her interest in hitting the books. She cut loose with lots of drinking and partying and let her studies slip. Her mother could do nothing to restrain Marijane from her constant carousing and late nights, but refused to let her throw away her opportunity to became a lawyer.

"What my mother put up with me in college and high school was unbelievable. I could not be held down. It was a remarkable clash of wills," Marijane said. "I would come home drunk as hell from law school and the next morning she would drag me and drive back to school. If it wasn't for my mother, I wouldn't have made it. She pushed me and made sure I got there. And I was thinking, Jesus, what kind of little princess am I?"

Eventually, she hunkered down and graduated from law school but was disillusioned about the profession before she even got her diploma. Marijane's onetime noble aspirations to become a lawyer began to falter as she looked around at the kinds of jobs that graduates were taking and was afraid she would be bored. It seemed that too many lawyers were desk-bound in soulless, boring jobs, doing paperwork, writing contracts, handling business over the phone. Professors and other lawyers told her that most lawyers never spent any time in the courtroom. "Law school almost killed my ambition. People's attitude was so blasé and defeatist. The work wasn't even that hard," she said. "After law school I was terrified. I wanted to be a trial lawyer. I'm not good at paperwork." She pressed on and passed the bar exam in 1973, still unsure about what she would do next. Marijane wasn't eager to jump into a law career. Instead, she thought about putting aside her law degree for the moment and looking for a job that might be more fun. She considered applying to a racetrack to be a hot walker, a person who walks horses around to cool them off after a race or workout. But something more exciting came to mind as she was reading the newspaper classifieds. She came across an ad placed by Ringling Bros. and Barnum & Bailey Circus. The circus was in Milwaukee, and they were hiring. They needed entry-level assistants and showgirls. So Marijane literally ran away to join the circus, meeting up with the traveling show and going on a brief tour of the Midwest. Marijane worked as a "ta-da" girl, which meant she stood in sparkly outfits and swept her arms and hands to introduce performers and punctuate acts as the band played "ta-da!" "I was a lot thinner and a lot better looking back then," she said. "I loved performing." It seemed glamorous, especially working with someone like the world-renowned animal trainer Gunther Gebel-

Williams. But the circus job was lousy work for lousy pay. She got $60 a week and had to buy her own food, which was sold by the circus at inflated prices. Life on the road was isolating and lonely. "It was just so shabby unless you were a star. This was just a rebellion for me." She quit after about three months and returned to Chicago to look for a job, giving up her brief stint in show business. Being the spoiled girl who always got her way, Marijane quickly got frustrated at not having a job and having nothing to do during the day. During a princess moment, she yelled at her mom, "I don't have a job. Do something about it." Her mom phoned a nun who knew a judge she could call to ask a favor. The judge, who had a lot of friends in positions of power, called Marijane and asked whether she wanted to become a public defender or a state's attorney. She asked which paid more, and the judge said public defender. "It was like twenty grand or something. That was a lot of money at the time," Marijane told me. So she decided she would become a public defender because the starting salary was slightly higher. The judge said it was a done deal. That was how people got government jobs in those days in a city known for its patronage system and a process at the courthouse known as the "Committee on Help." You had to know someone to get in.

Her career as a public defender began in the appellate division, but she soon got restless. Spending time researching cases, writing briefs and sitting in an office was too boring. She wanted to be in a courtroom doing trials. She moved to juvenile court and got a taste of the action. "I learned how to try cases and I got to know the judges," Marijane recalled. "I learned the power of people being afraid of me." When she moved to adult court at one of the suburban branches and finally got to do jury trials, she knew she had found her calling. Her original plan was to work for the public defender's office for about five years and then move on, perhaps to private practice, perhaps to something else altogether. She had no particular love of her clients or any kind of bleeding-heart resolve to save them, which made her different from many of the public-spirited lawyers in her office. But she got hooked like a drug addict, seduced by the courtroom, enlivened by the victories, emboldened by her success. "It's the only place, except on the back of a horse, where I live in the now. It's like a high," she explained when I asked why she likes being in the courtroom. She used a circus metaphor to describe the feeling of being on trial, quoting Karl Wallenda, patriarch of the renowned family of acrobats. "He said that the wire is everything. All else is waiting." As her confidence and legal skills grew, Marijane wanted only the hardest cases. "I never considered myself a public defender," she said. "I considered myself an anarchist under contract." She wanted to be a winner at all costs, to turn upside down the way she was perceived and treated in court.

After more than two decades as a public defender, Marijane Placek was a well-known fixture around Twenty-sixth and California, a lawyer and provocateur whose imperious personality and courtroom manner were admired by some, derided by others. Yet no one, it seemed, could contest her desire and commitment to win. And that was what her boss considered when Marijane demanded she be assigned the Aloysius Oliver case in the late summer of 2001. "I like her because she takes these on, and she fights until the end," Murder Task Force chief Shelton Green told me. "Any time they try a case against Marijane, she's going to make them work for it." In her twenty-four years with the office, Marijane had tried hundreds of murder cases and only one of her clients got the death penalty. And that case was later overturned on appeal. She wasn't about to let Aloysius Oliver tarnish that record.

Aloysius had a criminal record that began when he was a teenager, having served time in prison for theft, aggravated battery, drugs and weapons convictions. He may have thought of himself as a tough guy on the street, but that didn't matter to Marijane, who let Aloysius know who was boss when she first met with him at the county jail. "I don't get friendly with clients," she explained when I asked about her relationship with Aloysius. She was all business. She didn't smother him with warmth, tell him how badly she felt or that everything was going to be all right. In the county jail library, Marijane and Aloysius sat at a table near the back of the room, making sure they were out of earshot of other inmates and guards. Marijane laid out the rules. "I'm going to talk, and you're going to listen," she told Aloysius, who was overwhelmed by this brusque and imposing woman. "I don't want you to tell me anything right now. I don't want to hear your version of the truth. You can tell me the truth later. I'm in charge of your case now. This is *my* case."

She instructed Aloysius to keep his comments, thoughts and ideas about how to handle his case to himself because she knew that defendants like Aloysius often were too eager to talk, usually to their own detriment. They were frightened, confused and overwhelmed. They wanted to offer excuses, alibis and stories. They would make up lies that they couldn't remember later or their accounts would unravel with inconsistencies, which could derail a case. Marijane also was worried that Aloysius might start talking about his case with other inmates to fuel his own ego. An accused cop killer had special status in the jail, which invited bragging and bravado. Marijane also made it clear to Aloysius that she wasn't there to do him special favors. "I'm not a social worker. I'm not going to call your mother for you," she told him. "I'm not going to bring you food. I'm not going to bring you anything." But it was also a ploy to set a tone. Marijane's role was to play the bad guy. Assistant Public Defender Ruth McBeth would be the good guy. Ruth was the perfect foil. While Marijane could be domineering and vociferous, Ruth was unassuming and soft-spoken. While Marijane kept a safe personal distance from clients, Ruth allowed herself to get more personally invested. Ruth felt a greater sense of compassion for clients and a responsibility for their well-being. "Marijane calls me the softie," Ruth told me during an interview one afternoon after court. "And I guess it's true."

Ruth was clearly not as comfortable in the spotlight as Marijane, and spoke about herself in modest, unadorned terms. Her style was more earthy than flashy. She wore her brown and silver hair long, and sometimes came to the courthouse in flowing dresses and delicate lace blouses that, along with her wire rim glasses, gave her a sort of an upscale, modern hippie look. She told me that she was born in Bangkok on the Fourth of July, 1960. Her father had taught English there as a second language for a program funded by the U.S. Agency for International Development, and her mother was a high school math teacher. Ruth, her parents and younger sister came back to the states when Ruth was still a little girl and settled in Union Lake, Michigan, a suburb of Detroit. Ruth said that her childhood was rather ordinary. In high school, she joined the debate team where she got her first taste of delivering arguments in a public forum. When I asked why she chose to pursue a career in law, Ruth couldn't point to a defining moment or specific influence that inspired her, saying that the profession simply piqued her interest. Ruth studied economics at the University of Michigan and then went on to law school at Washington University in St. Louis where she met her husband, Jeff, now a civil lawyer. She was drawn to criminal law and wanted to be a lawyer with a social conscience. "That's where my personality lies. I like to fight for the underdog," she said. I asked Ruth if she could explain where that desire to help the downtrodden came from, and she told me that it simply felt natural. "To me, it just seems like the right thing to do. Why wouldn't you want to do that? Why would you need a justification to do that? I wanted to have a life with meaning." Ruth said that most of her law school classmates did not share such altruistic motivations. "People would tell me they were just waiting to be rich." Ruth chose public service over the promise of riches, and joined the Cook County Public Defender's Office in 1986, starting out in the appeals division. She later moved to the felony trial division and eventually was promoted to the Murder Task Force in 1998 where she and Marijane began teaming up on cases together.

Because she often felt a closer connection to clients than Marijane, Ruth took responsibility for making sure Aloysius Oliver was comfortable and got what he needed in jail while awaiting trial. She brought him books, was in regular contact with his mother and relayed messages between the two. Marijane showed little interest getting close to Aloysius. But her coldness was calculated. Liking clients carried too many risks. For one, she feared it could cloud her judgment in making sound, objective decisions about handling their cases. The other risk was to herself. "If I wind up as your buddy or your pal and establish a relationship with you, I might wind up getting close to you, and if I lose, you'll wind up dead and I'll end up crying," she explained. Marijane wasn't too concerned about becoming attached to Aloysius because when she met him, she immediately decided she didn't like him. She felt he was too cocky. Ruth had a different take. She liked Aloysius and found him engaging, thoughtful and vulnerable.

"Does it matter if you like the guy or hate the guy?" Ruth responded when I ask how she felt about Aloysius as a person. "No. He's charged with murder and you're there to represent him. But my problem is that I tend to like the clients. If your relationship is only about the case, then they never really have a complete relationship with you. You have to find where a person is at and learn about them a little more." Ruth would learn much more about Aloysius in the months to come, because knowing and understanding him would become pivotal in his defense. The stakes were too high for Ruth not to get personal. Aloysius was eligible for the death penalty if convicted of killing Officer Eric Lee. Neither Ruth nor Marijane dwelled on that possibility with him so early in the process. The prospect of execution could crumble any man, no matter how tough he thought he was. "Certain clients you don't want to tell right away," Marijane later said. "You don't want to scare them." But Aloysius knew what he faced, and he was scared.

CHAPTER FOUR

Welcome to Our World

SHELTON GREEN WAS DYING FOR A SMOKE to go with his morning cup of coffee. "You better close the door," he told me, pulling a Winston from a crumpled pack and lighting up. "You don't mind, do you?" Smoking wasn't allowed in his government office, but Shelton was the boss, and this was his domain. He closed the door as a courtesy to the others who shared space in this wing on the eighth floor of the courthouse annex. As long as no one complained, Shelton allowed himself and the handful of other smokers in the unit to discreetly get their nicotine fix. And sometimes they needed it bad around here.

Shelton, fifty, was chief of the Cook County Public Defender's Murder Task Force, also known as the Homicide Task Force. He supervised a team of thirty lawyers who handled nothing but murder cases in a city that had 666 homicides the year Aloysius Oliver was charged with killing Officer Eric Lee, 35 more homicides than the previous year. It was a particularly violent period, with Chicago recording the highest number of murders for any U.S. city, topping even New York. Added to that was another 151 murders in the suburban areas of Cook County, which fell under the jurisdiction of the office. If a homicide resulted in an arrest, the suspect would most likely be represented by a public defender; about eight out of every ten murder suspects in Cook County ended up with a court-appointed lawyer. By default, the public defenders were assigned to handle some of the ugliest, most challenging and seemingly hopeless cases for a group of defendants who got what amounted to tens of thousands of dollars in free legal services—all at the taxpayers' expense. Public defenders joked that they were the best lawyers money can't buy. I had come to visit Shelton this morning to get an introduction to the task force. "Public defenders don't get a lot of social acceptance," Shelton told me, his words drawn out and slow, revealing his southern roots. "The prosecutors hate them, the judges hate them, even the clients hate them. They take abuse from everyone." Shelton explained that working in such a maligned profession required a thick skin, and lawyers who made it to the task force had to be fearless, especially on a capital case where the stakes were the highest and their clients' lives depended on them. "You've got to have a 'fuck you' attitude," Shelton said. "Fuck you all. Fuck it." He paused for a minute, and then explained his burst of profanity, "Hey, they're trying to kill your client."

Fearlessness was indeed an important trait for lawyers who earned a place on the task force, and Shelton didn't want timid people working there. It was not a place for people who wanted to be liked because you constantly had to question authority—cops, prosecutors and judges, those symbols of goodness and righteousness in society. "You have to be willing to take on loser cases and fight your ass off on them," Shelton said. "Before we let you on the task force, we want you to know what you're doing."

The lawyers in Shelton's unit were driven by different motives—a sense of justice, a sense of competition, a sense of compassion. Some were addicted to the thrill, the drama, the intense nature and hyperreality inside the courtroom where life-and-death issues played out every day. Others hung on because it was a stable and protected civil service job, immune from the financial fluctuations and uncertainties of private practice. The pay wasn't bad, either. Lawyers were unionized, and the most experienced senior attorneys in the unit earned $80,000 to $92,000 a year, plus pensions and generous health insurance benefits. Supervisors got a few thousand more.

Shelton made one thing clear to me early on: public defenders were not, as many assumed, a collection of bleeding-heart liberals, ex-hippies, cop haters, anti-death-penalty crusaders or bureaucratic automatons. Some were conservative, some even favored capital punishment, as long as it wasn't for their clients. What they all shared was an obsession to win. "You've got to be a little nuts to do this," Shelton said. "I think we do it for part of the same reason people jump out of airplanes—for the rush. You will never have a rush like the one when a jury comes back and says, 'not guilty.' "

Yet the words "not guilty" rarely brought much joy to anyone besides the defendant, his family, his friends or his lawyers. The public certainly didn't feel the same way and was more likely to feel cheated, believing that someone who probably did a crime got away with it. It was as if public defenders had tricked the system and employed technicalities to subvert justice and aid the criminals. For that reason, victories among public defenders were rarely shared with outsiders. "When they win cases, they can't be too happy or go bragging about it," Shelton said. "Our victories are celebrated within our own office. You can't go out celebrating after you got someone off who was charged with raping and killing a fourteen-year-old girl." In the Murder Task Force office, lawyers taped hand-written and computer-generated notes to doors and bulletin boards announcing their courtroom triumphs. Many of the notes contained clip art cartoon animals with exclamations such as "Congrats!" "Hurray!" and "Great News!!" When Shelton was a rookie public defender, his wife, proud of her hardworking husband, would hang a banner outside their home congratulating him when he won big cases. "But after a while, even your family doesn't want to say, 'We're happy for you,' " Shelton said. "You like to share your victories. You like to brag and you can't. People look at you funny and ostracize you if you do."

Public defenders are not perceived as the good guys in the world of law and order or in a national culture of fear where authorities are supposed to be tough on crime. To some, they are heartless bastards who trick and scheme and hurt good people so that very bad people can walk away free, never to face the consequences of their crimes. To others, public defenders are merely functionaries necessary to keep the criminal justice system moving along. Their clients often insult them by demanding "real lawyers," or by referring to them as "PDs," which stands not just for public defenders, but also "penitentiary dispatchers." Day after day, Shelton's lawyers labored as advocates on behalf of some of the city's most vile and vicious killers and knew, as they marched into their offices each day, that their work was neither popular nor much appreciated by a crime-weary public. "Most people don't seem to care much about what we do," Shelton said.

Yet most in Shelton's office savored the work. Tough cases were fun. They were intellectual challenges. They were personal battles against state attorneys. "I've heard attorneys here say, 'I want a case where there's no chance of winning.' That way, you can't fuck it up. But if you win, it's a miracle," Shelton said.

Each of the lawyers in Murder Task Force, like the rest of the 468 lawyers in the Public Defender's Office, was consistently booked with cases and new ones kept coming. Inside their shared offices, the floor space was sometimes like an obstacle course of files, boxes and books piled along walls, in corners and spilling from shelves. Shoes, pants and jackets—some belonging to the lawyers, others on reserve for their clients to wear during court appearances—were scattered in office corners and in closets, as well. Some lawyers kept bottles of chemical hair remover, which they sometimes used on clients' faces for a quick shave before court appearances. Although their workspace seemed disorganized and their caseload impossible, this was hardly a group of bureaucratic slackers. Murder Task Force lawyers handled an average of twenty-seven clients at a time, with at least a third of those being possible death penalty cases. Someone was always in a trial or preparing for one.

Their clients were a snapshot of the worst of the city, and there was a repetitive nature to the people they represented—drug dealers who shot down their rivals, gangbangers who killed each other for being in the wrong neighborhood or flashing the wrong hand signals, mothers and fathers who beat or suffocated their crying babies, maniacal serial killers, contract killers, spurned lovers, sexual predators, armed robbers, the mentally ill and the mentally challenged— most of them guilty, all of them too poor to hire their own lawyers. It wasn't uncommon for the task force to inherit cases that were first handled by private criminal attorneys who either gave up or relieved their clients of their life savings, making them eligible for a public defender. "If you're in the middle class, you're fucked," Shelton explained. "Private attorneys come in at the beginning of a case and we would save all the files for ourselves because we knew they would drop them. There were certain lawyers you expected to do this."

When a public defender on the task force got a case, it was rarely the culmination of a mystery or whodunit that was solved through painstaking detective work. Like the Oliver case, the crimes were often committed in front of witnesses, the suspects already confessed, and there was usually physical evidence linking them to the crimes. Rare was the instance where some innocent was plucked off the street in a case of mistaken identity or the victim of an elaborate frame-up or conspiracy among police, prosecutors and others. Rare, but not unheard of. The past decade proved that wrongful convictions slipped through the system, that innocent people were sent to death row, that police lied or coerced suspects into confessing to crimes they did not commit, and that DNA could not just help convict, but was a powerful tool for exoneration, as well. So-called forensic experts proved they were fallible human beings who could and had made mistakes despite their best intentions. Those kinds of developments fueled the lawyers' passions even more. The task force lawyers fought for their clients not because they loved them or necessarily felt sorry for them, but because they wanted to win. The lawyers who aspired to work there, and those who made it to the task force, came from all walks of life and both sides of the law.

Shelton Green was a kid from the country who came to the big city and never looked back. A native of rural Tennessee and self-described hillbilly, Shelton came from a family of farmers. His parents moved several times, back and forth, to Chicago to get factory work between the planting and harvest seasons down south. They eventually settled in Chicago's Uptown neighborhood on the northeast side, an area that drew other southern families and later became a dumping ground for the mentally ill who were discharged from state hospitals and institutions in the early 1970s. In his new urban environment, Shelton was drawn to street life and lured to delinquent and miscreant behavior. "I can identify with clients more than the other lawyers," Shelton admitted to me in explaining his troubled youth. "I have a certain degree of empathy with them."

Shelton and his buddies got their kicks by shoplifting from the block-long Goldblatt's department store at the busy intersection of Lawrence and Broadway, the nexus of Uptown. They showed their youthful bravado by scrapping with local street gangs, fighting over territory, girls or whatever seemed to be a worthy conflict. After one of his pals was run over by a car driven by a member of a gang, Shelton sought retaliation. He got a nine-shot revolver, tracked down one of the guys in a bar and shot him in the leg. Shelton was arrested and faced a year in a juvenile detention home. It was 1969, and a turning point in Shelton's life. Around the same time, his brother, Richard "Ricky" Green was killed in Vietnam. Shelton wanted to do something to honor the brother he adored, as well as extricate himself from the criminal justice system and a life that surely could have evolved into more trouble. With the help of his mother, Shelton was able to work out a deal with a judge to join the army rather than spend his days in the juvenile home. Shelton became a sniper with the army's 173rd Airborne Brigade Reconnaissance Team and saw combat in Vietnam. He also earned his high school equivalency diploma through the army and thought that he might try to become a lawyer when he got back to the states.

Shelton came back from his tour of duty two years later, went to Chicago-Kent College of Law and began his career as a lawyer. Like many of his colleagues, Shelton joined the Public Defender's Office with the intention of moving on to something better. "I wanted to get a few years of experience as a trial attorney and then go into private practice and get rich," he said with a laugh. But he got hooked. Like other neophytes in the office, Shelton began by defending small-time drug peddlers, prostitutes, junkies, thieves and all manner of petty criminals. He earned a spot on the Murder Task Force in 1985 and became its chief ten years later. Running the office was a promotion that Shelton accepted with mixed feelings. He didn't much care for the administrative tasks and playing the politics that came with being a supervisor. He also didn't want to lose his edge as a courtroom lawyer and made a point to take on cases to stay involved. When he talked about why he so loved being in the courtroom, his voice rose up and swelled with passion. "You're onstage and everyone is listening to you," he said. "You've got a man's life in your hands. You're arguing against the majesty of the state. And when you're up there giving your closing argument, man, it's an adrenaline rush."

It was a rush that Shelton likened to flying on a chopper into a hot landing zone, or LZ, in Vietnam, an all-encompassing surge of energy mixed with fear and excitement when you're under fire. Shelton still had a taut, military physique that filled out his white oxford dress shirt, and he looked studied with his wire-rimmed glasses and neatly trimmed salt-and-pepper beard. "Man," he said, "there's nothing like it." Shelton had a few of his own cases coming up, including a case in which his client was charged with raping and eviscerating a teenage girl. "To me, it's a fight," Shelton said. "I'm not that concerned whether they did it or not."

And that's how it was for the lawyers in task force. One of the most dogged fighters worked across the hall from Shelton in a room whose walls and furniture gave off the stale odor of years of cigarette smoke. When I walked in to meet him for the first time, Woody Jordan was sitting with a pile of papers in front of him, a poster of Black Power activist Eldridge Cleaver behind him and a cloud of smoke above him. Next to a yellow-stained ashtray was a pack of Kools. He was wearing a UCLA T-shirt, blue jeans and tennis shoes. Woody was small, thin and compact, with short brownish silver hair, an olive complexion, large-lidded eyes and big ears that flared from his head. He had a streetwise air about him. He spoke fast and was raw in his language and manner. He also spoke loudly, as if he wanted everyone in the room, and the next room, to hear what he was saying, as if he were delivering a closing argument every time he talked. It was difficult to have a discreet conversation with Woody, but he didn't seem to care or harbor any secrets among colleagues in the office. He was a guy who spoke in exclamation points. One morning I saw him walk into the office and shout, "Let's set some killers free today!"

Woody was frustrated on that first day I stopped by to talk with him. He'd been trying to come up with a strategy for saving the life of Hector Nieves, a convicted killer whose family recently told

Woody that they wanted nothing to do with him and had no interest in whether he lived or died. "I can usually find something good in my clients," Woody said. "But with Hector, it is impossible." Nieves was convicted of beating a homeless man to death with a chunk of wood. The killing was part of Nieves's repeated pattern of getting drunk and then getting violent with his homeless brethren when he needed money to buy more hooch. Nieves had killed other homeless men in New York, crimes that had gone unsolved for years because there were no witnesses and few cared to pursue the cases. But one day Nieves walked into a New York police station and announced his wish to confess to five murders. At first, the cops thought he was crazy, just another homeless drunk looking for a place to sleep. Eventually, someone listened and checked out Nieves's story. Detectives found there were unsolved murders just as Nieves described. Not only that, Nieves ended up confessing to three more murders in Chicago, which eventually got him here with Woody as his lawyer. When he read Nieves's confessions from New York, Woody got a sense of who he was.

Hector Nieves was so unlikable and so remorseless that not even his mother would agree to speak on his behalf to try to spare him from the electric chair. "The problem with Hector," Woody said, "is that he hasn't done anything good in his life. Ever." Despite his best efforts, Woody couldn't get anyone to come to court for the sentencing hearing. "His family was in Puerto Rico. I offered to fly them up, but they were all too busy," Woody said. "That's not unusual for a lot of the guys I represent. To their families, they're already dead." By this time, Nieves was so embittered, so hateful, so unconcerned about anything that when Woody introduced him to a black assistant public defender who was helping him on the case, Nieves blurted a racist insult that left even the hardened Woody aghast. "He turned to her and said, 'I don't need you, you nigger lesbian bitch,' " Woody said. "For the rest of the day, during the jury selection and throughout the trial, it was very difficult for me to keep focused. Hector didn't care what was going to happen in that courtroom. But it wasn't going to change what I did." In a sense, however, Woody was relieved because it allowed him to feel nothing for a man who apparently felt nothing for himself or for anyone else. In the event that Nieves got the death penalty, Woody might be able to take it just a little easier. "I thought to myself, Thank you, Hector. You just made my life a whole helluva lot easier. I hope they fucking kill you. You deserve it."

Still, it could never be easy, no matter how repulsive the client, to be the lawyer whose client got a death sentence. Woody was lucky so far. Up to this point, none of his clients had been sentenced to death. But the ride was always rough. It took everything Woody had to try to save a life, and he had to do it whether he liked his client or not. The Nieves case had been long and convoluted because of multiple murder charges and convictions in two states. And even though Nieves had been sentenced to death on one case, Woody, as his public defender, was fighting to prevent death in another. They couldn't kill Nieves twice, of course, but death penalties meant long appeals, and it was always possible the sentences could be overturned. In anticipation of his sentencing, Woody ordered psychiatric tests to determine whether Nieves had mental problems and an MRI to see if he might have brain damage—anything that might be considered a mitigating factor to spare his life or explain his behavior. If the guy was diagnosed with some type of psychiatric malady, it could save him.

Woody Jordan didn't become a lawyer with the intention of saving people like Nieves. He just wanted a stable, well-paying job that provided for a good life, the kind of life he had growing up on the South Side of Chicago in the 1960s. His father was a civil engineer and his mom was a homemaker. Woody told me that he was a troublemaker during his teenage years. He worked construction jobs by day and was drawn to street life by night, a life that included hanging out, getting drunk and occasionally stealing cars. "I did a lot of shit when I was younger and I grew up real fast," he told me. But Woody was smart enough to know that an education was his best hope for a future. And he didn't want to go to Vietnam, either. College would protect him from the draft. So in 1968, Woody enrolled at the Illinois Institute of Technology in Chicago where he initially planned to follow in his father's footsteps and become an engineer. But his grades in the science and engineering courses were not up to par, and Woody changed his major to accounting. He figured accounting was a decent, albeit lackluster way to make a living. But his life took a few unexpected turns. When he was a sophomore in college, Woody got his seventeen-year-old girlfriend pregnant and decided that he should marry her. He was nineteen at the time. Not long after Woody got married, his wife's brother, who was in a Chicago street gang, was shot dead during a confrontation with a rival gang member. Woody attended some of the court proceedings with his wife and became fascinated with the process. He watched the defense lawyer argue the case and pictured himself in the courtroom doing the same thing. "It struck me that I could do that," Woody told me. "I thought I could get that guy off."

Believing he'd make a good lawyer, Woody decided to try law school after earning his undergraduate degree in accounting and was accepted at Loyola University Chicago. He did not pursue a career in criminal law at first, however. Woody instead started in the starched white-collar world of corporate law, where he thought he could make a comfortable and lucrative living. Jobs in corporate law and tax law were plentiful, and he had an easy time finding work. Woody worked for the accounting firm of Arthur Andersen and as a tax accountant for McDonald's. He toiled over such legal matters as researching the Internal Revenue Code for his clients, poring over long-winded tax documents and preparing mountains of tax returns for individual McDonald's restaurants that were owned by the company. "I didn't fit there," Woody told me. "It was painful."

So he quit and got a job with the public defender's office, starting out in the municipal court doing the usual drug, prostitution, robbery and theft cases. He was promoted to the Murder Task Force in 1990. "It was a great career move." He fit in beautifully, his manner, attitude and fearlessness made him a natural. Inmates at the Cook County Jail would come to know Woody by name; he understood life on the street and wasn't afraid to go out there to dig up witnesses and do his own detective work. Newly arrested criminal suspects often called Woody directly, asking for advice and help. But if they weren't accused of murder, Woody had to break the bad news. "I tell them, 'Hey, homes, your bullet may have just missed getting me as your lawyer by a couple of inches. If they ain't dead, you're out of luck.' "

Woody's years as a public defender separated him in many ways from the so-called normal world. "This is such a closed world. It's very insular," he told me during another visit to his office. When friends or colleagues would ask Woody how he was doing, he'd often remark in a wry voice "Another day, another dead body." Yet he thrived in this world, and like Placek, thought it was fun. "There's enough shit here to run a TV series for ten years," Woody said, "and it will all be true."

Woody's comment about another dead body every day was no exaggeration. Rarely a day passed when there wasn't another defendant downstairs in violence court being arraigned for murder and getting a public defender appointed to represent him. The cases were distributed around the office like a deck of cards. Like the homicide detectives who caught the cases on the front end, the lawyers got them the same way. It all depended on whose turn was up. Just the other day Woody's colleague, Bob Strunck, was dealt an accused serial killer. He was appointed to represent Ronald Macon Jr., charged with raping and killing at least three women and discarding their bodies like trash in alleys and near Dumpsters. There had been a string of thirteen rapes and murders on the city's South Side for the past six years. Police said that Macon confessed, explaining he drank booze and smoked crack with the women before killing them. Prosecutors would seek the death penalty. Bob would likely seek a deal to spare Ronald Macon's life. Bob, like Woody, was a lawyer whose oratory was as loud in the office as it was in the courtroom, and whose vocabulary was packed with four-letter words that served as frequent adjectives—both positive and negative. He had a square face and wore rectangular glasses and had a still-thick head of black hair flecked with gray. Bob had the air of a guy who'd been doing this a long, long time and knew all the angles. "Everyone's sanity in this unit can hang by a thread on any given day," he told me, explaining that he'd been on the job as a public defender for more than twenty years. "The honest truth is that some of these people you like, and some of these people you would never want to meet on the street."

Bob, a lifelong Chicagoan, was a sports nut who tacked and taped posters of the Chicago White Sox on the walls, and had schedules, calendars and magazines scattered everywhere among his legal files. When he wasn't talking about one of his cases, he was talking sports. If he wasn't a lawyer, Bob believed he would be a sports announcer or color commentator, a skill he developed calling football and basketball games while attending Santa Clara University in California. As a boy growing up in the early 1960s, he took the train to Wrigley Field to watch the Chicago Cubs play. His mother taught at a school a block from the ballpark, a perfect location for a boy who loved baseball. Bob's late father, James E. Strunck, was a criminal court judge who had the unenviable and tortuous job of presiding over one of the early death penalty cases in Chicago after it was reinstated in 1977. The elder Strunck was a pilot in the Pacific during World War II, and later served as a state senator and corporation counsel for the City of Chicago. The younger Strunck knew when he went to law school that he could not be a corporate lawyer or practice the kind of law that would keep him inside an office. He wanted to be a trial lawyer. "I didn't want to be working in a sweatshop law firm," he explained. "I'm not capable of working at menial tasks for eighty hours a week kissing some partner's rear end." And so he didn't. After graduating from Chicago-Kent College of Law in 1979, Bob got a job with the public defender and started out at branch court at Eleventh and State Street, next to the old police headquarters building. "There was no air-conditioning, the windows were open, and you could hear the El train go by," Bob recalled. "The court call was hookers and shoplifters. It was then I realized that junkies came in all different forms." Working branch court gave him the bug to stay on as a public defender. "I got the typical training. You walk right into the courtroom on your very first day. It was total baptism by fire," he said. "It was fun. It was a blast. Over there you can try a lot of cases and win them and all of a sudden you think you're F. Lee Bailey."

Winning cases built his confidence, and he worked his way up to the task force, where he had been for the past ten years, representing all manner of murderers. "What's amazing is that I've been a public defender since 1981 and the stories from the defendants rarely change. It's as if when you're interviewing someone it's like listening to a library of cassette tapes."

Back in his office, Shelton Green explained to me what it felt like to be in this exclusive club of lawyers who, on the whole, lost cases much more often than they won. "We know we're going into the courtroom against all odds, with the deck stacked against us," Shelton said. "It's like climbing Mount Everest. You go into court and get a not-guilty verdict, it pumps you up for a long time." Shelton once commented to a reporter in a courthouse hallway that the public defenders in his office were better trained and harder working than the state's attorneys. "I was later confronted by one of the state's attorneys in the hallway who heard what I said and took issue with that. I said, 'Fuck you. We *are* better. These are some of the best fucking attorneys in the country.' "

CHAPTER FIVE

How Can They Defend These People?

LATE ONE SUMMER MORNING, one of Marijane Placek's clients stepped up to the witness stand and began to tell a story so horrific that it left spectators in the courtroom gallery with their mouths agape. Some walked out nearly gagging, others left with tears in their eyes. I remained in the back of the courtroom and continued to listen.

The defendant's name was Joan Tribblet, one of about twenty other clients Marijane was representing besides Aloysius Oliver at the time. Tribblet was a thirty-year-old mother of five children who was charged with murder. Sitting beside the judge and leaning into a microphone, Tribblet spoke in a steady, emotionless voice as she recounted how she and her boyfriend choked and beat their fifteen-month-old daughter because she wouldn't stop crying. Tribblet admitted holding her daughter in a stranglehold, and said her boyfriend smacked the baby with a ruler on the back of the head. After the beating, the baby stopped crying. When the couple realized the child was dead, Tribblet said they panicked and tried to conceal what they had done. Tribblet blamed her boyfriend for coming up with the plan to dispose of their baby, whose name was Oncwanique. "He said we had to cut up the body and get rid of the body parts," she testified, not a hint of pain in her voice. "I placed her in his arms and I told her I loved her and would miss her and then I kissed her." As Tribblet said this, I heard sighs and snorts of disgust in the gallery. Marijane nodded for her client to continue.

Tribblet went on to describe how her boyfriend went into the bathroom to slice up the baby's corpse. As he went about the task, Tribblet said she was busy in the kitchen doing her part. She prepared a flour batter and heated up a pan of oil on the stovetop. She then coated the baby parts with the batter, fried it up, and gave it to her boyfriend to toss off in an alley where dogs could eat it. The courtroom was silent, the judge, the staff, the people in the seats stunned at what they were hearing.

When the smoke and stench from the cooking overwhelmed them in the apartment, Tribblet said she and her boyfriend decided to put the rest of the body parts in plastic bags and store it in the refrigerator for later disposal. And if that were not awful enough, she borrowed a neighbor's blender to liquefy the rest of the remains and later returned the blender to the unwitting accomplice.

There may never have been a case so hideous in this courthouse. More spectators got up and left the room before it was over. No one knew what to say. Marijane knew that if jurors ever heard this story, they'd be overwhelmed with revulsion and would want to send Tribblet right to the death chamber. That's why she advised Tribblet to own up to her role, plead guilty and testify against her boyfriend, Everette Johnson, which she was doing this morning. Tribblet was a tiny woman who looked like a lost teenage girl.

As gruesome as it was, the only thing that mattered to Marijane was that she proved her client didn't intend to kill the baby, that it was an angry act of discipline that had gone too far. It was an accident, Marijane argued. What Tribblet and Johnson did to cover it up was grotesque but irrelevant to the murder charge. The dismemberment was postmortem, a legal distinction that meant it was not an aggravating factor in the act of killing. Although Tribblet was convicted of murder through her plea agreement, Marijane was able to save her from a death sentence, getting her sixty years in prison, of which she would likely serve half. That was considered a victory. Tribblet would be an old woman before she got out of prison, if she survived that long. And she would have to live with the memory of what she had done. The term *victory* was relative, of course. There was little reason to celebrate anything about this case.

"That wasn't even one of my worst cases," Marijane told me later that day after leaving the courtroom. "I get baby killers all the time.

The worst case I had was the rape of a three- and five-year-old. The guy tossed the kids out the window afterward. The children were very badly raped. We had thought the fall killed them, but he had choked them with their own pajamas, which were wrapped so tight they were embedded in their throats." She recounted the story dispassionately, as if she were talking about what she had for lunch. She had told it many times before, and long ago had learned to shield herself from the feelings that would impede her ability to represent such people.

The man charged with committing that crime was Frank Redd, who in 1984 was arrested for strangling Leola Bea, three, and Aretha Bea, five, who lived in his building. A forensic pathologist testified that the girls suffered excruciating pain during the attacks. The youngest had sustained the worst injuries in a rape that he had seen in his eighteen-year career. During the trial, a schoolteacher who had taken her third-grade class on a field trip to the courthouse, brought the children in to observe the proceedings. Marijane and the prosecutor looked at each other in disbelief. "I mean, the victims had their vaginas split open because of the size of his penis," Marijane explained. "And the teacher was going to bring in the class to listen to this?" Marijane and the prosecutor agreed that it was not a good idea to have children in the room. "I took the teacher aside and I said, 'Do you know what this case is about?' " Marijane said. The teacher said she understood that it was a violent case, and told Marijane they needed to learn about it, and refused to take the students out of the courtroom. "I said they shouldn't ever have to learn about that. This is an aberration. This is nothing that a third grader has to know about." The class stayed for an hour or so, taking with them a story that surely would have horrified their parents. "This case was absolutely horrendous," Marijane said. "This guy was a piece of shit."

Lawyers in the Murder Task Force often traded stories about their cases and clients, people they sometimes called without apology, as Marijane did, pieces of shit. They routinely represented defendants accused of gruesome, evil acts. "This place is the concentration of the worst of Cook County," Task Force attorney Woody Jordan said one afternoon when I stopped to visit at his office. "You can really develop a warped sense of humanity. Working with some of these people is almost the closest thing to working with the devil. Some people in this world are just evil." In a career in which he's defended all manner of killers, Woody was recently assigned to one of his biggest and worst. The client's name was Paul Runge. "This guy is a fucking Ted Bundy," Woody said, referring to the infamous Florida serial killer known for his handsome looks, intelligence and savagery. "I've never had a case like this. This fucking guy is a Jekyll and Hyde. There is definitely something wrong with him." What was wrong was that Runge, a father of four who drove a beverage truck, confessed to being a serial killer who raped, murdered, burned and dismembered his victims. The day Runge was charged, Cook County State's Attorney Richard Devine said, "Paul Runge is our worst nightmare."

Woody was one of four attorneys working on the case. When the public defender's office was assigned to represent him, Runge had been charged with killing six women and a ten-year-old girl, and was awaiting trial in two different counties. A convicted rapist who already was in prison for escape, Runge was linked to the murders through DNA. It would probably be two years or more before Woody could even hope to go to trial with the tangled mess of a case. The killing began in 1995 when Runge, who was out on parole on a conviction for raping a fourteen-year-old girl, killed his wife's friend, Stacy Frobel, by beating her with a dumbbell, according to prosecutors. He then sawed up her body and dumped the parts in Wisconsin, the state charged. The summer of that same year, Runge was accused of killing two sisters, Amela and Dzeneta Pasanbegovic, in their suburban Chicago home. Two years later, prosecutors said he started to murder again. This time he was accused of raping and murdering Yolanda Gutierrerez and her daughter, Jessica Munoz. He had gone to their apartment after seeing a sign at a grocery store advertising some items for sale. He looked around but said he had to go talk to his wife before buying anything. He returned a few days later with a knife and a roll of duct tape. Prosecutors said he raped mother and daughter and then cut their throats. He was also charged with raping and killing Kazimiera Paruch, forty-three, and Dorota Dzubak, thirty, in a similar manner. The case files and details, Woody said, were horrifying. Not long after his arrest, Runge confessed to all the crimes and was ready to make a plea deal to life in prison instead of death. In his videotaped confession, Runge said he wanted to do the right thing and admit to his crimes. "I need help," he said. "Something's wrong with me. I don't know why I do this stuff." Prosecutors were not going to let him off that easy. They wanted him to go to trial so they could seek the death penalty. "This is a waste of time," Woody said. "He's ready to go for life, and I'm ready to plead him."

So it looked like Woody and the others would have to go through the motions, which both frustrated and invigorated him, for this would be as challenging a case as he ever had. The case was mammoth in scope. Seven murders, two different counties, multiple police agencies. "You've got to understand. At this point, there are thirty thousand pages of documents. I hired a paralegal just to help me go through the documents," Woody told me, and showed me a stack of CDs on which the files were copied. "I've never had a case of this magnitude. This is a career case. I only have one more like this in me." Woody told me that starting a case like this, figuring out where to begin, was overwhelming. "What do you do when you get a case like this? You go down to Jean's and you get really drunk and you start processing the files." In spite of the horrific crimes for which Runge was charged, Woody and he got along beautifully. "He's one of the best clients I've ever had," Woody said. "And he's a fucking genius." He pulled out Runge's high school records from a file cabinet behind his desk. The records showed that he got Cs and Fs in school, but later tested with a genius IQ. "He's one of the most charming, intelligent clients I've ever had, and he understands that every continuance means he'll be alive another thirty days."

Runge gave two confessions, which would give the defense team a basis for picking apart the cases and comparing the different accounts. In the first, he said he and his wife committed the murder of Stacy Frobel, and he disposed of the remains. In the second, he said that he did it alone. Runge also confessed to killing all the other women by himself. Woody, who by now read most of the files, described details of the killing from memory and recited the pattern. Runge had sex with the women anally, vaginally and orally and slit the throats of each of them. "He slit it so deep you could see the spinal cord," Woody said. "He almost cut their heads off." In each case the police found accelerant used to set the mattress on fire.

The FBI had suspected Runge in the serial killings for years but didn't have the evidence to arrest him, Woody believed. Despite what seemed like a solid case, Woody was skeptical about the state's DNA evidence, a sample of semen they said was taken from the mouth of one of the victims. "This is what troubles me. The bodies were burned to the point that they weren't human," Woody said. "But there was semen in the mouth? It should have boiled off or been burnt off. I don't buy it. I'm not so sure that shit wasn't planted. Just think about it. How did the DNA survive the fire? That's bothersome."

That would be just one of the pieces of evidence he would question. But with a confession from a man who clearly appeared to be sick, why wouldn't Woody consider an insanity defense? "You don't want to try an insanity case in front of a jury," Woody said. "People don't like the concept of insanity. Crazy people scare them. They don't want them to walk free." A finding of not guilty by reason of insanity doesn't, of course, mean defendants walk free. They usually are sent to an institution for psychiatric treatment. And if and when they get better, they might walk free. That's what scares people.

When it came to clients whose crimes exceeded all boundaries of decency and evoked pure evil, Murder Task Force chief Shelton Green thought that insanity seemed like a good explanation. Yet proving it was another matter. Judges and juries rarely accepted such arguments, reluctant to conclude that mental illness absolved defendants of responsibility for heinous acts. Just because someone committed an insane act did not make him insane. So when Shelton put forth the insanity defense, he truly believed the client was insane, which was the case with Mark Johnson, the most frightening defendant he ever represented. "Every one of my clients had my home phone number except for this guy," Shelton told me. "He was scary.

My wife has received calls from serial killers and gangbangers, but I didn't want to put her in the position of dealing with this guy."

Johnson was a convicted rapist who was arrested in 1985 for the murder of Willie Robinson and the torture, rape and attempted murder of Robinson's niece. Johnson had offered to help Robinson's niece move furniture and boxes into her apartment. During a break from the work, Johnson sent Robinson out to a convenience store to get them all something to drink. Johnson then tied up the woman, raped and beat her. Robinson came back, interrupting the attack, and tried to stop Johnson. Johnson then killed him.

While in custody awaiting trial, Johnson confessed to another murder a year earlier, which had remained unsolved. He said he raped and killed a woman by slashing her throat. He described attacking yet another a woman in a seven-hour torturous ordeal during which he sexually assaulted her, tied and gagged her and cut her arms and chest. She managed to escape and call police. After learning more about Johnson's background, Shelton decided he might be psychotic and would make a good candidate for the insanity defense. It might be the only way to save his life. "He was maybe the craziest guy I ever met," Shelton said. "You would look him in the eyes and just see nothing there." One psychiatrist who examined Johnson reported that Johnson told him he killed eleven people since age fifteen, tortured animals as a child and said his purpose in life was to kill. How could someone who said that be in his right mind?

Yet for Shelton and his cocounsel Richard Scholz, it was not that simple. They had a client who certainly talked like he was insane, but they needed to prove he was insane at the time of the crime. At trial, the psychiatrist called by the state testified that Johnson was "a true sadist" who derived pleasure from killing. Yet as depraved as he was, Johnson did not meet the legal requirements of insanity. Shelton argued that his client's mind was truly warped. "What he did was not right," Shelton argued. "It's crazy." But the jury rejected the insanity defense and found Johnson guilty of first-degree murder and sexual assault. To try to save him from the death penalty, Shelton and Scholz dug deeper into Johnson's past to try to understand how his violent behavior was spawned. Johnson told them stories of a dysfunctional childhood, of a mother who beat him bloody and then rubbed his naked body with alcohol while saying she loved him. He told them about an older brother who sexually abused their sister. Johnson testified at his sentencing hearing and told the jury about the beatings, about the sexual abuse, about growing up always fearful. He said he knew he deserved to die, but he wanted to live. Against that, prosecutor William Merritt called Johnson "a vicious, sadistic, brutal individual" and held up grisly photographs of a murder scene that sent one juror out of the courtroom sick. The jury voted to give Johnson the death penalty. "He was the only case I got death on," Shelton said. "His wires were crossed. He had been so abused that love meant pain and was expressed in injuries. To him, hate was when someone tried to love and kiss and comfort him."

"Did I ever tell you about the Johnny Campbell case?" Marijane said to me one afternoon. No other case of Marijane's attracted as much media attention or inspired as much public vitriol against her or any of her clients. The Tribblet case was bad, but Campbell was worse because the victim, a four-year-old boy, suffered excruciating pain long before he died. Campbell was charged in 1987 with torturing and killing his girlfriend's son, Lattie McGee, a child who over the course of a summer was beaten, burned with cigarettes, stuck with sewing needles, starved and hung upside down in a closet instead of being allowed to sleep. The judge, Michael Getty, called it the worst example of torture he'd ever seen. Campbell was accused of suspending Lattie by his feet, stuffing a rag in his mouth and taping potato peelings over his eyes. Prosecutors said that the mother, Alicia Abraham, was preoccupied watching television, never bothering to help her suffering son. She faced charges of her own of being a silent accomplice.

Marijane hired Larry Heinrich, a forensic psychologist, to conduct psychological evaluations of Campbell and to assist her during the sentencing phase. "That was one of the first cases where I read the autopsy report and I got sick," Heinrich told me during an interview later. "I really had trouble reading the postmortem. I just couldn't read the details. I didn't know how I was going to deal with him. I try to be as open-minded as I can." The autopsy report said the child's body was broken in many places, ribs snapped, collarbone detached, broken pelvis, burn marks on his skin, ligature marks around his penis, an apparent attempt to keep him from urinating. He was malnourished, weighed only twenty-six pounds and had pneumonia. "It was clear to me that this was a disturbed man. Other than that, he was a really nice guy," Heinrich said. "I could feel compassion. He could talk about it with deep regret. If you met him, you might feel comfortable having your kids around him." Statements like that alienated some people from Heinrich. "I usually try not to tell people what I do for a living," he said. "They say, 'You try to save these people's lives? Arghhh!' "

Marijane, who handled the case with cocounsel Allan Sincox, worked with Campbell to get a plea of guilty. He admitted to the crime, and so the next step was to try to persuade the judge to spare his life. Campbell had a history of mental illness and was clearly sick. That helped Marijane in some way deal with trying to save him, knowing that he was not of a right mind. "All we wanted to do was save his life," Marijane said. "We wanted to plead him guilty. Then Bob Greene got a hold of it."

Bob Greene was the nationally syndicated columnist for the *Chicago Tribune*. He waged an unrelenting campaign in the newspaper, offering every lurid detail of the case and urging that justice be served. It was part of Greene's long-running campaign on behalf of abused and neglected children, which played out in columns that made readers cringe with their explicit and disturbing descriptions of these crimes. The public outpouring was extraordinary. Marijane said people even called then–first lady Nancy Reagan, pleading with her to make sure justice was served. Greene published all the dates and locations of court proceedings, including the sentencing hearing, which drew more than one hundred people into the courtroom. "It created a huge stir. Every seat in the courtroom was filled. People were searched out front and the cops found knives and throwing stars and all kinds of weapons. I wasn't sure if they were meant for the defendant or for us," she said. "We were threatened, we were spit on. But actually, when I talk about it, it makes me excited. That was the one case where I felt the most alive because I knew we could do it, I knew we could take them on."

Heinrich testified for the defense at Campbell's sentencing hearing, offering the theory that Campbell suffered from delusions that Lattie McGee and his brother, Cornelius, six, were homosexuals and that he believed he could beat such tendencies out of them. A voice told him the boys were engaged in homosexual acts. "He believed his actions were to stop deviant behavior," Heinrich testified. "He believed he was acting in God's name, under God's law, to stop these children." Heinrich concluded that Campbell meant no harm. "He didn't mean to kill Lattie. He had intended only to correct these kids."

Prosecutors found such a theory appalling and argued that Campbell suffered from a drug-induced mental illness and faked symptoms of insanity. Judge Michael Getty was under enormous pressure. His office received calls and letters urging him to impose death on each of them. But in the end, he said he would not give in "to the outrage of public opinion" and sentenced Campbell and Abraham to life in prison without the possibility of parole. The judge said the evidence of Campbell's mental illness at the time of the killing was overwhelming. The mother was spared because she was not in the room when Campbell delivered the fatal blows to the child. Speaking to the press afterward, Marijane said, "He isn't some sort of monster. I'm happy for society. We've been killing sick people for an easy solution.

"God, that was the greatest two weeks," Marijane said, looking back. "Everybody thought we would lose. I could smell the blood. I could smell the state bleeding. You could feel the blood flowing because we were making inroads and more inroads. Our strategy was absolutely correct and it was perfect. It was fantastic. It was one of the finest times of my life."

Later in the afternoon after Joan Tribblet testified about killing and cooking her daughter's remains, Marijane invited me along to Mi Tierra, a Mexican restaurant west of the courthouse, for an extended lunch with Ruth McBeth and Larry Heinrich, who had become friends of Marijane's after having worked for her as a forensic consultant for more than a decade. As they sipped margaritas and dipped tortilla chips in salsa, they talked about the Tribblet case as if no one else were in the restaurant. Marijane kept referring to it as "the battered baby case," alluding to the way Tribblet prepared the body parts. At one point, Marijane called it "the Kentucky Fried baby case," and her dining companions collectively grimaced and continued eating. If other customers in the restaurant heard the conversation, they either didn't catch the details or didn't let on. I was hoping no one heard.

Like cops, firefighters, emergency room staff and others who dealt in death and tragedy, public defenders in the task force used such gruesome humor to distance themselves from the ugly world in which they worked. It was the kind of humor outsiders might have found offensive, the lighthearted recounting of bloody shootings, stabbings, graphic descriptions of decomposed and mutilated bodies. It was like a game of Can You Top This? "We really have sick humor," Heinrich explained to me apologetically. Later, he elaborated. "Every lawyer who does this has to have a sense of humor. If not, it can be emotionally self-destructive. If you don't deal with it, you succumb to alcoholism, stress, divorce or suicide," he said. "You're really dealing with the worst of humanity. When you're in a job that people don't understand, you develop your own private world of humor. I don't think it's disrespectful or meant to be disrespectful."

But telling crude tales and joking about hideous cases went deeper than using humor as a safety valve. It was about being comfortable enough to talk in such a manner without fear of being judged. It was about sharing stories and describing unspeakable acts with colleagues who understood without requiring explanation or apology. These lawyers avoided sharing such stories with outsiders because they felt it trivialized their profession and marginalized them further. Marijane hated talking about her work with outsiders because she grew tired of the questions about the grotesque and macabre. People wanted to hear the tabloid versions of murder cases, not the legal intricacies. "Don't tell me you're interested in the criminal justice system," Marijane said. "You're interested in the salacious details. It's an insult when people ask. People really don't want to know about a case. They want to know the gore. They want to know something visceral. Nobody can understand what you're doing unless they're worthy to understand. It becomes nothing but a trite story. It becomes a dime novel. I've got a hundred and ten stories, and I won't tell anyone. These people don't deserve to hear the war stories, because they can't understand the truth of them."

And so this was why the public defenders and their colleagues had their lunches and dinners and drinks together. They created exclusive gatherings in which they could discuss their work and the horrible things they have encountered in an uncensored forum. Marijane likened it to a British tradition in which officers would come back from battle. "They would do all these uncivilized things in battle, and then they would retire to the club. And what would they do at the club? They would eat and drink and have a wonderful meal." So Marijane and her friends continued to feast and to recount their battles that day.

A month after Joan Tribblet confessed, Everette Johnson, her boyfriend, was found guilty during a bench trial. Prosecutors sought the death penalty. But Judge Lon William Schultz found that despite the horrific manner in which Johnson and Tribblet disposed of the bodies, the way in which the baby was killed did not warrant death. Still, the judge said mother and father displayed "combined malignancies of the hearts." He said, "Mr. Johnson and Ms. Tribblet opened a window for everyone to see into the deepest and darkest depravity of their flawed human souls." Johnson got one hundred years in prison, despite the state's plea for more time.

Marijane had since moved on. She had the Aloysius Oliver case to deal with, and was waiting to hear what her investigator had come up with after visiting the crime scene and searching for witnesses.

CHAPTER SIX

Scene of the Crime

RICHARD ENGLISH WAS MARIJANE PLACEK'S right-hand investigator and street-smart confidant. He was the man she sent out into the city's scariest places and into the most insular and seemingly impenetrable worlds to extract information from people who would rather not talk and had an inherent distrust of authority. English was built squat and solid with a tanklike upper body, round stomach, strong arms and bulky hands. He resembled a 1950s-era wrestler, like Dick the Bruiser, with short clipped brown hair. His knit shirt pocket was usually bulging with a pack of Lucky Strikes, a Zippo lighter, notepads and pens. He had a gentle voice and friendly face, and he spent most of his days driving around the city, knocking on doors, walking up dark flights of stairs and talking to people. People who knocked on doors with badges and notebooks were not always embraced enthusiastically. But English had a gift for getting people to talk, an easy nature and quick rapport that allowed him access to gang leaders, drug dealers and the people who spent their days and nights hanging out on street corners. Most of all, he had patience. When the time was right, people talked. And he was a good listener.

Not long after getting the Aloysius Oliver case, Marijane called her man. She told English what she knew about the shooting and asked for his help. Like Marijane, English loved a good challenge. English read the police reports before visiting the crime scene. "The biggest question in my mind was whether Oliver knew these guys were police officers," English told me. "You know, it happened in a drug area and you don't know who the people are around there." As he tried to envision the events that unfolded that night, English thought that the whole scenario seemed odd. "Why wouldn't Oliver have shot at the police right away? If he was going to shoot, it would have been then and there, wouldn't it?" he said. "Why didn't the cops shoot *him*? They were in the heat of the battle. They easily could have shot him."

With such questions in mind, English took a ride down to the scene of the crime, which was about three miles south of the courthouse. With him was Leo Negrone, another investigator from the public defender's office. The scene and the neighborhood already had been blanketed and picked over by cops, detectives and investigators for the State's Attorney's Office. Neighborhood residents were by now weary of answering questions and repeating the same story. English and Negrone would have to try to build alliances and gain confidence among the neighborhood residents and witnesses if they hoped to get anywhere.

English had been an investigator for the past fifteen years, and knew how to finesse people when he walked into a strange neighborhood. First off, he never acted like a cop, or let people think he was a cop, even though he carried an investigator's badge. Cops were often intimidating and could be bullies. An attitude like that might prompt people to retreat or refuse to cooperate. "Sometimes the state or the police use strong-arm tactics or threaten to arrest people or say something about children being taken away, so they can get what they want," English told me later during an interview. "If you talk to people as if they're people, you will get better cooperation than the police will."

English knew the streets well, their dangers and the toll they could take. His son, Richard "Ricky" Jr. was shot six times and nearly killed about fifteen years earlier in their neighborhood when he was walking on the street and confronted by two gang members who demanded Ricky declare his affiliation. "I'm not in any gang," Ricky told them. He tried to persuade them that he was just minding his own business. One of the gang members dared the other to shoot Ricky, and he accepted the challenge, firing shot after shot into the innocent man. Ricky dropped to the ground bleeding, his insides ripped up by lead. Paramedics got him to the hospital in time for doctors to save him, and he spent seventeen days in intensive care before going home. Police tracked down and arrested the two gang members, who eventually pleaded guilty. English came to every court hearing rooting for the prosecutors. Later, English's friends and relatives would question how English could work for public defenders after what happened to his son, how he could work on behalf of the kind of person who shot his boy. He didn't launch into any kind of speech or long-winded justification. "Somebody has to do the job," English said. "I like what I do." He was a man of few words and little explanation.

Before becoming an investigator for the public defender's office, English, the son of Mexican immigrants, worked as an elevator operator for the Cook County Sheriff's Department. His job was to control and supervise the security of the elevators where prisoners, guards, lawyers and county workers rode inside the jail and courthouse complex. It was a decent-paying job for the father of two daughters and a son. Through friends, he heard about an opportunity to work as an investigator with the public defender's office, and decided to switch careers. Not long after starting there, English met Marijane, who had asked him to translate for some Spanish-speaking clients. English said he would be glad to help, and they quickly became pals.

English slowly cruised down the alley behind Carpenter Street. The sound of glass and stones crunched under the car tires. He parked on an empty lot opposite Aloysius's backyard. He and Negrone walked around to get a feel for the place, to get a lay of the land to better understand the location of the buildings, the sight lines, the length and width of the alley and gangways, the height and condition of the fences, trees and plants. The neighborhood was tired and defeated looking. The streets were marked by a mix of poorly maintained homes and lots filled with trash and broken furniture. Some of the old wood frame homes appeared as if they were sinking into the ground, sitting on slight angles, strangely askew. There were no trees in front of the Oliver home, which was surrounded by a chain-link metal fence. To the north about a half block was the elevated train line, the Green Line, as it was called, running along Sixty-third Street.

After looking around, English was puzzled at how Aloysius could have shot Officer Lee in the head as he was running down the narrow gangway. He wasn't convinced that Aloysius knew he was being chased by cops, either. "Supposedly," he later told me with a tone of skepticism, "they were wearing their badges over their chest." English and Negrone brought a tape measure and camera and walked around the scene, snapping pictures and measuring the gangways and garage and distances from the alley. They wanted to test the geometry to see whether Aloysius could have fired at Officer Lee as he ran down that gangway. The gangway was narrow and short. English wondered how Aloysius could have taken such a clean shot at Lee. How could he have been able to run, turn around, aim and shoot Lee so accurately? "That's what's perplexing," English said. "I have my doubts. You have someone chasing you. They're behind you. Do you have time to stop and turn around, aim your weapon, fire and hit someone in the head?" But English was not there to prove or disprove anything himself. He was there to gather information. "How the lawyers use it, and what they do with it is up to them," he said. "You can't prejudge. You can't assume the client's guilty or not."

During the next several months, English knocked on doors along Carpenter Street and around the neighborhood. If anyone answered, which wasn't often, he'd ask about locating Tommie Leach, Aloysius's cousin and a key witness. Neighbors weren't much help or didn't let on if they knew something. Leach had already pleaded guilty to assault and battery charges in connection with the incident, and served less than a year in prison. He had no reason to cooperate with anyone now and was not eager to talk. He also was afraid of harming his cousin's case. The two were close, almost like brothers, and would do anything for one another. After quizzing more neighbors, English was able to find Aloysius's pal Damon Rogers a few blocks away in an apartment on Racine Avenue. When English came up to the door of Rogers's apartment, he saw several children running around the front. A woman went into another room to give English and Rogers some privacy, and they sat down.

Rogers explained to English that he already had spoken to the police, and he hesitated to recount the events of that night again. English said he needed his help, that things weren't adding up. Rogers sighed and agreed to tell the story once more. Rogers said that on the night of the shooting, he was summoned to the back of the Oliver house by a female voice, who turned out to be Johanna Harris. By the time Rogers got to the alley, he said, he saw Aloysius and Leach fighting with someone, but it was dark and hard to see their faces well. Rogers said he heard someone yell, "Let the man go." Rogers also told English that he never heard anyone identify himself as a police officer. But as the men walked down the alley, Rogers said he could see one of them was wearing a vest and a police star. Then he heard one of them say, "He's got a gun!" In fear for his life, Rogers told English that he fled, running toward the front of the house. He claimed to have heard a bullet whiz by his ear. He kept running because he thought he was going to get shot. As he ran, he said, he had no idea a cop had been killed. That was all he was going to say. English wrote it all down in a report that he would later give to Marijane and Ruth. Rogers signed the statement as true.

English still needed to talk with Tommie Leach to clear up the matter of whether the officers had identified themselves as they approached the group in the alley. A source told English that Leach was staying at his girlfriend's apartment, and he went over there hoping to persuade him to cooperate. English explained that he was working for the defense team and urged Leach to provide a statement of how the shooting went down that night. Leach said he didn't want to talk. He feared that no matter what he said, it would mean trouble. He knew that prosecutors were looking for him, and that if English found him, they would find him, too. He didn't think he could help Aloysius, even though he thought his cousin was getting a bum rap. If Leach thought Aloysius was innocent, English told him, he should say something now.

Reluctantly, Leach started to talk, cautious and halting. He told English that it was difficult to sort out the events that night because it all happened so quickly. "I don't want you to go to court and lie," English told him. "We're out here to find the truth. If someone lies for you, then you get caught up in the lie, too." Leach admitted to English that he helped Aloysius beat up the man behind the house and remembered a group of men coming down the alley telling them to stop. He recalled the men pulling out guns and said he ran. "By the time I got out to the front, I heard gunshots but don't know what happened," Leach said. "I saw no badges or anything else to tell me they were police officers." Leach also signed his statement as a true account.

If Leach could be believed, his story and testimony would be a major piece of evidence favoring the defense. If Aloysius didn't know he was shooting at police officers, he might be able to argue self-defense and get away with a lesser charge, maybe even an acquittal. But English wondered whether Leach could be a trusted, credible witness and stand up to the kind of rigorous cross-examination that the state would surely pursue. Never discount any theory. English had learned that any story was plausible, that the police might not be telling it like it was. He believed it was possible that Aloysius truly did not know he was shooting at police officers. "There were a lot of people out there. The cops say they had their badges displayed. I don't know if that was necessarily true," English said. "Somebody chased him. Did they fire at him first? Was it self-defense?"

When English first visited the crime scene, he stood in the back alley where Officer Lee was shot and heard the rumbling of the El train a half block away. The noise got louder, shaking the steel girders and screeching against the rails. It gave him an idea. Perhaps when the officers yelled out to announce who they were, a train came by and drowned them out. He later called the Chicago Transit Authority to get a schedule of the trains on the night of the shooting. "There were no trains running at that time," English said later. "So that was that."

Being the mother of a man accused of killing a cop was almost too much for Lillian Oliver to endure. Her home was a crime scene, and for days she watched out of the front window on Carpenter Street as television camera crews and reporters swarmed her neighborhood, looking for people to interview, getting backdrops for their live shots. Reporters kept knocking on Lillian's door, but she refused to come out. She found refuge at the dental school where she worked as a secretary. She asked Marijane and Ruth to meet her at a McDonald's on the other side of the city to discuss the case rather than at her home, concerned that they all would be harassed. She felt imprisoned, fearing not just the press and her neighbors, but police as well. Not long after her son's arrest, Lillian Oliver received a letter that threatened her life. She suspected that it came from a police officer, though she could never prove it. The fear and the attention finally became unbearable, and she packed up and moved to another apartment on the city's West Side with her two daughters and other son, hoping to be left alone.

After several months passed, Lillian had some time to think about it all. She realized that nerves, anger and disorientation caused her to speak too soon on the courthouse steps where she apologized for her son in front of the media. She had a different view of things now. She didn't think her son shot Officer Lee. She didn't want to believe it. She lived in a neighborhood where many residents didn't trust the police and told stories of dirty cops, claiming that young men were often rounded up, roughed up and shaken down for drugs and money. "You've got some decent cops," Lillian Oliver told me when I went to visit her at her apartment one evening after she got off work. "But to me, ninety-nine percent of them are no good. I've worked in an emergency room for ten years and I have seen kids come in beat up from the cops. Everybody's got their skeletons. Sometimes you don't know what to believe."

There was one vital piece of evidence that Marijane and Ruth were anxious to see. The State's Attorney's Office provided them with a copy of Aloysius's videotaped confession. Marijane popped it into a VCR in her office, hit the play button, opened a notepad and sat back. The camera was aimed directly at Aloysius in a medium shot. He sat at the end of a table, flanked by Detective Thomas Kelly on one side and Assistant State's Attorney Darren O'Brien on the other. He was wearing a loose T-shirt and his head was down. Aloysius had three white bandages on his face—one on the bridge of his nose, another on his left forehead and the other on the side of his right ear.

Aloysius looked down at the table as Detective Kelly read his rights, and then he explained what happened that night as he sat on his back porch. He sounded tired and resigned.

"I saw a person down there taking a leak by my garbage can," Aloysius said. "I was really upset that he was in our backyard . . . and I grabbed my gun."

He continued in a low, monotone voice. "I walked to the person who was pissing in my yard. I grabbed him by the shoulder. I asked him what the fuck he was doing in my backyard . . . He didn't say nothing. He was saying somebody was chasing him."

Aloysius told the detective how he asked Johanna to get his brother and friends over to help and then began to beat the man. "I pushed him down and kicked him." His friends joined in the beating and then Aloysius saw three men coming up the alley. The men started running toward Aloysius, who then took off.

"Did any of those men say something to you as they were running up the alley?" Kelly asked.

"After I started running, they was like, 'He's got a fucking gun. Freeze. Police.' "

"Did you freeze?" Kelly said.

"I was already running."

"Why did you run?"

"I was afraid."

"Afraid of what?"

"I was afraid of getting shot or going to jail."

Aloysius said he ran down the alley by a garage and turned.

"Were you trying to get away because the police—you thought the police might arrest you for beating up the Hype?"

"Yes."

"Is that why you shot the police officer?"

"I wasn't trying to. I was just . . . I wasn't trying to shoot the police officer. I just . . ."

Aloysius said he continued running and remembered being surprised by another officer in the gangway. "He was like, 'Freeze, motherfucker.' And I was like 'You the police?' He was like, 'Yeah, I'm the fucking police.' And he grabbed my wrist and twisted it and took the gun."

Aloysius said he freed himself, ran off and tried to hop over the gate but fell before the other officers finally subdued him.

"I see you have some bandages on your face. How did you get hurt?" Kelly asked.

"Falling down."

"Are you making this statement because it's the truth or because of the bandages on your face."

"Because it's the truth."

"How have we treated you since you've been here?"

"Fine."

"Did you get something to eat?"

"I got three sandwiches and two Pepsis."

"Were any threats or promises made to you?"

"No."

The screen went black. But then the image came on again, and the detective announced that Aloysius wanted to add something to his statement.

"I wanted to say to the officer's family and to his partner that I wasn't trying to kill him. I wasn't even trying to shoot him," Aloysius said. "I know it ain't going to bring him back, but I'm sorry."

After watching the confession on video in her office, Marijane offered her review. "That's bullshit," she told me. "He didn't know his rights. There's such a tremendous amount of fear. This whole thing is refined to an art."

Ruth said Aloysius's statement seemed contrived. "It's so staged, yet the jury is going to believe it," she said in a resigned tone.

Marijane and Ruth knew they had a tough one. Yet just about anything could be negotiated at the courthouse. So Marijane had a conversation with Assistant State's Attorney David O'Connor to see whether the state would consider not seeking the death penalty if they worked out a plea. "What can we do about this?" she said, feeling out whether they could make a deal. O'Connor's answer was simple and direct. "I can't do anything."

It was a cop killing, after all, and the office was not prepared to make deals on this one.

If they were going to proceed to trial, Marijane and Ruth decided they would want another judge. Dennis A. Dernbach, who was assigned the case, was an ex–state's attorney, and, in the defense team's opinion, more likely than others to impose death. They wanted to take a chance in getting a more sympathetic judge. The court allowed one change of judge and would make another random assignment. They got Judge John J. Moran Jr., a nine-year veteran of the bench who had a reputation as a fair-minded and reasonable man.

The case slogged through the system for the next several months with the usual series of status hearings and filings of motions. Ruth visited Aloysius regularly at the jail. Marijane let Ruth handle many of the visits because she sensed that Aloysius was put off by her bold personality and bossy attitude. "I think he took offense at me," Marijane said. "But you have to let him know who's in control. I think he's panicked." When Ruth visited with Aloysius, she saw a small, frightened man. She was convinced, after speaking with him, that Aloysius felt pressured to confess on the night he was labeled as a cop killer. "It was a nightmare for him," Ruth told me. "It was Kafkaesque." Aloysius told Ruth that he received anonymous letters at the jail threatening his life. One of the letters said that there were people on the inside who could get him. But Aloysius decided not to request protective custody. Inmates in protective custody were marked as either homosexuals or snitches, and Aloysius wanted neither of those labels. He would ride it out in the general population.

Ruth developed an easy rapport with Aloysius and started to like him, seeing an intelligence and curiosity that made him easy to work with. He impressed her by talking about books and literature, discussing writers such as the English poet and philosopher John Milton. Aloysius asked Ruth if she could get him a copy of *Paradise Lost*, Milton's epic, dense and notoriously difficult poem about heaven and earth and the origin of sin and evil. This surprised Ruth because most of her clients asked for thrillers and dramas, not seventeenth-century poetry. Aloysius told her he was interested in deepening his understanding of good and evil and seeking spiritual strength. *Paradise Lost*, he told her, addressed the larger questions that he grappled with throughout his life. "He was struggling with the issues of what he had done with his life," said Ruth, who had read Milton in college. "Aloysius struck me because he wanted to delve into serious literature." One weekend not long after that visit, Ruth got on her bicycle and rode to a used book sale near her home where she searched for a copy of *Paradise Lost*. She had to find a paperback version because hardcover books were prohibited in the jail. Inmates had slipped drugs, money and notes inside the hardbound covers, and could use them as heavy weapons. By luck Ruth found a copy at the used book sale and brought it to the jail the following week.

About eight months after his arrest, Aloysius got his first chance to avoid the death penalty in exchange for a plea of guilty. To Marijane and Ruth's surprise, O'Connor offered him natural life in prison without the possibility of parole, though the prosecutor did not explain why the state changed its position. Marijane and Ruth met with Aloysius and asked what he thought. There wasn't much discussion. Aloysius flat out said no. He told his lawyers he wanted to fight this charge. To him, life in prison was the same thing as a death sentence. He wanted all or nothing. He was too young to spend the rest of his life in prison. The decision was his. If that's what he wanted, Marijane told Aloysius, she was willing to try for an acquittal. She loved the idea of going to trial and told Aloysius she and Ruth would argue his case vigorously. Even though Aloysius shot a cop in front of several witnesses, she would argue that there was more, much more, to the story and all kinds of possibilities for a defense. Marijane always kept in mind that a few rogue cops had tortured confessions out of suspects before, and others were convicted for consorting with drug dealers and gang members. Moreover, she was practicing law within a broken capital punishment system in which seventeen inmates were freed from death row because of wrongful convictions. This would not be a slam dunk for the state. Marijane wouldn't allow it and was determined to work all the angles.

On September 23, 2002, a year and a month after the shooting, Judge Moran cleared the way for Aloysius to go to trial. During a brief hearing, the prosecutors withdrew their offer of life in prison. The offer had been on the table for months, but the state had set a deadline this day for a decision. Aloysius would take his chances. A murder case moved slowly through the system, often taking two to three years before coming to trial unless attorneys worked out a plea deal to dispose of it early. Cases didn't unfold as they did in the movies either, where lawyers appear to be working on one big case to the exclusion of all others and are constantly visiting and updating their clients in jail. Marijane got new murder clients every few weeks, and the cases stacked up. She called many of them "routine," which meant that they involved clients with criminal records who killed each other and ended with plea deals or very brief trials. On the big ones, like Aloysius, there was much to do because it was a death case. The rules were different. As much as they prepared for their trial, they were also preparing for the sentencing and the appeal in the event they lost. The lawyers started by poring over the paperwork filed by police and would file discovery motions to get more—the investigative reports, lab reports, property receipts, logs, any piece of writing generated about the case. "You look at the documents, and then you look for the point of least resistance," Marijane explained. "So what do we have so far? He was there. He had a gun. Why would everyone lie about it?"

They also filed the motion to have Aloysius's confession thrown out. This required a hearing in which they would get to question witnesses and see who the state would be using to testify. "It's like scouting your opponent. You get to see their witnesses and you get to question the cops," Marijane said. And question the cops she would.

CHAPTER SEVEN

Confession or Coercion?

THE BENCHES INSIDE JUDGE JOHN MORAN'S sixth-floor courtroom were filled with police officers, some in uniform, others in their civilian clothes. Aloysius Oliver sat at one end of the defense table, closest to the judge and farthest away from the gallery and the cops who leered at him. Aloysius kept his head down and avoided looking at the throng that wanted him dead. Ruth McBeth took one last look at the notes scrawled on her yellow legal pad, stepped out from behind the defense table and began her argument to get Aloysius's confession thrown out. She told Moran that her client had been abused from the moment he was arrested. "The force used by the police went beyond what was necessary," she said. "The abuse that he suffered included kicking and striking and punching at the police station by Chicago police officers." Ruth delivered her opening statement calmly, evenly and without fanfare. Her oratorical style was the opposite of Marijane's. She was straightforward with a delivery that had little variation in tone or volume. Ruth posed a question for the judge: If Aloysius's injuries from resisting arrest required a trip to the hospital why, then, was he not taken to the hospital until after he confessed? "He did not receive any medical treatment at any hospital by any medical personnel until after that videotaped statement," she said.

David O'Connor, the assistant state's attorney, buttoned his jacket and stood up to rebut her argument. He was trim, with thick, short brown hair combed to the side in such a way that it made him look much younger than his years. His posture was straight, and he walked with graceful strides. He looked at the defense table with an expression that seemed to say this story of police beating Aloysius is preposterous. The explanation for Aloysius's injuries was simple: police officers chased down and captured a fleeing killer who had just shot Officer Eric Lee and tried to fight off another officer as they wrestled for Officer Vincent Barner's gun. "It was a struggle over that gun and towards life that ultimately caused Officer Barner to be striking and hitting Aloysius Oliver in that gangway," O'Connor said. "It was at that time that one of the officers heard Officer Barner's yells for help and came running in and tackled him off the gate." Once at the police station, O'Connor said that Aloysius volunteered to give statements to the detectives after being questioned. He was not bullied, coerced and certainly not beaten up, as he now claimed.

As its first witness, the state called Detective Tom Kelly, who took Aloysius's videotaped confession. Kelly spoke with a classic Chicago accent, pronouncing his vowels a little longer than necessary so that the Chicago sounded like Chi-CAAH-go with a nasally tone. He testified in by-the-book cop talk, having done this hundreds of times in his thirty-four years as a police officer. Kelly told the judge that the first time he met with Aloysius was about 11:30 p.m. in an interview room of the police station at Fifty-first Street and Wentworth Avenue. He noticed that Aloysius had three "abrasions" on his face.

After introducing himself and Detective Jim Riley to Aloysius, Kelly said he read Aloysius his Miranda warnings from a preprinted page. Aloysius sat at one end of the table and offered his first response to their questions. He denied the shooting. "At the end of that conversation we took Mr. Oliver to the washroom on the second floor, allowed him to use the bathroom, also allowed him to wash his face," Kelly said. "We then gave him several bandages and told him if he wished to place them on the abrasions, he may do so at that time."

After that interview, Kelly said he went to talk to other witnesses and police officers involved in the case and came back to see Aloysius about 4:45 a.m. He told Aloysius that other witnesses were giving statements, and asked if Aloysius was ready to tell the truth about what happened. Tired, worn and apparently seeing no way out, Aloysius said he was ready to talk. Kelly came back with Assistant State's Attorney Darren O'Brien, and they took the videotaped confession from Aloysius around 7:20 a.m. Kelly told the court that Aloysius was treated well while in custody. He got three bologna sandwiches, Coca-Cola, coffee and some cigarettes.

"Did he ever claim to you at any point in time that he was forced to give a statement?" O'Connor asked.

"No, sir."

"Was any form of psychological or mental coercion ever utilized against the defendant?"

"No, sir."

O'Connor concluded his inquiry. "Did you or your partner, or any other police officer at Area One Violent Crimes ever strike, slap, punch or knock the defendant against the wall?"

"No."

Marijane was getting that look on her face, her mouth in a frown, her eyes locked on O'Connor as he walked back and forth in front of the bench while questioning Kelly. When O'Connor said he was finished with the witness, Marijane pushed back her chair, looked at O'Connor with a scowl and came out roaring, her voice filling the room in an accusatory tone.

"Detective," she said, walking toward Kelly, "you were based at that time out of Area One, correct?"

"Yes, ma'am."

"And there were numerous detectives in the area, correct?"

"Yes."

"And you chose to, in fact, handle the interrogation of Mr. Oliver, correct?"

"I didn't choose to. I was told to."

And this was how she began. She came in fast with the questions, asking the detective how he got to work that night, what time his shift began, whether he went to the scene, did he remember the timelines. She had a way of asking the same question a thousand different ways, asking questions with the kinds of minutiae that could wear down her witnesses, not because they couldn't answer the questions, but because of the incremental and seemingly inconsequential nature. But they weren't inconsequential. She could ask a witness to state his name, age and address and somehow trip him up.

Kelly braced himself, answering politely and calling Marijane "ma'am" when he addressed her. He appeared to be drawing from a reserve of strength to help him tolerate Marijane's forceful and relentless questioning. She asked Kelly about seeing the "abrasions" on Aloysius's face. He said he thought they were not serious enough to require Aloysius to go to the hospital.

"So . . . you saw no reason for Mr. Oliver to be taken to the hospital, correct?"

"That's correct."

"Yet he was taken to the hospital, correct?"

"Yes, ma'am."

Marijane nodded her head, pleased with his answer.

Kelly recalled interviewing Aloysius again around 4:45 a.m. Marijane noted that Aloysius was not wearing pants at this time and was sitting in his underwear. Kelly said he couldn't remember when the pants came off, why they were off, or who took them from Aloysius.

"Now, specifically, questioning a man without any pants, that is an oddity, isn't it, or do you, you know, are pants taken all the time?"

"It would vary from case to case, ma'am."

Despite Aloysius's repeated denials of shooting Officer Lee, Kelly said that he never believed him and continued to question Aloysius to get to the truth.

"And specifically, you were willing to go to any means to get the truth, correct?" Marijane said, loudly and insultingly.

"No."

"Would that—would lying be part of the means to get the truth?"

"I did not lie, and I don't know what you characterize by *means*."

Kelly shifted in his seat as Marijane continued her cross-examination. Marijane hammered Kelly again with detailed questions about the time of Aloysius's arrest, the questioning of her client and whether he was beaten at the police station. Kelly's initial calm demeanor shifted to irritation.

Marijane caught Kelly looking over at the state's attorneys.

"Don't look at them!" Marijane barked.

"I believe I can look wherever I want," Kelly said, annoyed, his face turning red. "What's the question, ma'am?"

Marijane's coarse and hard-charging theatrics in the courtroom prompted police officers in the gallery, as well as the Lee's family, to shudder with disgust. Lee's widow and mother shook their heads as Marijane continued to question Kelly.

Marijane moved in again, asking about the videotaped statement and Aloysius's injuries. "So, the defendant never stated to you during any conversation that any officer punched him in the face and that's how those injuries came—when the officer was trying to take away a gun?"

"He stated he sustained the injuries when he was arrested," Kelly said.

"He didn't say how he sustained those injuries either in the videotape or to you, correct?"

"Correct."

"Did you ever ask him?"

"No."

"That's because you really didn't want to know because that would affect your ability to take a statement, correct?"

"Objection to the form of the questions, judge," O'Connor said.

"Well, let me ask you this," Marijane continued. "Those three small lacerations, you never asked him how he got them, correct?"

"No."

"Why?"

"Because I felt like I knew how he got them."

"Was that at the hands of the Chicago police?"

O'Connor again objected loudly, and the judge said to move on.

Marijane said she was finished. O'Connor was allowed to re-cross-examine Kelly and got right to the point. "Detective, did this defendant at any time during the time you were in his presence, from the time that you first met him until the time that the videotaped statement was taken, did he ever claim that anyone abused him?"

"No, sir."

As the hearing drew to a close, Ruth called up law clerk Joseph Runnion who was working for Marijane and Ruth at the time Aloysius was arrested. He and Ruth visited Aloysius in the jail library on

October 19, 2001, two months after arrest. During the visit, Runnion noticed Aloysius had a scrape on the right temple, a swollen left elbow and swollen fingers on his left hand.

"How would you describe those injuries?" Ruth asked.

"They looked fairly painful. I mean, they looked like they were fairly fresh."

Three hours after the hearing began, Marijane was ready to make the closing argument. She walked directly over to Moran. "Judge, the simple facts are this: what we have here is we have injuries to a defendant. We believe that the State of Illinois law is that unexplained injuries do, in fact, constitute signs of abuse." Why, she asked, was Aloysius sent to the hospital after his interrogation when no one at the police station thought his injuries were serious enough before then? She pointed out Detective Kelly's failure to remember specifics. "What this court constantly heard was a repetition over and over and over again, in fact, of him stating he didn't remember, didn't remember, didn't remember," she said. "This is not a gentleman whose memory can be relied on as to whether or not he gave Miranda warnings."

O'Connor dismissed it all. "When you consider the totality of circumstances, when you consider the tape, when you consider the words that the defendant utilized, when you consider the defendant's explanation as to what occurred there, you can't help but come to the conclusion that it wasn't any form of injury that caused him to give the statement," he said. "And counsel keeps suggesting that his injuries are unexplained. They are not unexplained at all. They were part of an extensive struggle over a gun after the defendant had apparently already shot one police officer."

Judge Moran didn't need to retire to his chambers to ponder his decision. He made it right then and there. He concluded that Aloysius was properly given his Miranda warnings, understood them and knowingly waived his rights. He was treated well in custody by being given food, drink, cigarettes, bathroom breaks and bandages. This was backed up by Aloysius's own words on the videotape on which he said he was treated well and gave his statement voluntarily. Moran concluded that Aloysius's injuries were unrelated to anything that happened at the police station and were received at the time of his arrest.

"The fact that the detective didn't feel that those injuries were sufficient to require a trip to the hospital and some other person, presumably the lockup keeper, thought that they might, is of no significance," the judge said. "Reasonable people can differ."

He paused and looked at the attorneys. "Motion is denied."

When Judge Moran made his pronouncement, Lee's widow sighed. "Thank you, Jesus," she said.

Back in her office after the hearing, Marijane told me she was neither surprised nor deterred by the judge's ruling. The confession alone was not going to make the case. Aloysius's videotaped statement might instead work in her favor. "You've got him on tape saying 'I'm sorry. I didn't mean it.' That confession could be mitigating," Marijane said. "Sometimes a confession can open doors to a defense." Even though they lost the motion, it was still a good day in court. "The motion is like a chess game. It's never a waste of time," Marijane said. "You're talking to the appellate court, the judge, you're setting yourself up for trial. You're trying to do a show to intimidate the witnesses and show them, 'You're my bitch.' " But there was another reason Marijane seemed more buoyant than disappointed. A source who worked in drug court had passed along a potentially explosive tip: Two of the officers who were at the scene when Officer Lee was shot were in trouble with the department. The source had information that officers Corey Flagg and Broderick Jones had been suspended for misconduct, possibly for shaking down drug dealers and consorting with known criminals. If those cops were indeed dirty, the whole case could be turned around. Their credibility as witnesses would be gone, their reasons and motivations for being in that alley behind Carpenter Street would be in question. The defense might have some potentially damaging material if they could confirm this and bring it out into open court. So Marijane and Ruth drafted a motion to subpoena the officers' personnel records and files from the police department's Office of Professional Standards (OPS). These records, if they confirmed their suspicions, would discredit the officers as witnesses to the shooting and could create the kind of doubt that might get Aloysius acquitted. But this also inspired Marijane to float a disturbing theory that Officer Lee could have been gunned down by one of the allegedly dirty cops because Lee knew too much and might have helped bring them down. Lee had a spotless record and excellent reputation. "He was one of the last honest cops in the world," Marijane said. "Perhaps he knew something."

It seemed far-fetched and far-reaching, but creating a defense and creating doubt was what this game was all about. "We're thinking we can build some kind of scenario," Marijane explained. But persuading the judge to order the files opened and placed in the public record was another thing. Rarely were OPS files made public. Cops were protected in ways the public was not from having their files released. "We can't do this without the OPS files going in," Marijane said. "They are sacrosanct. They are never, never allowed in. But this is too important."

Judge Moran got copies of the OPS files so that he could review them first and determine whether they were relevant. The files showed that the department sustained four complaints against Jones and two against Flagg. The complaints stemmed from a shakedown of a drug dealer in which the officers did not turn in drugs they seized from him. Marijane argued that the officers' misconduct would have direct bearing on their credibility as witnesses and that she had the right to use those records in court to impeach them. She also said that self-defense remained a viable option for this case. She wanted the police department to turn over disciplinary records, as well, to see whether these officers were ever charged with other matters, including excessive use of force. The idea was to find out whether the officers, as opposed to Aloysius, were the initial aggressors in this incident. Assistant State's Attorney David O'Connor argued they were not relevant, that the claim to self-defense was ludicrous. Plus, the officers in question were a half block away when the shooting occurred and might not be called as eyewitnesses anyway. Moreover, he argued that Marijane and Ruth were using a strategy that was improper and clearly a tactic to create an appellate or postconviction issue. Moran agreed and refused to allow the documents as evidence. This would not be the last that Moran would hear about these allegedly dirty cops, however. Marijane had a gut feeling that these cops were bad, that something in that group was not right. "How do I know? You can just look at them and tell," Marijane said. "We're a small community here. I don't know every cop in the city, but I do know the ones who handle violent crimes, and you hear about others from clients. You get a gut feeling."

A few days later, Marijane was in her office flipping through a copy of *Equine* magazine, undeterred by the setbacks of the last several motions. She was ordering framed pictures of the famed racehorses Secretariat and Citation. "The horse race is sort of a role model for doing a trial," she explained. "The race is divided into quarters. Citation got faster and faster each quarter. The jockeys had to hear, smell and sense their animals. They're trained to do that. That's what we're going to do."

CHAPTER EIGHT

Everyone's Entitled to One

FINDING AND INSPIRING LAWYERS to represent the poor has been a challenge as old as the legal system itself. While the Sixth Amendment to the U.S. Constitution guarantees the accused the right to counsel in a criminal prosecution, it says nothing about who's going to pay for it if the defendant has no money. Defendants who could not afford representation long depended on the goodwill of lawyers who worked for legal aid organizations or those who offered *pro bono* services. But the number of clients far outweighed those available to represent them. From its earliest days, the U.S. court system drafted lawyers into service to represent the poor. Judges who made these appointments often considered it more of a favor than a fundamental right of the accused. They needed to keep the system moving. It wasn't until 1914 that Los Angeles created the first public defender's office, which offered a range of legal services to the poor. Chicago wouldn't establish its own public defender system for another sixteen years. Until then, criminal suspects without the means to hire a lawyer were lucky to get any legal representation at all.

Chicago lawyers were not especially eager to volunteer for such work, and often found themselves involuntarily recruited, as Lisa J. McIntyre, author of *The Public Defender: The Practice of Law in the Shadows of Repute*, points out in her sociological study of the Cook County public defender system. In the early 1900s, Chicago judges appointed lawyers to represent indigent defendants, though usually without pay. It was, the judges reasoned, part of a lawyer's civic duty. Only lawyers who handled death penalty cases could hope to earn any money, and the pay was usually no more than $250. Had Aloysius Oliver been charged with killing a police officer back then, his chances of getting a decent, experienced attorney would have been slim. Experienced attorneys stayed away from indigent defense work, often complaining about the lengthy time commitments of these low- or no-paying cases. So the jobs went to younger lawyers eager to get experience in the courtroom. Defendants didn't always see this as a favor, and resented their unpracticed lawyers because they felt they were getting second-rate representation. Cases lingered, and suspects languished in jail much longer than necessary awaiting trial or disposition of their cases.

In 1912, the Chicago Bar Association attempted to recruit attorneys to join the Committee of Defense of Indigent Prisoners Accused of Crimes. The few lawyers who volunteered sincerely believed in service for the poor, a cause for which many of their so-called reputable colleagues would not dare take part, discounting such work as unsavory and beneath them. But the need for such defense lawyers became greater in the years that followed. By the 1920s, Chicago had developed its notorious reputation as a crime-infested city, fueled by Prohibition, the city's thirst for booze and vice, and the criminal entrepreneurs who were only too happy to provide them. The city was plagued by bootlegging, gambling, corruption and gangland violence. Organized crime brought bloodshed to the streets. Splashy newspaper coverage added to the terror, and crime control became a hot political issue. The citizens of Chicago demanded justice.

But justice was slow to come. Police and politicians were often in the back pockets of the very mobsters they publicly denounced and vowed to arrest. Many citizens of Chicago viewed their leaders as corrupt, even though these same officials declared major efforts to crack down on crime. In 1921, Kickham Scanlan, chief justice of the Cook County Criminal Court, declared that Chicago "was beyond a doubt one of the most lawless communities in the entire country." Members of the Chicago Bar Association criticized the police for misleading the public about their so-called war on crime. A growing number of lawyers charged that police officials misplaced their fervor to clean up the city by going after masses of poor defendants to create the perception that they were fighting crime. Such criticisms would be repeated in the years and decades to come as other politicians declared their own wars on crime. It was always a numbers game. Tally up lots of arrests, call the press and make it appear as if they were winning the battle against crime. Invariably, these crackdowns occurred in the poorest neighborhoods, with a disproportionate number of minorities going to jail and overcrowding the jails.

As arrest and conviction rates rose, there was a growing public perception that poor defendants could not receive a fair trial. Prosecutors were suspected of convicting innocent people to appease the public, fuel their own political ambitions and advance their careers. Amid this growing atmosphere of distrust, a group of reform-minded lawyers and business leaders formed the Illinois Association for Criminal Justice. In 1929, they published a devastating report called the Illinois Crime Survey, which concluded that the Cook County Court system was an utter failure. The association formed a judicial advisory council, and one of its first recommendations was to create a public defender's office. Early in September 1930, the Judicial Advisory Council announced that it was seeking an attorney to head the office. On September 25, Benjamin C. Bachrach was appointed the first public defender of Cook County. He was fifty-six years old, from the South Side of Chicago and highly regarded among criminal lawyers. His name was well known, for he assisted the renowned defense attorney Clarence Darrow in the Nathan Leopold and Richard Loeb murder trial of 1924.

Bachrach accepted the position, saying he felt it was time to perform a public duty at a financial sacrifice. He set up an office in the Criminal Courts Building and hired five assistant public defenders. Early reports were favorable. Bachrach's lawyers worked hard and disposed of cases efficiently. Even though many of the clients were found guilty or pleaded guilty, they said they were treated fairly by the law. Chicagoans hoped that the public defender would not coddle criminals or provide undue sympathy. Rather, they wanted these lawyers honestly to provide what the accused deserved—a proper defense. If clients were guilty, their lawyers would advise them to plead out, thus avoiding unnecessary trials.

Four years after the inception of the public defender's office,

Philip J. Finnegan, chief justice of the criminal court of Cook County, wrote a favorable assessment of the new system, describing an efficient operation run by lawyers who equaled any private lawyer in experience and skill. Finnegan noted a remarkable change in the administration of justice in the courts. Northwestern University Law professor Newman F. Baker praised the office in an editorial in the *Journal of Criminal Law and Criminology*. Baker wrote that the city was blessed to have both a spirited prosecutor and a public-spirited defender. "In the past, the administration of criminal justice was too much a sporting contest," he wrote. "The prosecutor too often forgot he was not a persecutor—that he should not attempt to convict the innocent. The defendant's attorney went too far in the opposite direction. He forgot that as an officer of the court his duty was to see that justice was done—not to win cases for persons whom he knew to be guilty."

Based on the records at the courthouse, the public defender was making a demonstrable difference in moving cases through the system by decreasing the number of trials and working out guilty pleas. But they were not just adept at disposing cases. They were winning them, too. In 1934, public defenders won not-guilty verdicts in 251 out of 635 jury trials. Chief Justice Finnegan estimated the public defenders saved the county about $400,000 in court costs. Finnegan said that public defenders deserved their due, even though he knew it would be a hard sell. "The public generally has never been much excited about the misfortunes of the poor if they become entangled with criminal law. Whether or not they secured a fair trial, were convicted or found innocent, was a matter of supreme indifference."

Such indifference made government intervention all the more important in guaranteeing representation for the poor, yet it wasn't until 1964 that the *Gideon v. Wainwright* decision firmly established the right to counsel for those who could not afford it. The U.S. Supreme Court unanimously concluded that states have a constitutional obligation under the Sixth and Fourteenth amendments to provide representation to indigent defendants in felony cases. Thus, public defenders were not just on hand to help keep the system moving, they were the right of the defendant.

These were noble ideas. Yet public defenders still were expected to help make the system efficient, and some of their clients believed that this efficiency was created at their expense. Defendants felt, rightly or wrongly, that their cases were being hustled through, that their public defenders gave up their cases without a struggle to please the judges and clear the dockets. Critics said the job of the public defender was not to defend, but to sort through their defendants, categorize them according to the nature of their charges and help the court dispose of the cases in a businesslike manner as quickly as possible. Public defenders were and still are offended by the idea that they were merely functionaries of the court system.

Cook County Public Defender Gerald Getty, who presided over the office from 1954 to 1972, often found himself having to defend his position as the poor man's lawyer. Getty's most famous case was the defense of Richard Speck, one of the country's most notorious mass murderers who, in 1967, killed eight nursing students in Chicago. The murders tested Getty's resolve amid mounting public pressure and criticism. He put on a vigorous defense without apology and received dozens of angry letters from the public. "In the name of God, what are you trying to do?" "How can you sleep nights?" One letter writer called Getty "the worse [sic] person that ever walked."

Getty explained how he was able to sleep nights in his autobiography *Public Defender.* "I thought that by defending Speck, I was helping make democracy work. Before the trial was over, a lot of other people thought so, too." Getty realized that the court system would be made a mockery if he had not put forth an honest and earnest effort to defend Speck. Though Speck was found guilty, Getty said he felt he proved something important. He proved that despite the heinous nature of the crime and the public call for his lynching, Speck could still receive a fair trial. "We tried this case to the best of our ability," Getty said afterward. "I feel we tried it in the best traditions of the legal system." What Getty said he proved was that the system could be fair and honest, that even though he was technically a "loser" in court, he made the prosecution prove its case. By offering Speck a first-rate defense, as was his obligation, Getty also helped reinforce his guilt. There was no reasonable doubt. Getty was satisfied for having done his job and the prosecution and the public was satisfied that a serial killer was convicted. It helped secure the legitimacy of the court in the eyes of the public. "We often do not take the time to remember that a poor man should have the same chance of maintaining his life and liberty as his rich counterpart," Getty wrote.

And so it was in Cook County, where more than half of all criminal cases were represented by the public defender. When Getty was in office, up to 70 percent of the public defender's caseload came from the city's poor, black neighborhoods on the South and West sides. Not one for political correctness, a notion that had not yet developed, Getty wrote, "The Italians, Irish, Puerto Ricans, Polish and other ethnic groups haunt the office in descending order." The Chinese, he added, rarely got into trouble, and if they did, they were more likely to pay for their own lawyers. His clients fell into what he called the most vulnerable group—men between eighteen and twenty-six years old. Getty represented several thousand clients during his career, though only about 30 percent ever went to trial, and the other 70 percent pled guilty, which was fairly typical. He took 1,100 defendants to bench trials and 412 to jury trials, and estimated he won about 65 percent of those cases. As noble as Getty's self-portrait was in his memoir, he was forced to leave the office under an ugly cloud of suspicion, scandal and allegations about his office and personal life. It all came crashing down in 1972.

In February of that year, Getty, in an apparent attempt at saving himself a great embarrassment, announced to the press and public that he was the victim of an extortion plot. He said a woman who headed the public defender's juvenile division, along with a former investigator who had been fired by Getty, teamed up to blackmail him for $50,000. Both were arrested in the alleged plot. Getty was vague about exactly what they threatened to expose, leaving the press to speculate and dig deeper. Later, it was revealed that the woman, Carolyn Jaffe, planned to say that she had been having sex with Getty at the juvenile courts building. At the same time Getty made his revelation, Chief Judge John Boyle announced that he decided to take over the administration of Getty's office after uncovering serious irregularities in the office during a secret investigation. The judge charged that the Public Defender's Office was rife with financial mismanagement, unrestrained spending, improper influence and nepotism involving Getty's own relatives. Getty's daughter, for example, was hired as a secretary at a higher rate of pay than her colleagues, according to Boyle. Getty was forced to defend himself and said there was nothing improper in hiring relatives who were competent at their jobs and earning their pay. He was hardly a profligate spender. Instead, he was forced to run an office that was underfunded, not overbudgeted. While critical of Getty's administration, Boyle never said that the lawyers in the office were incompetent or not doing their jobs. The judge's charges did not seem compelling in a city where hiring friends and relatives was a longtime tradition. Still, with the sex scandal promising to escalate with journalists poking around for more dirt, Getty decided to resign. James Doherty, an assistant public defender and friend of Getty's, was appointed to take over the office. He inherited a firestorm.

Fueled by the allegations and revelations during Getty's administration, watchdog groups began to hold the office under even greater scrutiny after Doherty took over. In 1975, the Chicago Bar Association found that the office "fell far short of community needs for adequate representation of the poor." The problem was inexperienced lawyers, lack of resources, investigators and secretarial staff. Nothing came of that report, and Doherty continued to run the office for another twelve years without interference. But in 1987, a report from the Better Government Association (BGA) offered a much more stinging assessment of the public defender based on anonymous interviews with assistant public defenders, judges and other employees in the court system. The report called the office a bastion of favoritism for hiring in which judges appointed or helped friends get in, saying they "have brought the seamiest aspects of Chicago politics into the criminal justice system in Cook County." The BGA went on to describe the public defender's office as a patronage system that controlled hirings, firings and promotions based on clout, family relationships and recommendations by powerful lawyers and politicians. "Taxpayers don't get the best lawyers available for the money," the report said. Lawyers often got their jobs through the "Committee on Help," a group of powerful and politically connected judges and lawyers. When someone applied for a government job, the person doing the hiring wanted to know who sent you, a notion immortalized in the title of the book, *We Don't Want Nobody Nobody Sent* by political science professor and Chicago historian Milton Rakove.

Further, the report said that the office used phony statistics, exaggerating the number of cases it handled, and had people on the payroll who never showed up. The lawyers complained that raises and promotions were arbitrary and they seemed to be rewarded not for their skills, but for their willingness not to make waves. Worse, some judges viewed the public defenders assigned to their courtrooms as their own employees, as if they could order the lawyers around. Many public defenders, the report contended, feared standing up to the judges for fear of losing their jobs. Public defenders who participated in the study had a list of complaints about their ability to do their jobs effectively. They were given little time to prepare cases and felt as if they were going through an endless mill. They had no training on the job and were initiated through baptism by fire. They couldn't even get basic supplies like pens, staplers or scissors. "You have to know someone just to get a legal pad," said one. The legal library was woeful, and the investigators were ill trained and poor at their jobs.

The report made the Cook County Public Defender's Office seem like an out-of-control disaster. Morale there was already low when less than a year later another devastating report came out by the Chicago Council of Lawyers. It found that lawyers had little motivation to provide effective counsel. Because of a lack of leadership in the office, lawyers had few role models to emulate. The lingering effect of political hiring and favoritism made it worse. The best lawyers were not being recruited or hired. "Decades of political hiring and administrative neglect have substantially impaired the Office's ability to provide effective representation," the report declared.

James Doherty, clearly in over his head with years of accumulated problems in the office to contend with, finally stepped down as chief public defender. Rather than resign, however, he was able to stay with the office in a lesser administrative job. A lawyer named Paul Biebel was named acting chief to preside over an office that had grown to more than four hundred lawyers with a budget of $21 million. (Biebel would later become chief judge of the criminal courts.) During his stint as interim public defender, Biebel was credited with initiating sweeping changes in the office, successfully lobbying the Cook County Board to increase the public defender's budget to bring in seventy new lawyers over a two-year period. He increased diversity in the office with more women and blacks and initiated a nationwide minority recruiting program. He brought in more training and computers and expanded the law library. The county eventually hired a permanent replacement, Randolph Stone, a former public defender in Washington, DC.

Doherty continued working until he retired, but he was deeply hurt by the criticisms for which he felt he did not bear responsibility. "That was all a bad rap," Marijane Placek said to me in Doherty's defense. "Doherty was truly a tragic figure. He became the fall guy. He was the accidental public defender. He was not an administrator, he was a lawyer. The reports and the criticisms broke his heart."

It broke his heart because Doherty truly embodied the spirit of the public defender. He was an idealist who, despite more than thirty years in the system, remained committed to his youthful visions when many of his fellow lawyers succumbed to the cynicism, frustration and burnout that sent public defenders packing to work at private law firms or change careers altogether. Doherty advocated change within the system, championing reforms that led to police being compelled to turn over evidence favorable to the defense, even if the defense was unaware of it or didn't ask. As a young lawyer he wrote a poem that is passed around to this day called "Defender's Credo," which reads, in part:

With every fibre of my being I will fight for my clients . . .
I will seek acclaim and approval only from my own conscience

And upon my death if there are a few lonely people who have benefited,
My efforts will not have been in vain.

Before leaving his post, Doherty made one important change that
would leave his mark on the public defender's office. He created the
Murder Task Force. His suggestion to form this new, elite team of
lawyers came in response to criticism from the American Bar Association and other groups who denounced the office's practice of shuf-
fling clients from lawyer to lawyer in a fragmented fashion, which
was known as the horizontal defense. It meant that defendants
would have different lawyers from bond court to trial. Most public
defenders were assigned to specific courtrooms and took all manner
of cases, sometimes juggling more than one hundred clients at a
time. The system encouraged plea bargaining and discouraged
many lawyers from investing much time in a case because it was
likely to be reassigned. Clients felt that their public defenders were
just pushing them through the system with little regard for the outcome. Murder cases were too serious to be handled in such a manner. Under Doherty's plan, the new task force would match each
murder client with a lawyer to shepherd him throughout the
process. This would free lawyers from the crushing caseloads that
usually left insufficient time to investigate them more thoroughly.
Now they could mount a more sophisticated defense and work more
closely with clients, giving the lawyers the opportunity to visit them
in the jail and get out on the streets to investigate their cases.

In 1974, Doherty approached a young public defender named
William Murphy and asked whether he was interested in heading up
the task force. Murphy had been a public defender just a few years
but already had developed a reputation for winning tough cases. He
found his home in criminal court after a brief career as a corporate
lawyer, which had bored him so badly he considered leaving law altogether. Murphy's salary dropped from $18,000 a year to $6,700
when he became a public defender. He didn't care. He was single,
without responsibility to anyone but himself, and was hungry to do
something exciting. He loved being in the courtroom arguing cases
and was drawn to Doherty, a fatherly figure who became a mentor

and confidant. Murphy was in awe of Doherty, who stood six feet tall, weighed about 240 pounds and had a voice that carried for blocks. "He was my hero," Murphy recalled during an interview. "And he was truly a great criminal defense lawyer."

When Doherty proposed the idea of forming a task force, Murphy was not enthusiastic, but he listened because he respected his boss. Murphy thought the plan would fail, just another layer of bureaucracy that would be difficult to manage and would take away his time from the courtroom. But Murphy decided to give it a try, telling Doherty he would do it as long as he could take charge in shaping the new unit and handpick its members. Murphy wanted to recruit strong lawyers with a competitive spirit rather than the most experienced ones. It was about personality as much as legal prowess. He wanted lawyers who could go for the kill, who wouldn't get pushed around and wouldn't become sycophants to the judges. "Let's do it and see how it goes," Murphy told Doherty. He scouted lawyers by watching them in court and during basketball games after work with their colleagues. He looked for aggressiveness and stamina.

Murphy assembled a team of seven lawyers that would forever change the way public defenders in Cook County handled murder cases. The initial group was mostly white males, Irish or Jewish, and under thirty-three years old. They had shaggy hair, mop tops and beards, and looked as if they'd be more at home at a peace rally than inside a courtroom. There was one woman. After distributing the caseloads, each lawyer ended up handling about thirty to thirty-five cases at a time. One of the first recruits was Bob Queeney, a relatively new lawyer whose first job as a public defender was visiting the jail to interview clients who never saw their lawyers until court calls. "My job was just to show them that we were on it, that someone in the office cared about their case," Queeney told me. In many ways, Queeney embodied the stereotype of liberal public defender back then. He came of age in the '60s, and was a self-described advocate of social justice who was inspired by the story of Sacco and Vanzetti, the Italian anarchists whose controversial murder trial in 1921 became a cautionary tale about the mixture of politics and crime. When Murphy asked whether he was interested in joining the task force, Queeney thought it would be a great chance to make some waves. "The public defender's office, for a long time, received a lot of bad publicity and ill will," Queeney said. "Part of it was that some judges would make your life miserable. It was just a tough fucking business. You had too many cases and it was real hard to win cases. Judges bullied public defenders and treated them with contempt. Most were quite openly hostile to you if you went to trial or defended vigorously. They would blame you and punish your client."

Another recruit was Todd Musburger, a public defender who started out in the juvenile division, graduated to "guns, cars and hookers," and then sex crimes. Like many of his brethren in the task force, Musburger became a public defender because he wanted to help the downtrodden. "Assisting people who were at the lower end of the strata struck a chord with me," explained Musburger, who had taught public school and worked as a juvenile probation officer before becoming a public defender. Stuart Nudelman, a Jewish kid who came from a family of "Roosevelt-era liberals," was also a perfect fit for the group. "We were really taught to fight for the underdogs when I was growing up," Nudelman told me. "I wanted to give something back, and I thought being on the task force was the ultimate job in the public defender's office."

Richard Kling, recruited after the task force was formed, may have been the most liberal and public spirited of them all, given his background. His father was a member of the Communist Party who was investigated by the House Committee on Un-American Activities and went underground for five years. Kling marched for civil rights and participated in protests during the 1968 Democratic National Convention in Chicago. He joined the public defender's office in 1971. Murphy knew right away that Kling would be a great fit for the group. "It was really a team that was fighting together for the downtrodden, the underdogs, for justice and for truth," Kling recalled.

Fueled by their idealism and hungry to make names for themselves, the lawyers in the new task force shot out of the gates and started winning cases. Two years after the task force was formed, Murphy reported that it was winning as much as 75 percent of its cases. Winning didn't necessarily equate with an acquittal, but was measured in defendants either being acquitted or being convicted of a lesser charge. As the task force started to get more public, more lawyers wanted to get on and demanded they be allowed to join. "A lot of people got jealous in the public defender's office," Murphy said.

Queeney felt charged up like never before, as if he had a new kind of permission to dig into cases even harder. "I never left any stone unturned. I just took it real fucking seriously," he said. "There was this idea that we were identified as being special. And we would believe it."

"These guys were the best in the building," Musburger recalled, clearly proud of his association with them. "I felt a real high sense of duty, both to the group I was with and to my clients. We had a special distinction and that ruffled some feathers, even within the public defender's office."

"Judges weren't used to that kind of fight," Kling said. "We were obstructionists. We tried to save people's lives. They didn't like the fact that we filed more motions and more creative motions and novel motions and theoretical motions. They didn't like it."

One of the few women to work on the task force during those early years was Andrea Lyon, who eventually was promoted to unit supervisor. "It was definitely a boys' club back then," said Lyon, who went on to become a law professor and head of DePaul University Law School's Capital Resource Center, which assists poor defendants. "I didn't have anyone to emulate. On my third or fourth day there, someone left autopsy photos of a naked woman on my desk. I just took them out to the secretary and said I think someone might have left these here by mistake." Lyon was a self-admitted do-gooder who often developed close relationships with clients. "I used to get into disputes with some of the lawyers in the task force who felt I was too touchy-feely. But I felt the job should be a reasonable mix of ego and idealism."

That idealism carried through in the courtroom. Many judges

were not used to seeing such aggressive public defenders and expected, more often than not, to get plea agreements rather than demands for trials. Even state attorneys were used to the idea of public defenders eager to make deals, and everyone getting along and moving on. One judge called the task force lawyers "cocky and aggressive" in an article in the *Chicago Reader*. A prosecutor was less charitable, concluding the task force members cared only about winning, having developed a callousness to crime and violence that ran deep. "I call them the Vulture Squad. While the body is fresh, they hover over it," Michael Ficaro said at the time. "They have a tendency to let the good cases come through, selecting the cases they think are weakest and trying to get them to trial."

During the nascent years of the task force, a petite blond graduate student from the University of Illinois walked into the office to ask for help on her master's thesis. She was going to study the task force to analyze its new methods of representation and effectiveness. Her name was Beth Lynch. She met William Murphy to ask for his cooperation in her research. "I immediately fell in love with him," she recalled. "And eventually I married him." She completed her research project, which found the new system to be highly effective. The fifteen murder defendants she interviewed felt they were treated fairly and had confidence in their lawyers. According to her report, 73 percent of the clients said that if they were able to hire their own lawyer, they would hire the public defender currently handling their case.

While supervising the task force, Murphy won the biggest victory of his career and sent a strong message that his unit meant business. His client was Denise Watson, a twenty-three-year-old nurse's aide who was charged with twenty-three counts of murder and arson in 1976. Watson was accused of setting fire at the Wincrest Nursing Home, sparking what authorities said was the deadliest fire in the city in decades. The blaze began in a portable wardrobe, and smoke rushed down a corridor to a chapel inside the home where mass was being held. Because many of the residents were frail, infirm and in wheelchairs, they could not easily escape, and staff could not escort everyone out quickly enough. Some were trapped in the chapel and died of shock and smoke inhalation. Watson escaped the burning building and was hospitalized for smoke inhalation for three days. After she was released from the hospital, police picked her up for questioning and began to interrogate her. Detectives believed Watson set the fire as an act of revenge after a supervisor told her she was going to be fired. While at the police station, Watson broke down and confessed, saying she had a history of fires that seemed to follow her around. At first, Murphy thought he surely had a losing case. "I went down to the jail with my law clerk," Murphy recalled, "and I said, 'Why'd you do this?' And she started telling me from the very beginning why she gave the confession, and I pulled out a tape recorder. She told me everything. They tricked her into confessing."

The prosecutor on the case was William Kunkle, one of the top attorneys in the office who later would go on to prosecute serial killer John Wayne Gacy. Murphy's strategy at trial was to discredit Watson's confession. He argued that Watson was not in her right mind. She was ill, fatigued, frightened and would have confessed to anything to get out of the police station. Murphy decided to have Watson testify in her own defense, confident that this smart woman would make a favorable impression on the jury. It worked. Watson was acquitted on all charges.

News of cases like that got around. Lawyers from around the country called to apply to the task force, as well as seek advice to learn more about this special unit. In a journal Murphy kept on and off during his time as a public defender, he wrote, "We're the best, second to none . . . every judge and prosecutor knows we won't be pushed around." But they would soon by pushed to their limits. In 1977, Illinois reinstated the death penalty, and the stakes got higher. (The U.S. Supreme Court in 1972 had voided all state death penalty laws, declaring them racially discriminatory and haphazardly applied.) The responsibility of having a client's life in their hands and the emotional strength it took to work on such cases was unprecedented. Task Force lawyer Richard Kling recalled how he and his colleagues reacted to the news. "It changed the whole mentality of the office," Kling told me. "We realized they were trying to kill our clients. It makes all the difference when you're sitting in the courtroom and you hear somebody say this person should be killed. And I had the misfortune of having the first death penalty case after it was reinstated."

Kling was assigned to represent Lonnie Yates, an ex-navy man charged with killing Veronica Lee, a seventeen-year-old honor student and church choir member who was stabbed thirteen times with scissors and hit on the head with an iron after she came home and interrupted a burglary. Yates allegedly stole seventeen dollars and change from the burglary. He was found guilty, and Kling had to find a way to save his life. He was working in uncharted territory without guidance because no one in the office had done a death penalty case before. He carefully chose a jury he believed could understand the frailties of the human mind. He tried to humanize his client and have Yates's family testify on his behalf. He pleaded with the jury, telling them killing was wrong, "no matter who the killer." "It was a horrible, horrible case," Kling said. "I still remember the address of the crime: 3146 West Franklin. This is not something I talk about, and it's not something I regularly think about, but I can remember it clearly as if it were 1979." The jury recommended death, and Judge Sylvester Close agreed, offering these chilling words to Yates: "An electric current will be sent through your body until you are determined to be dead." Kling responded: "The act Yates committed is no more brutal and calculated than what you have just done."

To Kling's relief, Yates was never executed. His life was spared after the Illinois Supreme Court sent back his case due to improper arguments by the prosecutor. He was resentenced to one thousand years. But many more cases would come back to haunt prosecutors as Illinois's death row began to fill up and evidence emerged that some of the condemned should not have been there at all.

CHAPTER NINE

Death Takes a Brief Holiday

ALOYSIUS OLIVER FACED THE PROSPECT of the death penalty at a time when the Illinois criminal justice system was the shame of the nation. The state's administration of the death penalty was under attack as never before following an extraordinary period during which thirteen men were freed from death row after new evidence showed they were wrongly convicted, some of them coming within days of execution. Governor George Ryan, a Republican and longtime supporter of capital punishment, found the system so frighteningly flawed that he declared a moratorium on all executions and urged the legislature to enact a series of reforms. No one would be put to death in Illinois, the governor insisted, until he could be morally certain that no innocent person was in danger of being wrongly executed because of shortcomings in the system. Ryan set up the Governor's Commission on Capital Punishment in January 2000 to make recommendations for revamping the system.

As important as these proposed reforms were, the governor's critics questioned his motives. He made these unprecedented recommendations while he was under investigation on corruption charges, and many believed he was desperate to save his legacy should his reputation become tainted by criminal charges. His popularity in his home state plummeted at the same time he was earning international praise for his work as a death penalty reformer. The scandal notwithstanding, two years later the governor's commission came up with eighty-five recommendations to overhaul—not abolish—capital punishment, establishing rules for police interrogation procedures, pretrial investigations, DNA evidence collection, jury instructions, judges' training, lawyer qualifications, disclosure of evidence, use of depositions and sentencing protocol. State lawmakers eventually passed a series of measures intended to serve as a system of checks and balances, including changes establishing who is eligible for death, and requiring the taping of all interrogations and confessions. The new rules followed many of the commission's recommendations. By the time the reforms were passed, another four men were exonerated because of wrongful convictions, bringing the total to seventeen since 1987.

After the reforms were passed, many public defenders as well as longtime opponents of capital punishment complained that it still was not enough. To their thinking, eliminating the death penalty would have been the best and most humane course of action. "When you release all these people from death row, I mean, what the fuck? Something is wrong," Shelton Green said to me when I asked about his reaction to the reforms. "People thought everything would be better with the reforms, that it was fixed. It ain't." Other task force attorneys were equally dismissive. "The death penalty is inherently corrupt," Bob Strunck complained when I asked his opinion. "Don't reform it. Abolish it. It's like trying to put liposuction on a pig. They've got to put the death penalty out."

But Marijane Placek, in spite of spending a career trying to save clients from death, was not as passionate about eliminating it as some of her colleagues. "When the death penalty is for *my* client, it's not appropriate. But I still believe there's a necessity for the death penalty," she told me. "Not for deterrence. That's a joke. It doesn't stop people from killing." The death penalty, she reasoned, was appropriate for a handful of violent, incorrigible prisoners who continued to kill while in prison. Death would be appropriate, for example, in the case of Henry Brisbon, known as the I-57 killer, who was convicted of murdering three people off the Interstate-57 south of Chicago in 1973. "He stuck a shotgun up one woman's vagina and blasted," Marijane said. Brisbon was sentenced to one thousand to three thousand years in prison, believed to be the longest term ever imposed in Illinois. (There was no death penalty at the time.) But in October 1978, eleven months after his sentencing, Brisbon used a homemade knife to subdue a guard and stab another prisoner to death. When Brisbon was tried for the crime in 1982, Illinois had restored capital punishment, and he was sentenced to death. "There are certain people, if you're talking about true punishment, who have to be put down," Marijane said. "Jail will just enable people like him to be kings."

As part of the reforms, Marijane was appointed by the Illinois Supreme Court to sit on the Capital Litigation Trial Bar Committee, which was created to qualify lawyers for handling death penalty cases. The committee would certify both prosecutors and defense attorneys. To qualify as a lead attorney, the lawyer must have at least five years of criminal litigation experience, have tried at least eight felony cases, including two murder trials, and have at least twelve hours of specialized training for death penalty cases. The court also said that lawyers must be in good standing with the Illinois Bar Association and be familiar with the ethics, practice procedures and rules of the trial and appellate courts. Marijane was honored to be chosen for the committee but unimpressed by its impact or that of any other reform measure. "It's a sham," she said. "The reforms are all just cosmetic. I think Ryan has his heart in the right place, and I give him a lot of credit. But it's meaningless." Marijane's colleague, Bob Strunck was equally skeptical. "This whole idea of qualifying lawyers is farcical. Anyone knows they can screw up a capital case," he said. "When I first started this job, I thought the death penalty was great. My thought process was that there was good and evil, right and wrong. It really changed for me when I started seeing all this shit." Marijane was insulted by the suggestion that ineffective defense lawyers were responsible for many of the wrongful convictions. "Some of these reforms give the public the idea that there are all these incompetent attorneys out there," she said. "That's just not true. The reforms don't do enough and can't about the problems— the lying, the prosecutorial misconduct, the problems with DNA. Are many people being sentenced to death because their lawyer fell asleep in the courtroom? No. There was lying, and it wasn't on the defense part. It was about prosecutorial misconduct."

Prosecutorial misconduct was responsible for some, but not all, of the wrongful convictions. In 1999, the *Chicago Tribune* began publishing a series of in-depth investigations that helped spur Ryan's re-

forms to the Illinois capital punishment system. The paper's first series was called "Trial and Error: How Prosecutors Sacrifice Justice
to Win." Reporters found at least 381 instances nationwide in which
homicide convictions were thrown out because prosecutors con-
cealed evidence favorable to the defense or knowingly presented
false evidence. Illinois had 46 convictions reversed. Later that year,
the *Tribune* followed up with "The Failure of the Death Penalty in
Illinois." It examined 285 death cases since capital punishment was
reinstated in 1977 and found a system "riddled with faulty evidence,
unscrupulous trial tactics and legal incompetence." The paper cited
cases in which defendants were represented by disbarred or suspended attorneys or were convicted with the help of jailhouse infor-
mants, out-of-date crime lab techniques, racially imbalanced juries
and questionable prosecutorial tactics. In Illinois alone, twenty-six
death row inmates received a new trial or resentencing because of
inept attorneys. While defense attorneys shared part of the blame
for losing winnable cases, not one lawyer in the Cook County Murder Task Force had a death row case sent back because of incompetence or misconduct. Most of the problems occurred in rural parts of
the state where there were no public defenders and courts appointed
relatively inexperienced lawyers. In overturning one case, an Illinois
Supreme Court justice wrote the defense attorney provided "legal
assistance that would border on the comical if only it were make-
believe." The *Tribune* continued its crusade with another series in
2001 called "Cops and Confessions." The paper found at least 247
murder cases in Cook County since 1991 in which police obtained
incriminating statements that were later thrown out or failed to lead
to a conviction. It described how cops cleared cases by breaking
down suspects, including children and the mentally challenged, by
persuading them to make dubious confessions. Defendants often alleged mistreatment, but their cases were difficult to prove without
evidence other than their word against the police.

No other single person did more to discredit police interrogation
tactics in the last twenty years than a man named Jon Burge. Mention
the name around the courthouse, and virtually everyone would nod
knowingly. If ever there were a contemporary symbol of police brutal-

ity, it would be Burge. He was in command of a detective unit in Area Two on the city's South Side. The unit was suspected of torturing confessions from more than sixty suspects, including at least ten who were convicted and sent to death row, during the 1980s. These suspects told stories about being beaten, burned and subjected to electric shocks, having alligator clips attached to their ears, noses, mouths and penises. Some said plastic bags or typewriter covers were put over their heads to nearly suffocate them. One man said detectives shocked him, squeezed his scrotum and put an airtight bag over his head until he confessed. Afraid of more pain, many suspects acquiesced and admitted to crimes they did not commit. Burge was fired from the Chicago Police Department in 1993 for his role in the torture ten years earlier of a man accused of murdering two police officers. The suspect, Andrew Wilson, complained that he was beaten, kicked, suffocated, burned, and given electric shock with two different devices to his genitals, ears, nose, and fingers. Still, he was convicted and sentenced to death. Though his conviction was overturned, he was retried and sentenced to life in prison. There was never doubt over his guilt, just the methods police used to establish it.

In one chilling incident, a murder suspect named Aaron Patterson, who was arrested on suspicion of stabbing a couple to death, scrawled a desperate message in the police interrogation room after he confessed. Using the end of a bent paper clip, he etched a note into a metal bench that said he lied about the confession. "Police threaten me with violence. Slapped and suffocated me with plastic. No lawyer or dad. No phone. Signed false statement to murders." Patterson was convicted and sentenced to death, though prosecutors presented no physical evidence or eyewitnesses tying him to the killings. A key prosecution witness later recanted, claiming she was threatened by police and prosecutors and forced to implicate Patterson. Patterson was fully exonerated and released from prison. He became a community activist, though later he would be charged and convicted of drugs and weapons violations.

Another man, Madison Hobley, confessed to setting a fire that killed seven people, including his wife and infant son, and spent thirteen years on death row. Andrea Lyon, the former Murder Task

Force chief, represented him in a civil suit again the city of Chicago. The suit accused detectives under Burge's command of torturing Hobley and planting evidence, and claimed it was part of an ongoing conspiracy in the department. "It's the end-justifies-the-means problem. With this case, you can see how it happens," Lyon told me. The suit, which named six detectives, offered a window into the alleged tactics at Burge's station, though he was not specifically accused of anything. Six detectives were named. The detectives were accused of beating Hobley and placing a plastic bag over his head to cut off his air supply and forcing him to confess. Hobley claimed in the suit that detectives made up the confession and planted a gas can at the scene and lied at his trial. Hobley's case, along with the others, was indicative of large-scale problems. "Everyone knew what Area Two was doing back then," Lyon said. "I mean, a guy comes to court with twenty-seven stitches. We all knew what was going on. We really tried hard to show it to the juries. But it was your clients' word against the cops'."

Stories like those from Area Two demonstrated that cops sometimes crossed the line, and instilled a sense of rage in Task Force chief Shelton Green that drove him even harder to continue his work as a public defender. "What gets me is that some police and prosecutors lie and cheat and some of the judges know it and don't do anything about it," Shelton said. "That really pisses me off." To illustrate his point, Shelton showed me an article he kept in his office from the *University of Pittsburgh Law Review* called "The Blue Wall of Silence as Evidence of Bias and Motive to Lie: A New Approach to Police Perjury." The article, published in 1998, cited instances of police lying to frame suspects, lying about how they got evidence and lying to protect each other, often thinking they were doing the right thing. Shelton was especially angered by the prosecutorial hesitance to address police perjury. "I'm not saying they're all bad," Shelton said. "Most police officers are good people, and they come to believe that the defendant is guilty."

Marijane had the same attitude. She knew some cops crossed the line, but was careful not to indict them all. "I don't dislike cops. I think like us, they see too much bad stuff," she explained. "In doing their job, they might overreach. That's not an excuse. That's just one of the reasons I understand how things happen. A lot of the times, they're pushed into situations that are very ugly. It's not like *Law & Order* where you walk into a crime scene and an hour later it's solved. Real life is topsy-turvy." Marijane and Ruth McBeth were about to learn just how true that was.

Every year on December 18, the anniversary of her father's death, Marijane drove out to the Queen of Heaven cemetery in the far west suburb of Hillside to visit his grave. It was a ritual she never missed. She always went alone and would spend an hour or so talking to her dad about her life. She was standing there in the winter of 2002, sixteen months after Aloysius Oliver was arrested, when the moment was interrupted by the ring of her cell phone. Marijane never liked cell phones and had only recently, and reluctantly, bought one. Ruth McBeth was on the other end, and she sounded out of breath. "You're not going to believe this," Ruth said. "Omar is getting out." Ruth hurriedly explained that in forty-five minutes, Cook County State's Attorney Richard Devine was going to hold a press conference to announce Omar Aguirre, one of Marijane and Ruth's former clients, was being released from prison. Devine was about to admit publicly that Aguirre had been wrongly convicted of murder three years earlier.

Marijane and Ruth had no idea this was coming, or that anyone was even looking into the case. Ruth had received the call from Devine's office just minutes earlier. That left little time for the lawyers to get to the press conference or offer the media their take on the story. Without their input, Marijane complained, the state would put its own spin on events and try to diminish its responsibility. Marijane was furious that Devine planned to announce this wrongful conviction without the courtesy of giving the defense team more advance notice. There was no way she could get downtown for a press conference in forty-five minutes. She knew from the beginning that Aguirre never should have been convicted and had felt badly that she was unable to win for him. She wanted to be on hand to savor Devine's mea culpa.

Aguirre was a Mexican immigrant who could speak very little English. In 1997, police picked him up and charged him with torturing and murdering a fifty-six-year-old furniture dealer named Sindulfo Miranda. Miranda's charred body was found inside his burned-out Mercedes on the city's West Side. Three other men were charged with the crime. The police version was that the men abducted Miranda at a bar, bound him with duct tape and placed him in Aguirre's van while two others drove Miranda's car to an isolated stretch of street. They forced Miranda back in his car and set it ablaze, possibly while he was still alive. A dubious police informant implicated Aguirre, claiming he had heard Aguirre and the others plot the murder and saw the men with Miranda just before he was killed. Detectives said that Aguirre confessed after a lengthy interrogation and identified one other accomplice. The officer who interrogated Aguirre in Spanish also acted as his interpreter and wrote the report. After meeting with Marijane and Ruth, Aguirre said through an interpreter that he never confessed. He couldn't even read the officer's English translation of his confession, which was admitted as evidence in court.

"The case stunk," Marijane later told me. "I thought all along that it just didn't smell right." Her theory was that the murder victim was dealing drugs and was killed by rivals or unhappy business partners. Why would someone drive a late-model, nearly immaculate Mercedes to a hole-in-the-wall bar in an awful neighborhood? "But I couldn't bring in any evidence that the guy was a drug dealer," Marijane explained. "If it was a robbery, why would they burn up the car like that? A brand-new Mercedes?"

Investigator Rich English served as translator for Marijane and Ruth as they prepared for trial. He met with Aguirre several times to try to learn what really happened. Aguirre told English he was working on the day of the murder as a temporary laborer, but had given a different name to his employer because he was an illegal immigrant. That would make his alibi difficult to prove. The first trial ended in a hung jury. The second time around, a jury found Aguirre guilty, and the judge sentenced him to fifty-five years in prison. The other man he implicated, Edar Duarte Santos, pleaded guilty and got just twelve years. "It broke my heart when he was convicted," Marijane said. "I wish there was something I could have done." After Aguirre's conviction, Marijane said the state offered him a tempting deal to reduce his sentence and allow him to go back to Mexico. All he had to do was cooperate and testify against the others. Marijane and Ruth asked Aguirre if he wanted to talk, if he had anything to offer. Aguirre told Marijane, "I don't know anything. I didn't do it, so how would I be able to say anything or help anybody?" Aguirre went to prison still proclaiming his innocence.

Marijane was eager to find out how Devine was going to explain the wrongful conviction at his press conference. The media event turned out to be about much more than Omar Aguirre. Standing alongside of Devine were U.S. Attorney Patrick Fitzgerald and Chicago Police Superintendent Terry Hillard. They announced that Aguirre was one of four men exonerated for the murder of Sindulfo Miranda. A federal gang task force working with Chicago police said the murders were committed not by these men, but by gang members who were now charged in a series of drug-related kidnappings and tortures. What made the original case seem so airtight, they explained, was that all four innocent men either made plea deals or confessed. The FBI and U.S. Attorney's Office charged members of Chicago's Latin Kings street gang with the murder and charged the informant who implicated Aguirre and the others with making false statements. "As for our involvement in the original homicide investigation, I can tell you that our detectives followed the evidence as it existed back in 1997," Hillard told the press. "That evidence included an eyewitness account of a crime by a person who knew the offenders."

Later that evening, Marijane called her contacts at the *Chicago Tribune* and *Sun-Times* to make sure they got her comments on the case. She said that Aguirre was an easy patsy who could have no alibi because he was a day laborer and there were no official records to show where he was working. "This is what I said it was," Marijane said.

A month later came more big news. Two days before he was to leave office, Governor Ryan stunned the nation. Saying the capital pun-

ishment system was "haunted by the demon of error," Ryan announced he would grant clemency for all 167 inmates on death row,
commuting their sentences to life without parole. "Because the Illinois death penalty system is arbitrary and capricious—and therefore
immoral—I no longer shall tinker with the machinery of death." His
decision followed an emotional series of public hearings during
which victims' families were forced to relive the crimes for which
these prisoners were convicted. Prosecutors vigorously objected to
every clemency request but felt as if they were wasting their time. It
seemed Ryan had long ago made his decision, and many believed it
was political. The governor, still embroiled in a personal scandal
that would eventually lead to his conviction and imprisonment on
corruption charges, desperately needed to leave a positive legacy to
his administration. Devine said the governor had gone too far with
this blanket clemency. "Our position has been and remains that the
death penalty is appropriate for the worst of the worst, people who
have committed crimes so atrocious that they are no longer fit to be
among us," Devine said. That included killers of police officers like
Aloysius Oliver. Death row may have been empty now, but prosecutors had every intention of filling it up again. Oliver would have a
place waiting for him.

The Oliver case was scheduled to go to trial sometime after the following Thanksgiving, and Marijane and Ruth had to start rounding
up a list of experts to testify, including someone who could help
them sort out the shooting scenario and ballistics evidence. At a
forensics conference a few months earlier, Marijane met an interesting English fellow who gave a talk on ballistics and weapons identifi-
cation. His name was John Nixon, and Marijane liked him right
away. He ran a forensics consulting business in rural Indiana. She
was impressed by his credentials and enamored of his British accent.
Marijane took his business card and told him that she might need his
services someday.

CHAPTER TEN

Meet Mr. Nixon

BIPPUS, INDIANA, is a small farming town about 150 miles southeast of Chicago and a world away from the gritty urban streets from which Aloysius Oliver came. To get to Bippus from Chicago required a three-hour drive through the industrial belt and odiferous discharge from the steel plants and oil refineries along Lake Michigan from East Chicago to Gary, Indiana, and then straight across the state along State Road 30. After the city skyline disappeared in the distance the flatlands and farms took over the landscape, vast spaces with patches of woods and old wooden houses. Bippus, population about 250, was marked by the intersection of State Road 105 and County Road 800 North. There was not much in town besides the 7–7 Mini Mart, Bippus Farm Supply, Bippus State Bank, a post office and Tate's Table, a dinerlike restaurant. There was one striking similarity between Bippus and Aloysius's community. In both places lots of people carried guns and weren't afraid to use them. The difference was that in Bippus, it was legal to carry a gun for personal protection.

On the outskirts of Bippus, in a two-story reinforced concrete block building set back a few yards from his home, John Nixon ran a small company called Athena Research & Consulting. He named his company after the mythical Greek goddess of strategy, wisdom, intellect, truth and justice. In his advertisements, Nixon described his company as a supplier of premium quality technical and scientific services that "strive to emulate the high intellectual and ethical standards associated with the mythical Olympian Goddess Athena." Nixon hired himself out to defense lawyers, police departments, insurance companies, government agencies, defense contractors, weapons manufacturers or anyone else seeking his expert services in mechanical engineering, ballistics, firearms, explosives, weaponry, and even business practices. He came across as an intellectual man with a wry sense of humor and an obsessive interest in his work, traits which drew Marijane Placek to him right away. She decided to hire Nixon to test some theories about how the Oliver shooting unfolded. Maybe Nixon could find something that would raise doubt as to whether Oliver fired those fatal shots.

Nixon's place was at the end of a long driveway, with woods on one side and farmland behind the house and on the east side. It was the kind of place where people left you alone and you could shoot your guns, let your dogs run free and do whatever you wanted. Perfect for his line of work. It wasn't unusual for Nixon to walk out back and fire off a few rounds from one of his many test guns. Nixon seemed a little out of place in Bippus, which also was a long way from his native England. He was born and grew up in the Scottish Borders region, which he told me was the least populated part of the British Isles—cold, wet, windy, barren and hilly. "You could say that I was an English hillbilly." Nixon was in his early forties, stout and barrel-chested with short, wavy blond hair, blue eyes and a clean-shaven pinkish face. His accent hardly sounded hillbilly, evoking more of the proper-sounding Queen's English than some backcountry dialect.

His credentials were impressive. Nixon earned a first-class honors degree in mechanical engineering from the University of Greenwich, London, and a master's in business administration from Henley Management College, Brunel University, London. He also completed a four-year engineering apprenticeship with British Steel Corporation, and training in military tactics and technology at the Royal Military College of Science. His curriculum vitae listed anti-terrorism courses, studies in space technology, risk management, weapons and ballistics. He was the author of patents in munitions design and had been designated as a court-qualified expert in the United Kingdom, five U.S. states, as well as by the U.S. Federal Court.

Most interesting and most mysterious, Nixon listed on his résumé work for the British Ministry of Defence and the British government. He said he could not talk about specifics, but had conducted work in the areas of rocketry, missiles, explosives, guns and munitions. That was classified. His résumé listed nineteen research papers whose titles and subject matter were not to be discussed. "I can talk in broad terms about the work I've done there," he told me when I pressed him to elaborate on his background. "Guns, ammunition, rockets, explosives design, research, development, performance testing, midlife improvement programs and reverse engineering of foreign systems. Not giving away much there. Most specific projects, and most, if not all reports, are classified." Only someone with the proper clearance, he explained, would be allowed to review his work.

So what was a guy like this doing in Bippus? "I fell in love," Nixon told me. "My wife is from here." They met while Nixon was doing business in Fort Wayne, Indiana, about thirty-five miles to the east. She was a nurse, specializing in work with heart patients. "We knew each other for a few years; you know, that long distance thing is hard," he said. "I couldn't get work here right away. I had looked for work in defense, but I couldn't get security clearance because I was not a citizen." Instead of trying to find work, Nixon packed up and came to the United States to continue the consulting business he established in the U.K. several years earlier. Bippus was a welcoming place where he would be left alone. No one would flinch if he went out to the backyard and fired rifles or pistols, which he often did as part of his work. "If you *don't* have a gun around here, they think you're crazy," he said. "I don't like cities much, anyway."

Marijane and Ruth McBeth sent Nixon a package of background material to get him started on his analysis of the shooting of Officer Eric Lee. He pored over a stack of official police reports, the autopsy report, and viewed video depositions of officers Vincent Barner and Andre Green, as well as police video taken at the scene immediately after the shooting. This was a good start, but he also wanted to visit the crime scene himself.

Nixon was clearly excited about his work, and it showed in his eyes, which always seemed wide with enthusiasm. He was eager to show me the tools of his trade when I went to visit him one winter afternoon at ARC headquarters in Bippus. From the outside, the place looked more like a garage than a forensics lab. The front door led to an L-shaped room in which there was a workbench with a vise mounted on one end, some tables, boxes and plastic tubs. Off to the side was a large steel door on which was painted "Fort Knox," the trademarked insignia for the security company that custom built the door to a vault in which he stored his most valuable, dangerous and expensive professional equipment. It looked like the door to a bank safe, with twenty-four internal steel bolts to lock it in place. The door was almost a foot thick and led to a room with steel-reinforced concrete walls and two feet of steel-reinforced concrete under the floor. "It's for theft and fire protection," Nixon explained. "It exceeds the U.S. federal government's specifications for the storage of secret material."

He swung open the door and led me inside a 12-by-16-foot room that resembled a combination ballistics lab and gym locker room. "The judges want to know that the evidence I analyze is safe," he explained. "No one is going to get in here in a hurry." On one table, covered with plastic dustcovers, were a comparison microscope and a stereomicroscope, which Nixon employed for analyzing ammunition and firearms. On the opposite side of the room were shelves on which boxes of ammunition were stored, including the type allegedly used by Aloysius Oliver when he shot Officer Lee, a brand called Sellier & Bellot, which Nixon pulled out to show me. "It's Czechoslovakian-made," he said. "It's popular with crooks because it's cheap and it's good quality. It's made by very cheap labor. I order mine online." He had both soft-point and hollow-point bullets, which expand on impact, thus doing more damage to flesh and organs.

Nixon pointed to a series of cabinets on the far wall. On top was a massive weapon on a tripod that looked like it belonged in a war zone. "It's a 50-caliber rifle," he said. "It's a really powerful rifle, single-shot bolt action. I'm actually storing it for someone." He opened one of the cabinet doors to reveal scores of other rifles, shotguns and handguns, some of which he owned, others he was borrowing or were being analyzed for court cases and lawsuits against manufacturers, a big part of his business. He also got calls from television producers seeking to check the accuracy of scenes and plots involving forensic evidence. He had consulted for programs such as *CSI: Miami* and *Law & Order*. "A lot of people get their idea of what it's like to get shot from the movies," Nixon said. "And it's just not like that at all. You don't go flying back." He demonstrated the usual overly dramatic scene of a man getting blown away, throwing himself backward as if he were being pummeled in the gut by a battering ram or blown by a hurricane-force gust.

Recently, Nixon was hired on a case in which a man who was hunting wild turkeys was mistaken for one. Another hunter, thinking he was going to bag a bird, blasted toward the man with a 12-gauge shotgun from about 40 yards. The man who was mistaken for the turkey was fortunate to have escaped serious injury. He got hit in the back with just four pellets, and only two penetrated his clothing. Still, the victim sued the other hunter, claiming he was thrown 15 feet by the force of the blast and suffered neck and back injuries from whiplash. Hired by the defense, Nixon conducted mathematical calculations to prove that the victim could not have been hurled back as violently as he claimed. To illustrate the point to a jury, Nixon decided to make a video. With the tape rolling, he got a 12-gauge shotgun and blasted toward a 50-pound bag of salt from 40 yards away, the same distance from which the man had been shot. The bag of salt did not fly back. "So I sent my report and the video to the plaintiff's attorney. By the time I got there to testify, the case was settled," Nixon said. "If a fifty-pound bag of salt doesn't fly back when shot, how could a two-hundred-pound man? It just doesn't happen that way."

Nixon was often called upon to examine such cases, to analyze and calculate the impact of gunshot wounds to prove or challenge legal claims. He told me that when he worked in England, the government performed shooting tests on pigs, goats and sheep in an effort to understand how various firearms damaged the flesh. Nixon reviewed thousands of these animal wounds and became proficient at what he called the science of wound ballistics. "A lot of what I do is to put things in perspective, because juries get their ideas of what happens through television," he said. "You get some weird things."

To hammer his point home once more, Nixon went upstairs to his loft-style office above the vault to show me a police training video of an actual shooting. The scene was captured by a hidden camera inside an interrogation room of a Los Angeles police station. The video showed a man who had been arrested on drug charges impatiently waiting in the room to be questioned. A cop walked in and asked the man if he wanted some water. The man said yes and unscrewed the cap of a bottle of water. He took a sip, put the bottle down and looked around nervously. The cop came back in for a moment, then left. The man then reached into his pants, pulled out a .45 pistol, placed it to his own temple and shot. His head jerked back just slightly, and blood poured down his hair. He did not go flying off the chair or into the wall. "See, it doesn't happen that way," Nixon explained enthusiastically. He had seen the video so many times before that it didn't faze him as it might someone like myself who had never seen such a disturbing image of a fatal shooting on tape. I felt chilled, as if I had just watched a snuff film.

Whether a body flies when hit by a bullet might or might not be relevant to the shooting of Officer Eric Lee. But analyzing ballistics, bullet trajectory, distance and accuracy would play an important part in re-creating what happened that night. Marijane and Ruth wanted Nixon to test whether it was possible for Aloysius to shoot Lee in the way police described. The facts were these: Lee was struck twice in the head in the dark by a man who was not a trained shooter. Both slugs passed through Lee's head and were never recovered, which meant that there was no physical evidence to link Aloysius's gun to the shooting. Could someone else have fired the shot that killed Lee? Marijane and Ruth wanted to raise that possibility.

Nixon decided he would have to drive to Chicago to visit the shooting scene on the same date and hour during which the incident occurred. He wanted to measure the light conditions, walk through the alley, the yard and the gangway to get a feel for how it was that night. So on August 19, 2003, Nixon loaded his pickup truck with video and laser measuring equipment and headed to Chicago. The public defender's office lent Nixon an investigator to accompany him to the scene. It was not a safe area, day or night, and a blond-haired Englishman toting expensive equipment around there by himself was not safe. As if to punctuate that point, within minutes of Nixon's arrival he got robbed. As he was unloading equipment from his truck in the alley behind Aloysius's house, Nixon stepped out of sight from the truck for a moment. Someone swiped a few hundred dollars' worth of laser measuring equipment within seconds, despite the presence of an investigator and two cops nearby in a squad car. Undeterred, Nixon continued his inquiry, walking around the area with his Sony digital video camera in the remaining daylight, and again, at the exact minute of the shooting when it was dark, around 9:15 p.m. Nixon retraced Aloysius's steps. He stood at the northeast corner of the garage where Aloysius would have stopped during the chase to shoot toward Officer Lee, who was moving north down the alley toward the back gate.

According to Nixon, the measurements from the scene showed that the distance between Lee and Aloysius at the time of the shooting was about 10 yards. Aloysius was standing on ground 15 inches lower than that upon which Lee was standing. He noted that Lee was 6 feet tall, and Aloysius was only about 5 foot 7. The autopsy showed one bullet entered Lee's head 4.4 inches below the top and 1.3 inches above the ear, and exited the left side 2.2 inches above the ear. Nixon did some math, and according to his calculations, the bullet traveled upward .9 inches, right to left. Using the measurement of a typical male head thickness of 7 inches, the bullet traveled at an upward angle of 7.5 degrees to the horizontal. The bullet also traveled slightly from back to front. The entry wound was 67.5 inches above ground level. Nixon concluded that if Lee's head was oriented normally, Aloysius would have had to shoot from his hip. If Aloysius had shot from shoulder height, Lee's head would have had to be tilted to the left at a 5.5-degree angle. All of these measurements would matter because they could prove or disprove the placement of the shooter relative to the victim and offer clues to where the shots came from.

The lighting that night was another issue. There were two streetlights in the area, one 17 yards north of the tree closest to where Lee fell, and one 15 yards south of the tree. Nixon took measurements with a light meter and through the lens of his camera, which was a model designed to work in low light with reliable accuracy. By any standard, it was dark and not easy to see from where Aloysius stood to the alley. The two bullets that hit Lee entered within inches of each other. Since Aloysius fired both shots from the same location, that meant that Lee's orientation would have had to have changed by about 90 degrees from one bullet to the next. Nixon believed that Lee was likely looking in the general direction of Aloysius while chasing him, and so the first shot to hit him was in the ear. Once hit, Lee's head or body would have had to turn 90 degrees, possibly turning for cover, and he was hit by the second bullet, which caused the final, fatal wound.

So what did it all mean? To Nixon, it raised the question of whether Aloysius could possibly have made those shots in those conditions. He wanted to test the theory further and bought the exact gun that Aloysius used in the shooting, a stainless steel Sturm, Ruger GP100 revolver with a six-inch barrel. He loaded it with the Sellier & Bellot cartridges and did some shooting in light and in dark conditions, using one hand, as Aloysius would have done. Target shooters generally use two hands to stabilize the gun and shoot with greater accuracy. One-handed shooters, especially with large guns such as this one, were hardly ever accurate. Based on his visit to the scene, his measurements, the police reports and his own experience, Nixon concluded that there were a number of issues related to the accuracy of Aloysius's alleged shots. The Ruger revolver and ammunition, Nixon said, were capable of placing successive shots within one inch of one another at a range of 10 yards. However, such accurate shooting would normally be accomplished by a relaxed, skilled shooter using a two-handed hold, controlling his breathing and trigger operation, shooting at a stationary target in good light, and having plenty of time to aim.

None of that characterized what happened the night Lee was shot. Nixon said Aloysius was clearly not a trained target shooter, and held the gun with one hand as he raised the weapon to shoot. Aloysius had just run about 15 yards and was most likely scared and breathing heavily. He was shooting toward a moving target across his field of view from left to right, and given the light conditions, it was extremely unlikely that he could see the gun sights to even attempt a proper aim. Oliver could not possibly have made such an accurate shot by design. "If anybody says he did it deliberately, it's fantasy land," Nixon said.

Out in his backyard, which abutted an empty farm field, Nixon offered to demonstrate his theory to me, first in good lighting conditions, and second, in the dark. He had the same .357 revolver in his lab, and loaded it up with the same Czech-made ammunition. He walked to one end of the yard and posted an 8½-by-11 sheet of white paper with a circle on a target stand and paced off ten steps away from it. Nixon put on a red pair of "ear defenders" to muffle the sound of the blasts. Even from 10 yards, he couldn't hit the inner rings of the target. Trying to shoot successive shots accurately was even more difficult due to the tremendous recoil of the gun. Nixon reloaded the gun, handed it to me and suggested I try it. The gun was sleek and felt heavy in my right hand. I used my left hand to stabilize my grip. I aimed, pulled the trigger, saw a flash and felt the gun kick back. Nixon told me to make two successive shots as fast as I could. Neither hit the paper. I tried again, and again until I emptied the chamber of its six rounds. Nixon explained that if a shooter pulled the trigger twice, as fast as possible, there would be no time to reposition the gun to aim properly. Later, in the dark, with just some light coming from the kitchen window of Nixon's house behind, he asked me to try again. It was even more difficult to make the shot. After firing once, the muzzle flash temporarily disoriented my eyes. Nixon made his point. It was a tough shot once. Twice? Nearly impossible. "A running man, breathing heavily, fires two shots, single-handedly, double action, rapidly, in the dark, at a man ten yards away who is also moving. Hits him twice in the head, just an inch or two between bullet holes. Astronomical odds of achieving this," he said.

Marijane was thrilled when Nixon told her his theory. But she wanted to test it out herself. As a licensed gun owner, she'd handled a few weapons in her time. Marijane learned to shoot with her father, who had taken her to a farm to shoot pumpkins when she was a girl. She arranged a field trip to Indiana to do some shooting and have some fun. She gave Nixon a list of weapons that were involved in some of her other cases, too. She brought along Ruth and attorney Andrew Northrup, and met Nixon at a shooting range in Northwest Indiana, about an hour from Chicago. "Everyone is so liberally antigun," Marijane said when I asked about her interest in weaponry. "I want our attorneys to see what they are and how they work. Guns are a tool. I don't think guns are the evil that people think they are. It's the people. We have people in our office who don't know the difference between a shotgun and a rifle."

Nixon loaded up his truck with a cache of weapons and ammunition. After he arrived at the range and began unloading pistols, rifles and semiautomatic weapons, the range master sauntered over, and Marijane thought he was going to make some inquiries about their arsenal, perhaps suspecting that they were planning some kind of terrorist attack with all that firepower. The range master smiled and asked if they needed help carrying all those guns over to the range. Nixon, who had a handgun strapped to his side, said no thanks. The ballistics expert and the lawyers spent the afternoon shooting revolvers, semiautomatics and even the .50-caliber gun Nixon had on loan called the Desert Eagle, an Israeli-made weapon. Nixon had the lawyers shoot the .357, and it was clear that even under range conditions, they could not hit the target. It was just too difficult.

Nixon wrote up a final report with his conclusions and prepared an animated re-creation of the shooting that he hoped to use in court if called to testify. With Nixon's report and theory in place, Marijane and Ruth had secured an important dimension to their defense. First, they would point out that there was no forensic evidence proving Aloysius fired the gun that killed Officer Lee. Second, they would demonstrate that it was unlikely Aloysius could have intentionally aimed and landed two shots in Lee's head. Thus, Aloysius's contention that he never meant to shoot Lee might hold more weight. He might have just been an unlucky shot.

CHAPTER ELEVEN

Steal the Flag

FOR THE FIRST TIME IN ANYONE'S MEMORY four cop-killer cases, including the case against Aloysius Oliver, were expected to go on trial at the Cook County Courthouse in a single year—2003. Public defenders from the Murder Task Force represented every one of the accused and faced battles with the state's top prosecutors who sought the death penalty in three of the four cases. (The fourth defendant was too young.) To the state's attorneys, these cases were clearly defined battles between good and evil, between killers who had complete disregard for the law and those sworn to uphold it. "Cop-killer cases are different," Task Force chief Shelton Green told me. "The first thing is that the victim is different, and the state's attorneys will wrap that American flag around themselves so tight. There's an approach I call 'steal the flag' with these cases. That's what we try to do—steal the flag."

Stealing the flag meant preventing prosecutors from monopolizing the ideas of truth and justice simply because the victim was a police officer. "Any time your victim falls into that hero category, you can pretty much expect the state attorney will talk about their duties and service to the community, and they will wrap themselves in the flag," Shelton explained. "They will put out the concepts of American justice before the jury, as if they own it. You want to make that argument before they do. You're just trying to steal their thunder a little bit, to make those jurors think." Shelton said that Marijane was a master at playing steal the flag. "I remember in one closing argument, she said to the jury that not everyone could be a policeman or a fireman and spend all day doing heroic things," Shelton said. "She told them that 'you have a chance today to save a life and be a hero.' So you sort of put the jury in that hero category, to make them believe that they can be heroes. I thought that argument was brilliant."

When an accused cop killer was on trial, officers would descend on the courthouse to attend hearings, listen to motions and fill rows of seats in the courtroom in a show of support and solidarity. Defense lawyers complained that packing the courtrooms was a form of intimidation that frightened jurors into voting for convictions. This had, in fact, become an issue during the last such trial two years earlier. Jonathan Tolliver, a low-level drug dealer and gang member, had been charged in the shooting death of Officer Michael Ceriale, a rookie patrolman who was on a drug stakeout in the Robert Taylor Homes public housing complex. Police officers filled the courtroom nearly every day of the five-week trial. Jurors struggled to agree on a verdict for ten tension-filled days. They had difficulty sorting out the facts because of conflicting testimony and allegations of perjury among some witnesses. The panel was deadlocked by a single holdout who could not be persuaded to budge. Cook County Judge Dennis Porter finally declared a mistrial. The lone holdout later told the *Chicago Tribune* that the sight of all those police officers in court was intimidating. "Should I tuck tail and give up my belief and save my hide, or should I vote on what I saw, what the judge instructed me to do?" the juror said. "Believe me, it was hard sitting in that courtroom."

The juror explained he was reluctant to convict because he believed prosecutors had no physical evidence against Tolliver and that witnesses, many of whom were gang members and drug dealers, changed their stories because they were coerced by police and prosecutors to make incriminating statements. Private attorneys Richard Steinken and Melissa Brown, who defended Tolliver, believed that their client had been convicted in the court of public opinion long before the trial. Three months after the mistrial, prosecutors tried Tolliver again. The jury that heard the case this time returned a guilty verdict after five and a half hours. The verdict assured that the state's attorney's conviction rate for cop killers remained at 100 percent. Cop killers were not supposed to get off. Ever.

* * *

On June 20, the first cop-killer case of 2003 got under way at the Cook County Courthouse. Woody Jordan and Bob Cavanaugh, another veteran of the Murder Task Force, were assigned to defend Kevin Dean, forty-two, a convicted car thief and drug addict who was charged with shooting Officer James Camp during a struggle over the officer's gun. The prosecution's version was that Camp and his partner, Kenny King, both working in plainclothes, were walking through a housing project when they noticed a parked car with a punched-out door lock. Two men were sitting inside. When they got closer and peered inside the car, the officers also noticed that the steering column was damaged, leading them to believe that someone had broken in and stolen the vehicle. Camp went to the driver's side and King walked around to the passenger's side to have a word with the two occupants and prevent either from bolting. Dean swung open the door and popped out of the driver's side. He began wrestling with Camp and shot him in the face with the officer's own 9 mm pistol, the prosecution contended. A uniformed officer who pulled up to the scene saw what was happening and shot Dean five times when he tried to flee. While recovering in the hospital under guard, Dean gave police a statement implicating himself in the crime. The state filed notice that it intended to seek the death penalty. One of the prosecutors working on the case was David O'Connor, who in a few months was going to prosecute the Aloysius Oliver case.

When Woody and Cavanaugh first got the case files, they sat down in the office they shared to brainstorm. It was clear to them that Dean and Officer Camp wrestled over the gun and that the shooting was probably not deliberate. "As soon as I read the report, I thought we could win it," Woody recalled. "We knew the cop had his gun out, and we just reenacted the struggle." Dean and Camp were rolling around in the snow, struggling over the gun, Woody said. Officer King ran over and dove into the fray like a football player, knocking Dean and Camp. "That set the gun off," Woody said. "It was just a big struggle. That's an accident." And that's how they planned to make their case. Dean did not intentionally shoot the officer. That alone could spare him the death penalty. They also could argue that Dean might not even have known Camp and King were cops when they first confronted him. After all, they were in plainclothes. The officers, however, said that their badges were out. "There was no evidence that their badges were out," Woody said. "There was no blood on them. There was no blood on the badges because they were tucked in their clothes somewhere."

But the defense still had to explain Dean's hospital-bed confession. Woody and Cavanaugh would try to discredit the reliability of that statement. Dean was still woozy from medication when he confessed, Woody said. "It was a miracle he even lived. The police took a statement from Dean in ICU that, in effect, said that he knew it was the police he shot. The surgeon later said that Dean was so heavily drugged, he could not have known what he was saying." The deeper they got into the facts of the case, the more Woody and Cavanaugh thought they might be able to win. But as the trial neared, Woody began to get preoccupied with something else. His wife had been having respiratory problems, and doctors suspected she might have lung cancer. She had been going through a series of tests and was scheduled for a biopsy. Woody asked for a continuance, but the judge would not allow it. Cavanaugh, who had not been feeling so well himself because of back pains, handled the first two days of jury selection. Woody went with his wife to the doctor. "They do a biopsy on her left lung and it's brutal. I mean, a biopsy is like digging a hole," Woody said. "I had to have my eyes closed. It was like digging out a bullet. Later, I said to my wife, 'I don't know if I can go back and do this case.' And my wife said to me, 'Get the fuck outta here and go do it.' "

The biopsy results came back a day later and confirmed the worst. Woody's wife had lung cancer. Woody was numbed and did not know whether he had the strength to continue the trial. "I asked myself, 'Am I up for this?' And she said to me 'I'm not going to die in two weeks, so go there.' " Shaken, Woody reluctantly left for the courthouse. "I'm driving there, and I'm scared," he said. "And then as soon as I walked in that courtroom, I saw all these cops. And I said to myself, 'Who the fuck do all you cops think you are? Who the *fuck* do you think you are?' " His resolve grew even stronger. His adrenaline was never higher. He wanted to fight.

Officer Camp's partner gave tearful testimony about the day his friend died, describing how they worked their patrol together that day, ate a fish lunch and then afterward came across the car they suspected was stolen. Before he knew it, King said he saw Camp fighting on the other side of the car with Dean, and then heard a shot. He ran over from behind and grabbed the gun from Dean, who tried to point it at him. During cross-examination, Cavanaugh suggested that King jumped on Dean's back, sending all three men tumbling to the ground and causing the gun in Camp's hand to go off in his face.

Earl Carter, the officer who came upon the scene during the struggle testified that as he drove up, he saw three men wrestling on the ground. He heard a shot, and one of the men stopped struggling. He said Dean rose up, fired a shot at him and ran off. Carter yelled for Dean to halt, and then fired five shots after Dean refused to stop. The wounded Dean was not holding a weapon when police found him collapsed down the street. Against his lawyers' advice, Dean decided to testify in his own defense. His version of the story was that yes, he was sitting in a car he had stolen. Two strangers approached the car, which made him nervous. One yanked Dean out of the car and put him in a chokehold. Dean said he could barely breathe. "Then all of a sudden, some heavy weight hits, and I heard a gunshot." Dean said he remembered nothing about giving a statement to police in the hospital.

When it came time for Cavanaugh to deliver the closing argument, every seat in the courtroom was filled. He began by telling jurors that Dean never intended to kill Camp. It was an accident. When Camp's partner jumped in to help during the tussle, he caused the gun to go off, either by Camp's hand or his own. Cavanaugh suggested that King, realizing he could have been responsible for the death of his partner, told investigating officers that Dean had killed Camp to cover himself. Cavanaugh made his move to steal the flag. He urged jurors to do what was right, to send a message to the dead officer that they did the responsible thing by acquitting Dean for a crime he did not commit. "You say, 'James, we did our duty,' " he said. "Because of what you did and what that star stands for, we found him not guilty of your murder." Police officers shuddered and sneered when Cavanaugh invoked the dead officer's name. It was an insult. They stared Cavanaugh down when he returned to his seat. Assistant State's Attorney Steve Rosenblum dismissed Cavanaugh's theories as ridiculous. The shooting was no accident. Dean simply didn't want to go back to prison for stealing a car, and deliberately shot Camp in the face after getting hold of the officer's gun. "He turned it and executed him," Rosenblum said.

After closing arguments ended, the attorneys waited. And waited. Nearly seven hours passed. Around 8:00 p.m., the jury foreman informed Judge Henry Simmons that they might not be able to reach a verdict. The judge ordered the panel to continue deliberations and sequestered them for the night. Jurors resumed deliberations the next morning. Late that afternoon, Woody and Cavanaugh were summoned back to the courtroom. The jury had reached a decision. Again, every seat was filled with anxious police officers, reporters and family members. Dean's mother sat up front. Woody, who was planning to handle the sentencing phase of the trial, was worried. He was already making notes for the opening statement he planned to use at Dean's sentencing hearing, thinking about how he was going to try to save him from the death penalty. The jury foreman handed the verdict to Simmons, who examined the paper, looked out at the gallery and read the finding: not guilty of first-degree murder. The moment just hung there. Everyone in that room was stunned.

"Thank you, Lord," Dean's mother said. Dean's other family members hugged each other as prosecutors and police sat in silence. No one had been acquitted of murdering a police officer in this city as long as anyone could remember. Cavanaugh and Woody seemed just as bewildered, looking at each other in disbelief, but restraining themselves from showing any kind of joy. While Dean escaped the first-degree murder charge, the jury convicted him on various other charges, including disarming Officer Camp and possession of a stolen car. He still faced thirty years in prison for each charge instead of the death penalty. Cavanaugh told Woody he did not feel comfortable leaving the courtroom with all those cops around.

"We're going out the back door, and we're going to Jean's," Cavanaugh told Woody. "You deal with the press. Then we're going to have one beer and we're getting the fuck out of here."

Woody left the courtroom and stood before the assembled reporters, circumspect about the victory. "Mr. Dean is quite relieved," he said. "He realizes he is being punished for the crimes he committed and he has been acquitted of the crimes he should be acquitted for. It was a consistent verdict, both logically and legally." Later, State's Attorney Richard Devine, through a spokesman, said he was disappointed but had to accept the jury's verdict. "It sends the wrong message for the brave men and women of the Chicago Police Department who put their lives on the line for us every day." Mayor Daley was even more emphatic. "I'm extremely disappointed in the jury's verdict," he said in a prepared statement. "The men and women of the Chicago Police Department put their lives on the line for us every day, and they deserved better than this decision."

Woody and Cavanaugh walked two blocks over to Jean's on Twenty-sixth Street and ordered their beers. Cavanaugh left about fifteen minutes later after he finished his. Woody stayed and had two more. "You have to realize how emotionally charged that courtroom was," Woody said later. "These cops know your name, they know your face. We ain't celebrating around here." Yet Woody also walked away feeling sad. "I felt so sorry for Camp's partner," Woody said. "You could tell on the witness stand how badly he felt, how he blamed himself for what happened."

Like Aloysius Oliver, Dean claimed he did not know he was being approached by cops before the shooting, and Woody believed his client. Woody had been around long enough to know that plainclothes cops can look as menacing as the criminals they arrest. It was especially dangerous for cops of color. "My hat goes off to black cops. I mean, they are always in danger," Woody said. "Can you imagine being a black cop in this city? During a drug bust when they bust into a house, if they see a white face come through the door, they know it's the cops. Those cops have guts. That's real courage, man. If I was a black cop in this city, I wouldn't get married or have kids. Can you think of any job that's more dangerous?"

During the trial, Woody held back one piece of evidence he thought he might need to help save Dean's life if he was convicted of first-degree murder. It was a photograph that was shot near the driver's side of the car door. In the picture, there is a puddle of blood on the street. "The paramedics had said the officer was lying face-down in a pool of blood and had his vest on," Woody said. "Now we didn't have his badge in as evidence. The police had taken it and put it in one of those displays, I think, for those killed in the line of duty. But we had the plastic necklace. Now did Dean know these guys were cops? They were both black, they're at the Ida B. Wells housing project. So on the necklace there was no blood. The cops testi-fied they had their necklaces out when they came up to the car. They weren't. They were tucked under their vests!" How, Woody won-dered, could Camp have had his badge out over his vest and be lying facedown in a pool of blood and there be no blood on the badge holder? "We held that back because we felt that would be the only shot at saving his life," Woody said. "You've got to hold something back, especially in a case like this one where you think there is no hope."

Though Woody and Cavanaugh were surprised at their win, they shared no joy with or for their client. "He was one of those people who blames everyone else for what happened and just had no con-ception of accepting any responsibility," Woody said. "He was an asshole. You're not winning for him. You're winning for yourself. You might as well put a mannequin over there. You're playing the game for yourself." After going home that night, Cavanaugh called Marijane to tell her about the verdict and to let her know that one of the assistant state attorneys who lost the case was O'Connor, whom she would face at the Oliver trial. Marijane was pleased to learn of the defeat, which would put the prosecutor under even greater stress now.

Three months later, on September 11, 2003, the next cop-killer case went to trial. Hector Delgado, a teenage gang member, was accused of fatally shooting Officer Brian Strouse in an alley. Task Force lawyers Kathy Lisco and LaFarell Moffett represented Delgado and were scheduled to go to trial in two months. They felt that the atmosphere around the courthouse had been poisoned by ill will toward their colleagues after the Dean victory. The lawyers were especially disturbed by Mayor Daley's remarks and asked Judge Thomas Sumner to move the trial to another jurisdiction to avoid any influence from the outcry following Dean's acquittal. Lisco and Moffett argued that potential jurors could be influenced by the mayor's comments, forcing them to lean toward a guilty verdict for fear of offending the police. Sumner denied their request, but did lash out at the mayor's remarks as inappropriate. "People in responsible positions should hold their tongues," the judge said. "For many people, voting and serving on a jury is the only link they have to their government other than paying taxes. It is improper to criticize them." Sumner promised he would keep emotions from spilling into the courtroom and told prosecutors he planned to control the number of officers who attended the trial if he felt that their presence was making a statement to the jury. He vowed not to preside over a "circus." Still, officers posted fliers around station houses about the upcoming trial, urging their brethren to attend.

On the day the trial opened, police officers jammed the courtroom, as they did in the Dean trial. Delgado's lawyers planned to argue self-defense, acknowledging that the teenage Delgado fired his gun at someone that June night in 2001, but claimed he did not know it was a police officer and thought it was a rival gang member. Officer Strouse had been part of a surveillance operation that night in the Pilsen neighborhood, a community racked by gang activity and violence. While working the surveillance, Strouse heard shots being fired. He stepped out from behind a van, announced he was a police officer and was struck by a bullet. He never had a chance to see his assailant. Police arrested Delgado, who was sixteen at the time, after police found him hiding under a stairway at his gang's headquarters. Under questioning, he said that rival gang members fired the shots. Then he said that it was one of his own gang. Finally, he admitted that he shot at a figure in the alley who he thought was a rival gang member.

Prosecutors argued that no one in the mostly Hispanic community could have mistaken Strouse, thirty-three, who was white and wearing a bulletproof vest and badge, as a gang member. In her closing argument, public defender Lisco contended that Delgado was new to his gang and was afraid of being killed by rival gang members. He shot at someone in the alley in self-defense, she said, and should be found guilty of second-degree murder. "There's no dispute between the state and defense that he commited this act and that it was a crime," Lisco said. "The only dispute is what is the name of the crime."

"It's not defense," Assistant State's Attorney Brian Sexton countered. "He's playing offense out there."

The jury took just three hours to find Delgado guilty of first-degree murder. Since he was sixteen when the crime occurred, he was not eligible for the death penalty but could get life instead. Strouse's sister, Kathy, who was also a police officer, wept and then rested her head on the shoulder of a woman sitting next to her. The woman was Shawn Lee, the widow of Officer Eric Lee. She would soon be attending the trial of the man accused of killing her own husband.

The other pending trial was to decide the fate of James Scott, charged with killing Officer John Knight. Scott was accused of shooting the officer during a chase. The defense planned to make issue of the fact that Knight was driving an unmarked police car. As in the Aloysius Oliver case, Scott claimed that he didn't know he was being pursued by a cop and shot in fear and self-defense. Knight was being represented by public defender Michael Mayfield, another member of the Murder Task Force. Mayfield had assisted in other police shooting cases, but this was his first as the lead attorney. Both the Scott case and the Oliver case looked liked they could start around the winter holidays.

Ten weeks after winning what may have been his biggest case ever, Assistant Public Defender Bob Cavanaugh died. Members of the Murder Task Force were stunned. Only in retrospect did anyone realize that the usually feisty lawyer had left clues all along that something was wrong. During the Kevin Dean trial, Cavanaugh had mentioned several times to Woody that he was having recurring pain in his back, though he insisted on pressing on. Woody would see him bend over in pain and wince, but Cavanaugh never sought a day off or asked for sympathy. Woody figured it might be a muscle pull or injury. Cavanaugh was a martial arts enthusiast and former Marine who spent a lot of time working out and practicing his moves. Those back pains turned out to be more serious than Woody suspected. Cavanaugh, who was fifty-two, later explained that he had advanced kidney cancer. It was as if he staved off the illness to get though the Dean trial. "It wasn't until afterward that I learned he was urinating fucking blood," Woody told me. "I told him to see a fucking doctor. He was afraid of what he would find."

Shelton Green was crushed. "Bob Cavanaugh was one of the best damn attorneys in the unit," he said. Yet Cavanaugh still had the humility to feel that he was vulnerable and was unafraid to show his humanity. When he first got the Dean case file, Cavanaugh went in to talk with Shelton about his doubts. "He was a bit depressed and didn't think he could win," Shelton said. "I told Bob, 'You can win it. You can win this motherfucker outright. You can beat the shit out of this case, so go out and find something.' " Shelton was especially proud when Cavanaugh and Woody won. "When you win a case like that, it's a fucking miracle," Shelton said. "The next thing I know, Bob's dead. His wife had called me. He had told her to call me when he died. He knew he was going. That was the hardest funeral I've ever been to."

Woody had known Cavanaugh since high school, and the blow was almost more than Woody could bear. He remembered how much fun Cavanaugh was having with the Dean case, how much he loved the challenge, which clearly was the highlight of his nineteen years as a public defender. Judge Simmons, who presided over the Dean trial, told the *Chicago Sun-Times* that Cavanaugh was one of the best lawyers to step into his courtroom, an honest, skilled and prepared lawyer. "His death is a great loss for indigent clients and the profession."

CHAPTER TWELVE

Preparing for Battle

WITH A COUPLE OF MONTHS to go before Aloysius Oliver's trial, Marijane Placek and Ruth McBeth were feeling confident. They knew prosecutors were under greater pressure to win a conviction after the surprising loss in the Kevin Dean case. "The state must be in a panic," Marijane told me when I asked how the case was going. "I know they're scared." A meeting with O'Connor to discuss some upcoming depositions confirmed her opinion. O'Connor put another offer on the table. Would Aloysius be willing to take sixty years in exchange for pleading guilty? Marijane and Ruth looked at each other and said nothing. They told O'Connor they would take the offer to Aloysius and ask him to think about it. "When the state offers a plea like this, there must be something about the case that doesn't make it a death case," Marijane said afterward. "But I don't think the kid will take the plea." To Aloysius, an offer of sixty years was the same as getting life. "How old would he be when he gets out, eighty-eight? They don't live that long in prison," Marijane explained. "Look at it from his point of view. You're going to be in prison until everyone you know is going to die. When you get out, nothing will be the same. This is what he faces: you're either going to die or never get out of prison. I once had a guy who was offered twenty years, and he said to me, 'Why would I want to take it? When I'm forty, I won't be able to fuck.' "

Aloysius did not take the offer. He wasn't going to admit guilt. He wanted a trial. With all plea offers now behind them, Marijane and Ruth had to push forward with another part of their defense. In case they lost, they needed to prepare an argument to save Aloysius's life. They chose not to have the jury make the sentencing recommendation, and would go straight to Judge Moran, who they knew was a good Catholic and would not dispense a death sentence easily. "I like this judge a lot. I think he's an ethical man," Marijane said. "He's a remarkably strong judge and he is not afraid of the press or the political ramifications of what he does." She also was impressed by Moran's sense of decency. In his courtroom, Moran made a practice of acknowledging the victims of the crimes for which the defendants were charged, making sure their names were heard. Moran's father was a Cook County judge, and the younger Moran sat in the same courtroom in which his father presided. "He has a sense of propriety, and he will take his decision very seriously," Marijane said. "Not every judge at Twenty-sixth Street is like that."

Preparing for a death penalty hearing was like trying to buy life insurance. Writing the policy involved gathering everything the lawyers could find to persuade Moran that Aloysius's life was worth saving, even if he had to live it out in prison. Marijane and Ruth would have to go through what amounted to another trial in which the state would put on aggravation and the defense would put on mitigation. Prosecutors would present evidence and witnesses to paint an unflattering picture of Aloysius to justify the maximum punishment, evidence such as Aloysius's prior criminal record and possibly the family of Officer Lee to show how his death shattered their lives. The defense would put on evidence to seek a measure of mercy, to try to humanize Aloysius and to suggest his rehabilitative potential. To prepare for this possibility, Marijane had hired Julie Norman, a professional mitigator. Julie's role would be twofold: to investigate Aloysius's life and background, and to serve as a liaison between Aloysius and his lawyers during the coming months. "Julie is going to give me feedback about Oliver and she's going to tell me where his head is at," Marijane explained.

Mitigators had a tough job. They were hired to try to find the best in some of the very worst people, and some of the very worst were clients of the public defender's office. Mitigators developed extensive biographies of defendants to share with judges and juries, seeking to humanize those who were seen as inhuman. It was tricky work. Defendants' families weren't always cooperative or truthful when questioned in detail about their personal lives. Worse, they often didn't have anything good to say about the client. "I want to hear the good, the bad, warts and all," Julie told me. "Some of these families try to paint a case where the defendant had this wonderful childhood and everything was peachy keen. Then later it comes out they had this history of abuse, neglect or violence. You have to go out on the streets and you have to find people who don't want to be found."

Julie didn't look like the kind of person who would be knocking on doors and asking nosy questions in some of the city's most dangerous neighborhoods. She looked more like an elementary school teacher from the suburbs. Her face was soft, round and pleasant. She had a comforting smile that suggested you can trust me, but a gaze that could quickly change to don't fuck with me. She wore wire rim glasses and colored her collar-length hair a light platinum blond. Julie had the vibe of a compassionate soul, exuding kindness and understanding with a dose of street smarts, which served her well in her job. She was a natural for mitigtion work. A child of the sixties, Julie was a liberal-minded rabble-rouser and socially conscious do-gooder from Burlington, Iowa. She marched in Mississippi during the civil rights movement, was a member of Student Nonviolent Coordinating Committee and went to Washington, DC, to protest the Vietnam War long before it became fashionable. Her first job out of college was as a public aid worker in Chicago. "I started my job on the Monday after Martin Luther King was killed, and I remember crying all day," Julie recalled. "The whole city was burning. All summer there was rioting and I saw buses and cars getting overturned. I'd see my clients overturning cars and looting stores." The young, petite blonde from Iowa visited the city's most impoverished and dangerous neighborhoods, often by herself, to check up on clients. "Working at public aid broke my heart," Julie said. "The tragedy and the poverty, the people living on dirt floors."

About a year after moving to Chicago, Julie met a fellow social worker named John Peterson at a meeting of their local union. He had long hair and wore round John Lennon–style specs, and she thought he was really cool and handsome. They began dating and by

1970 were married. As much as she loved her work, Julie eventually got frustrated and burned out as a public aid worker. She decided to leave and take a job with the Illinois Department of Children and Family Services (DCFS), where she investigated child abuse and neglect, hardly a more uplifting career choice. "So then I saw people living in horrible conditions, which was bad enough, but they were being abused, as well," she said. Part of her job involved taking children away from unfit parents, an unpleasant task that also could be dangerous. During one home visit, Julie was nearly killed. She was following up on a tip about a mother who frequently left her children alone. Julie found the children by themselves and waited for the mother to come home. The mother came back drunk a short time later and asked Julie who the hell she was. Julie remembered the woman going into a bedroom and coming out swinging a hatchet and a butcher's knife. Julie dodged the attack and calmed the mother down, allowing her to vent about working long days to earn money for the children, about not being able to afford a babysitter, about her runaway drinking problem. They ended up in tears, hugging each other. Julie was the kind of person people liked to hug. Her nature was sweet, her ear sympathetic.

Julie's work was alternately satisfying and horrifying. Yet she wanted to do more, to delve deeper into the root causes and social forces that caused people such pain, to find ways to extract them from lives of desperation and violence. She decided to go back to school to open up more career possibilities. She earned a law degree and a master's degree in addictions sciences and became a licensed clinical professional counselor. Several years later, Julie began taking on cases as a mitigator, and Marijane was among the first to hire her based on the recommendation of a mutual friend. "I don't think Marijane liked me at first," Julie said. "I liked her, but I found that she could be intimidating." Marijane asked Julie to dig into the background of a murder defendant named Victor Nieves who was accused of raping and stabbing a woman to death and slitting her three-year-old daughter's throat. The Nieves case was as ugly as they came. He was accused of killing Vivian Vellez, twenty-two, who had been Nieves's lover at one time. Vellez's little girl survived the attack and was found clinging protectively in the arms of her dead mother.

Julie visited Nieves's closest family members—his parents, grandparents, cousins, everyone she could find. None of them believed Nieves was capable of such a crime. That wasn't surprising, because most families of the accused said that, but Julie found evidence that Nieves lived a straight life. He worked hard, stayed out of trouble and showed no violent tendencies. "I had a family meeting at his house and more than thirty people showed up for it," Julie recalled. "The parents were just one hundred percent behind him. He didn't have any background with gangs. He was a good kid." Julie asked the family members for childhood photos, which she would use to elicit sympathy from the judge and jury, to paint a more human picture of her client, to show him as an innocent boy, not a vicious killer. They came to Julie with envelopes and boxes stuffed with pictures of Nieves as an altar boy, as a Cub Scout, playing Little League baseball. "They were heart-wrenching photos," Julie said. The more time she spent with his family, the more Julie became convinced that Nieves was innocent. "He didn't do the crime, and we were going to present a case to explain why he couldn't do it," she said.

At the trial, Marijane and cocounsel Allan Sincox argued that Nieves had been framed for the murder by Vellez's boyfriend, who was jealous because they had been lovers. But prosecutors struck a blow when they brought in the little girl who survived to testify against Nieves. "I saw him kill my mom," she testified. "And then he cut my neck from here to here." The girl drew her index finger across her neck from ear to ear. Despite the girl's wrenching testimony, there simply was no corroborating evidence, and a jury found Nieves not guilty. "Marjane did just a fantastic job on the case. Oh, Lord, she did it," Julie said. "So we never had to use our mitigation."

While hoping for the same outcome in Aloysius Oliver's case, Julie nonetheless had to dig into his childhood and spend time with his family. She knew little about him and began by reviewing police reports on the shooting, reading witness statements and watching the videotape of Aloysius's confession. Her first meeting with Aloysius at the jail was brief. She saw a man in his late twenties, who looked like a teenager trying to grow a beard. He was thin and slight, and spoke in a soft voice, barely looking up at her. Aloysius wasn't in the mood for talking. He said that the jail chaplain had come to see him that very day to tell him that his cousin, Tommie Leach, had died suddenly. It turned out that Leach had a blood clot that traveled to his heart. He was supposed to testify for the defense to support Aloysius's contention that he did not know he shot at police. Aloysius cried when he told Julie about losing his cousin and dearest friend. He and Leach were very close and had been since childhood. Aloysius wept on and off during the meeting and barely spoke. Julie cut the interview short and offered to call his mother to let her know how he was doing and pass along his regards. Aloysius said he was grateful.

During her next visit to the jail, Julie tried to pry him open a little more. She learned a few surprising things that suggested that Aloysius was not a typical defendant despite his criminal record and the company he kept on the street. Not only was he a high school graduate, he enrolled at Chicago State University. Aloysius told Julie that he had planned to study accounting but dropped out before completing his first semester, pulled instead by the forces of the street. He had only one full-time job during his adult life, as inspector in a furniture factory. He earned $5.25 an hour and was laid off after about eight months. Aloysius told Julie that he never knew his father, and never had contact with him. He lived with his mother, Lillian, sisters Angela and Ashiyenetta and brother Andres in the home where the shooting occurred. Julie needed to understand his blood relationships and had Aloysius explain his family connections. Aloysius said he and Ashiyenetta had the same father, but that his other siblings had different fathers. He told her that the adults in the extended family were heavy drinkers and that they fought often. As he spoke about his family, Aloysius's eyes would sometimes fill with tears.

About a month later, Julie came back to the jail to check on Aloysius. He looked thin, weak and tired. He told her was depressed and hadn't been sleeping well, usually only two or three hours a night.

He was still mourning the death of his cousin and was scared about his impending trial. He was more talkative this time, however, and offered Julie what he thought might be some relevant information to help his case and explain why he had a gun that night to protect himself. Prior to the shooting, Aloysius said that he and his cousin, Tommie, were raising pit bulls at home to make some extra money. They were getting ready to sell the dogs when someone broke into the house and stole the pups. On another night, Aloysius told Julie that he was standing out front of his home with friends when a car drove by and someone fired three or four shots, shattering the windshield of a friend's car. The theft of the pit bulls and the drive-by shooting left Aloysius's nerves frayed. He told Julie that he didn't know who might be lurking around the neighborhood, armed and ready to shoot. That's why he got a gun. On the night those undercover cops came down the alley, Aloysius said he did not know who they were or what to expect. Julie listened, took notes and reported this to Marijane and Ruth.

A few weeks after Julie met with Aloysius, Marijane was up in her office telling Ruth she just learned the state brought in one of its top prosecutors, James McKay, to assist David O'Connor and Joe Magats in the Oliver case. "I think it's because we're scoring points," Marijane said to Ruth. "I think they brought him in to take control. He's kind of a bully." Ruth agreed they would be facing a tough adversary. "McKay is masterful," she said. "I respect him immensely. He's one of their best."

McKay was known around the courthouse as "Mad Dog" McKay because he was a fierce fighter, driven and unrelenting. Public defender Woody Jordan also thought he was the top prosecutor in the building. "You know the old saying about how you rise to the level of your competition? It's that way with McKay," Woody told me. "I've always loved doing cases against McKay because I know I'd have to do my best. He brought out the best in me, and I appreciate that." McKay had been with the state's attorney's office for eighteen years. He worked his way up to become chief of the felony trial division and chief of the narcotics prosecution bureau. He was working in narcotics when O'Connor asked him to assist on the Oliver case. McKay jumped on the opportunity because he loved heater cases. Like Marijane, he savored the battle, especially against lawyers in the Murder Task Force. "Marijane is good," McKay told me in an interview. "What I like about her is that she's not lazy. She tries cases. I respect those lawyers who work it and aren't afraid to try cases."

While McKay and O'Connor had reputations as skillful prosecutors, they had been criticized for the lengths they would go to win. In one case they did together, the Illinois Supreme Court ordered a new trial for a man convicted of killing a rookie police officer. The defendant, Murray Blue, was sentenced to death for killing Chicago Police Officer Daniel Doffyn in 1995. But the prosecution's methods, the court found, were at times overzealous and improper during the highly emotional trial. McKay and O'Connor placed a headless mannequin in the courtroom, which they had dressed in the dead officer's uniform, still stained with blood and brain matter, gruesome remnants from the slaughter. Jurors were given gloves and allowed to take the uniform into the jury room during deliberations. The Illinois Supreme Court justices described the prosecution's conduct during the trial as a transparent attempt to play to emotion rather than evidence. In his closing argument, McKay urged jurors to send a message to all police officers that they supported the badge and suggested their verdict vindicate the fallen officer's family.

As a result of the state Supreme Court decision, Blue got a new trial. He was again found guilty but got life in prison instead of death. The prosecutors may have gone over the top, but in their minds they knew Blue was guilty. To O'Connor and McKay, their work was an earnest effort to prosecute cop killers who deserved to be convicted. "We presented evidence that we thought was certainly admissible," O'Connor told me, looking back on the trial. "Yes, some of it was shocking in that regard. We make sure mistakes like that don't happen again." O'Connor seemed genuinely hurt that his sense of decency would be questioned. "Our reputations are everything," he said. "And any time someone tries to denigrate us, it hurts not only us, but our reputations as attorneys." McKay felt their intentions were pure. "At the time of the trial," he said, "we thought we were doing the right thing."

Marijane understood what it took to win a case and couldn't really fault her opponents for pushing the limits. That was part of the game inside the courtroom, seeing how far you could go. "McKay is a sneaky prosecutor," Marijane said. "But I don't think he would lie. I respect him as a lawyer. He's a warrior. It's because he's willing to show emotion, to show genuine passion. He goes in there on fire. You see, the thing is, those cases that were sent back, they were not about hiding evidence. They weren't wrongfully convicted guys. It was just about going a bit too far. They were all about the fight."

True to his reputation, McKay came out blasting during pretrial hearings in an effort to sink Marijane and Ruth's defense plans. He challenged their request to present John Nixon's video of the lighting conditions, as well as his computer-animated re-creation of the shooting as evidence to suggest that Aloysius could not have intentionally hit Officer Lee with two successive shots. McKay argued the animation was speculative and unreliable. Moreover, it did not matter whether Aloysius aimed or was a good shot. Simply pointing the gun in Lee's direction and shooting toward him made Aloysius responsible for the killing. McKay also tried to discredit Nixon as an expert witness, questioning the validity of his credentials and rolling his eyes when Marijane asked him about his expertise. Judge Moran ruled that portions of Nixon's video could be shown to jurors, but decided against allowing the animation. McKay made it clear that he would make the defense fight for every bit of evidence they sought to present.

Every December, Marijane threw herself a big bash to celebrate her birthday and Christmas, which fell in the same month. Like everything else in her life, Marijane's parties were not like other people's parties. She held it at a horse racing track. The track was like a second home to Marijane. "Everything I needed to learn I learned at the track or riding horses," she explained. Her father introduced Marijane to horseback riding when she was a girl, intending to tame his spoiled little daughter by teaching her about respect and patience. He drove her to a stable outside the city and signed her up for lessons. Marijane's dad explained that because she was an only child, she was destined to be the center of attention. He wanted her to experience something that would rein in her ego, and believed that teaching her to ride and understand horses would help. "You can't cry or pout to get an animal to do something for you," he told her. "You have to learn to work with the animal and understand it." Marijane immediately took to riding and as her skills improved, she began competing in equestrian events. She developed a deeper understanding of the animal and what it took to make a horse respond to her commands. Now she saw herself doing the same thing in court with clients, judges and opposing counsel, attempting to control and command them by sensing their strengths and weaknesses.

The day of Marijane's party was cold and cloudy, with the temperature about twenty degrees. It was near the end of the 2003 winter racing season at Hawthorne Race Track in Cicero, a worn-looking industrial and residential town southwest of Chicago, notorious in reputation for being the former home of Al Capone and his criminal empire. Hawthorne was not the most majestic track around, but it had a steady clientele of hardcore gamblers and race fans. Marijane had been going to races at Hawthorne since she was four years old and was as comfortable with a racing program—maybe even more—as she was with a legal brief. Her party was scheduled to begin at noon, one hour before post time for the first race.

As I drove to the track along Laramie Avenue, I could see the grandstand seats were empty, but there were hundreds of cars in the parking lot. Inside the clubhouse, the place was bustling, with most people sitting at tables or in rows of theaterlike seats that looked out on the oval track through tall picture windows. The horses snorted great puffs of vapor as they ran in the chilled air. Inside the warmth of the clubhouse, puffs of tobacco smoke streamed from the nostrils of men. On the upper levels of the building, companies and families were having holiday parties in private rooms. Marijane rented a large private room on the third floor of the clubhouse called the Cigar Suite, named after the famed thoroughbred. The room had windows overlooking the track and doors leading out to private box seats in the grandstand. On one wall was a bank of television screens broadcasting races from other tracks around the country. A buffet table under the TV sets held steaming trays of pasta, Italian sausage, meatballs in gravy, salad, toasted garlic bread and platters of bite-size tarts, brownies and pastries. Marijane arranged to have a private cashier with a tote ticket machine so guests didn't have to leave the room to make bets. She also paid for an open bar inside the room, and the bartender poured generous drinks. Marijane spared no expense for her guests, and her guests indulged. Her party outfit was on the wild side. She wore a wig of long braided tendrils adorned with beads, a sort of Rastafarian look. She was dressed in a casual outfit of jeans, loose blouse, and little makeup. Marijane stood up to greet everyone who came in with a bear hug and kiss. She walked around, carrying her bourbon on the rocks, and repeated the same line to everyone: "Are you having a good time?"

Marijane's guests came from the courthouse and beyond. She told me she only invited people she liked and trusted, and she didn't want colleagues from the office talking obsessively about work at her party. From the public defender's office I recognized investigator Rich English, who came with his son Ricky; Ruth McBeth, who brought her son Andrew; I also saw Shelton Green and Bob Galhotra, president of the union that represented the public defenders. John Nixon was at a table with Julie Norman and her husband, John. Nixon was busy studying the racing program in search of a winner.

As more guests arrived, Marijane's friend JD welcomed them into the suite and relieved them of the gifts they carried. He placed them into the coat closet on top of a growing stack of wrapped packages and cards. JD, short for James Daly, had known Marijane for more than twenty years. He worked part-time at the track as a handicapper, groom and hot walker, and did odd jobs around Marijane's house, including caring for her dogs. She told me that JD was one of her most trusted friends. JD was taut and thin, with a smoker's voice and the energy of a man who never seemed to rest. During the party he walked around the room, offered to explain the racing program to neophytes and volunteered tips on his favorites. When JD asked whether any of the guests wanted to go downstairs to watch the horses walk from the paddock out to the track, I went along and stood in the cold as they marched by and JD told us what he thought of each horse.

After we returned upstairs, Marijane held her racing program up and announced that everyone needed to pay attention to the sixth race. There, in the program, the sixth was listed as "Marijane's race." Marijane had been coming to the track long enough, and knew the right people in the front office, to get a race named after herself. "Everybody downstairs," Marijane announced. "We're going to have a group picture in the winner's circle."

About forty people put on their heavy coats and wound their way down through the inside of the clubhouse and marched through a set of glass doors out into the cold to watch the race, which was won by a horse named Cuban Leaf. Afterward, a track employee opened a gate that allowed the people to get on the dirt track and stand with Cuban Leaf and jockey Shane Laviolette in the winner's circle. Marijane took her place near the horse and jockey, flanked by her friends. After the photographer got her shot, everyone marched back upstairs to resume the party, this collection of lawyers, friends and relatives who made up Marijane's closest circle, drawn by her larger-than-life personality, her engaging manner and generosity of spirit. Marijane was cheery as ever. Christmas and New Year's lay ahead and she felt good. Jury selection for Aloysius's trial was a month away, and she felt like a winner.

On the morning of January 11, 2004, a group of fifty residents of Cook County were called to assemble on the third floor of the courthouse annex building. They gathered at the door of the main jury assembly room to make the long walk to courtroom 606. They were led to the elevator that took them down to the first floor. From there, they walked through the main lobby past the metal detectors, past the snack shop and up to the sixth floor where they were seated in the six rows of benches facing Judge Moran. The lawyers stood and watched as they filed in, scanning their faces, checking out their clothing and sizing them up.

"Welcome to Twenty-sixth and California," Moran said. The

judge stood up to address the jury, a sign of respect and a signal of their importance here. Moran ran a straight courtroom, and his serious voice and careful manner made it a place that demanded courtesy and decorum. Joining Marijane and Ruth at the defense table this morning was Andrew Northrup, the young lawyer from the forensics division. Aloysius walked into court for the first time in clothes other than his khaki jail uniform. He was wearing an oversized large gray suit that hung from his thin frame like drapery, his slacks bunching up around his ankles. He was just about 5 feet 8 inches tall and weighed a mere 130 pounds. His hair was trimmed close to his head and he had a thin mustache. Aloysius sat down between Ruth and Northrup, his eyes looking up and out at the jury pool.

Moran asked the potential jurors to introduce themselves and say what they did for a living. They came from all walks of life: a mechanic, social worker, school superintendent, music teacher, shipping clerk and a construction worker who said his sister had been murdered. Moran explained to the potential jurors that they would only be asked to hear evidence of the case and determine whether Aloysius was guilty or innocent. They would not be required to decide whether he should be sentenced to death if found guilty, which would be a relief to those who would not want such responsibility or were morally or philosophically opposed to the death penalty. Marijane placed a blue wristwatch with a rectangular face the size of a credit card on the table in front of her. Next to her legal pad and calendar book were a roll of Halls cough drops and a bottle of Evian water. She had been fighting a cold, which made it difficult for her to hear well. Several times she asked the potential jurors to repeat themselves.

Moran asked the potential jurors standard questions—whether they belonged to any clubs or organizations, what they read for leisure, had they seen or read anything in the media about this case, had they ever been the victim of a violent crime, and could they be fair to both sides? One after another told the judge they'd been victims or that someone close to them had been a victim of crime. Some in the jury pool had criminal records themselves.

The lawyers went through the process known as voir dire in which they began selecting a jury by eliminating potential jurors they thought might be biased or unable to give a fair hearing to the facts of the case. Marijane and Ruth knew they had to be careful about choosing jurors who might be predisposed to believing the police version of events, and on the lookout for people who might be less trusting of authority. People who lived in Englewood, in Aloysius's neighborhood where the shooting occurred, had a very different view of the police than residents of the more well-to-do Lincoln Park on the North Side. Ruth asked to remove a woman who had a number of police officers in her family. A man was eliminated because he had a six-page rap sheet. One potential juror had been convicted of second-degree murder. One said he had no faith in police officers. One said his son was shot and killed. Another said he had been shot a couple of times and lived. Marijane offered a challenge against a woman whose husband was a cop, but the judge denied it, saying she could still be fair. After about four hours of negotiations, the lawyers settled on a group of twelve jurors and two alternates. The case was ready to go to trial.

CHAPTER THIRTEEN

The Trial Opens

ON THE COLD GRAY MORNING of January 13, 2004, the jurors chosen to decide the fate of Aloysius Oliver began arriving at Twenty-sixth and California. As they walked west from the parking garage across the street to the courthouse, they passed television news vans and camera operators in bulky winter coats standing outside sipping coffee and marching in place to keep warm. The lawyers, judges, bureaucrats and the rest who had business here walked briskly toward the building and climbed the stairs to the entrance where they lined up before the metal detectors and then veered off to their various destinations. The morning edition of the *Chicago Sun-Times* offered a preview of Oliver's trial, declaring it a battle between "two of Cook County's most aggressive, experienced, and colorful criminal lawyers." Marijane Placek, never shy of pretrial publicity told the paper, "I have the personality of a bear. You don't know which way I'm gonna come from. Bears are either happy, jolly and playful circus pals, or they are killers." The other colorful lawyer described in the story, James McKay, declined to comment.

The hallway outside of Judge Moran's courtroom was already crowded with cops, many of whom wore sports jerseys over their blue shirts. Officer Eric Lee's mother, Anna, and widow, Shawn, were in a corner with a woman from the state's victim-witness liaison office. She held a box of tissues from which the crying women plucked sheets. Their faces looked tired and sad, showing the three years of grief and emptiness they had felt since Eric was killed. Each was wearing a memorial button with Eric's portrait.

Marijane and Ruth McBeth walked off the elevator onto the sixth floor wheeling a cart toward the courtroom and made their way though the groups of police officers, lawyers and others who came to see the trial. Neither looked up or around, their faces fixed and expressionless. Marijane wore a beige and brown tweed suit and green sweater, and Ruth was in a two-piece peach-colored suit. A few minutes later, the team of prosecutors stepped out of the elevator with two carts overflowing with large poster boards, plastic and paper bags of evidence, photos and large brown accordion file folders. Chicago Police Superintendent Phil Cline, dressed in his formal blue uniform, was in the hallway shaking hands with each of the Lee family members and offering his best wishes. Lee's family, friends and fellow officers filed in to take their seats on the left side of the courtroom facing the judge. Aloysius's mother and two sisters took seats on the right side. Colleagues from the State's Attorney's Office and the Public Defender's Office, eager to see how two veterans would handle their opening statements, came to watch but soon found that the room was filled to capacity and were turned away. A sheriff's deputy closed the wooden doors to Moran's courtroom, allowing only those with direct involvement in the case to enter. About a dozen people waited in the hallway, hoping to get a seat if someone left during a break.

Judge Moran, who was not one for small talk or speech giving, asked each side if they were ready to proceed and brought the jury in. The jurors took their seats against the wall to the judge's left. James McKay stood up, buttoned his dark blue coat and began. "On the night of August 19, 2001, Eric Lee was a peace officer trying to be a peacemaker," he said. "Little did Eric know that he was going to meet a man who had no interest in peace that night. Little did Eric know that he was going to meet a man that had no interest in law and order that night."

McKay walked over to the defense table and pointed, his voice rising. "Ladies and gentlemen, meet Aloysius Oliver. Cop killer." He paused for effect. "Because it was on that night, ladies and gentlemen, when this little man with his big gun, a .357 six-shot revolver, fully loaded, pointed that gun at Officer Eric Lee, a man he knew was the police, and he pointed the gun at that police officer and he fired twice."

The prosecutor's tone was sneering, revealing disgust for Aloysius. "As a result of Aloysius Oliver's actions on the night of August 19, 2001, the blood of a police officer, the blood of a peacemaker, the blood of Eric Lee, spilled on the alley behind 6330 South Carpenter. And the citizens of Chicago lost Eric Lee." McKay wanted jurors to hear and remember what Aloysius allegedly said before firing his gun: "Fuck the police. *Fuck* the police." McKay had saved that punch for the end. "That's what this man is all about." When he finished, the room was silent.

Marijane waited a moment, moved back from the defense table and walked toward the jury. She did not have notes, preferring, as always, to speak extemporaneously. She had rehearsed some lines the night before, but allowed herself spontaneity, feeding off the energy that inhabited the room. She scanned the jury box and began by saying that the defense had to prove nothing, that her job was to tell the rest of the story. "Because the first thing you have to realize is that this event happened in less time than, in fact, it took Mr. McKay to tell you about it," she said. And the rest of the story, she explained to the jury, walking toward them, would shine a light on police procedure. It would paint a picture of Aloysius's neighborhood at night, a neighborhood known for crime where, just a few days before the shooting, someone stole puppies from Aloysius's house, which put him on edge and made him suspicious of people around the backyard. "And this is, in fact, the circumstances that start the chain of events that brought about this tragedy," Marijane said. Her story was that Aloysius was frightened, and from his darkened yard he thought the man urinating in the alley was coming to terrorize his family.

"As much as the state would like to shout, 'cop killer' and point, that does not fall into the realm of evidence," Marijane said. Aloysius did not know that the men who came down the alley that night were police officers until after the shooting, she said. Once Aloysius knew they were police, he stopped firing his gun, even when he had a clear shot of a defenseless officer. Marijane took a breath and summed up. "What you will find is that this is nothing but a tragedy. That this is something that, in fact, was running on parallel lines: a man trying to protect his home and an officer trying to do his duty. Neither are wrong. This is a homicide. But when, in fact, you look carefully at the evidence, you will see it's not a first-degree murder."

The state's first witness was Shawn Lee. Her job on the stand was simple and brief: to identify her husband from a photograph and to confirm that he was indeed dead, setting a foundation for the prosecution's case. But her presence would accomplish much more; it would allow jurors to see her grief, to feel sadness themselves and understand what the trial was really all about. Shawn Lee was a beautiful woman in her thirties, with shoulder-length brown hair pulled back in a ponytail and large brown eyes. She walked up to the witness stand slowly, her body tense. She wept quietly, and her sorrow and longing for her slain husband filled the room. David O'Connor brought up a photograph of Eric Lee and asked Shawn to identify it. "He's my husband," she said through tears. Then O'Connor went back to his table, held out an autopsy photo facedown and asked that it be entered as evidence. He also asked the defense and the judge if he could spare the widow from viewing it, and stipulate that she would identify the corpse as that of her husband. They all agreed, and Marijane did not ask to cross-examine Lee. It was over in two minutes. Lee stepped down, wiping her eyes as she walked out of the courtroom.

The next witness was Lamar Logan, the drifter known as "the Hype" whose decision to urinate in Aloysius's backyard triggered the events that ended in Lee's death. He shuffled up to the witness stand seemingly oblivious or unconcerned that he was in a court of law to participate in an important trial. Logan looked as if he had been plucked off the street that morning and had not bothered to clean himself up. He was dressed in baggy cargo pants and loose shirt; his long black hair tied back with an elastic band. Assistant State's Attorney Joe Magats began by asking Logan a little about himself. Logan said he was thirty-one years old, "lived everywhere" and hadn't worked full-time in at least three years. He supported himself with odd jobs and had convictions for felony theft and possession of a controlled substance. Logan admitted to using several different names, including Marcus Lee, Lamar Lee, John Logan and

Mark Logan. Magats wanted to get all that out in the open now, so that the defense couldn't tell jurors that the prosecution tried to hide Logan's disreputable background or criminal history. Logan said he was not promised anything for his testimony and was cooperating on his own free will.

On the night he wandered down the alley behind Aloysius's house, Logan said he had downed six or seven 16-ounce cans of "211," a cheap malt liquor. He remembered walking behind Carpenter Street with four cans of beer in a bag and being stopped by three cops in plainclothes. They asked a few questions, searched him and let him go. He told Magats that he clearly could see the officers' badges and guns, and knew they were cops. He continued down the alley and when nature called, Logan said he stepped aside, trying to get out of the sightline of the cops, and ended up relieving himself in the most convenient spot by the gate of Aloysius's backyard. "I had to go to the washroom." He remembered two men coming from the yard, asking what he was doing there. One said, "Get him" and started beating him up. As he lay on the ground, Logan covered his head with his hands to protect himself from the kicks and punches. He yelled for help, hoping the cops he saw earlier would hear his cries. And then he saw figures run down the alley toward him. Logan said he heard a shot but did not see where it came from. He remained on the ground and saw a cop fall down in the alley, bleeding from the head. Logan tried to get up and run, but another officer told him to stay on the ground. "Before I know it, police all over," he said.

Magats asked Logan if he remembered telling a grand jury that he heard the people beating him say that the police were coming. "Did you give that answer?"

"I can't recall. I don't know what I said at that time. Might say yes. I couldn't remember. I was half, you know, hit upside the head."

When her turn came, Marijane stood up, scowling at Logan, walking as she spoke. "Mr. Logan, the assistant state's attorney asked you about different names you use, correct?"

"Yes."

"Are you in *show business*?"

The question prompted giggles in the gallery. Logan did not laugh, and answered, "No."

Marijane began an attempt to discredit Logan, speaking to him in her accusatory voice. "Do you ever tell these different names to police to, in fact, escape being prosecuted for crimes or escape who you are?"

"No."

"So you just tell these different names to the police because you just like telling the police different names?"

"Yes."

Marijane got Logan to explain to the jury that he never saw the actual shooting, but had only heard it. Logan's speech was difficult to understand. He mumbled his answers and squirmed in his seat impatiently during Marijane's aggressive questioning. "Could you please take your hand away from your mouth. I have a problem hearing," Marijane said. "And talk as loud as you can." She was not going to make this easy and again asked Logan whether he remembered anything about testifying before a grand jury two and a half years earlier. Logan became confused about when and where and to whom he told his story. He looked embarrassed and humiliated by the constant questioning for which he did not have satisfactory answers, and he explained that sometimes his mind became frazzled. "Do you remember even testifying before a grand jury two days after this happened?" Marijane said.

"Today."

"Not today. Before a grand jury?"

"No."

She asked if he had gone over his testimony today with the state's attorney, and he said he did. "And is it what you remember happening?"

"I know that already possible a head."

"Say again?"

"My head. I ain't look at it. I just seen it. Didn't look at it. Read it. I just know it's in my head already."

Logan was falling apart on the stand. "Do you remember anything about the night in question?" Marijane asked.

"What?" Logan said.

"Do you remember what happened on the night in *question*, any-thing?"

"The night in question?"

"Yeah."

"Night of what question?"

Marijane sighed loudly. She was irritated. She moved on, getting Logan to tell the jury that he did not remember what the cops looked like, nor did he ever hear anyone say, "Fuck the police." As she wrapped up the cross-examination, Marijane asked Logan why he stayed at the police station all night after the shooting, suggesting that he was not there by choice and was somehow bullied into being a witness.

"Were you allowed to leave the police station?"

"No."

"Were you under arrest?"

"No."

"How did you know you weren't allowed to leave the police sta-tion?"

"Because I was handcuffed to the wall?"

His remark sparked laughter in the gallery, and Marijane spun around with a surprised look and said, "I am sorry?"

"Handcuffed to the wall."

"Did they tell you what you were being handcuffed to the wall for?"

"No."

After the lunch break, the state called Officer Lee's partner, Andre Green. He was a large African American man with the build of a football player, a large torso and thick muscular legs over which he was wearing a sharply tailored dark navy blue suit. Marijane and Ruth moved to the other side of the courtroom to see him better. McKay handled the questioning, and his first goal was to establish that even though Green was working undercover the night of the shooting, it was clear that anyone would have been able to identify him as a police officer. Green told the jury that he was wearing a

FUBU brand football jersey and blue jeans with his badge displayed around his neck, and his gun and radio visible outside his belt. He said Officer Lee also wore his badge outside his shirt, and his gun and radio hung on his belt where anyone could see it. Both men wore bulletproof vests under their shirts.

When he first stopped Lamar Logan in the alley, Green said he dismissed him as a harmless drunk. "He seemed kind of like a bum. He reeked of alcohol," Green said. "He's mumbling and he seemed kind of disoriented, so I just let him go." A couple of minutes after Logan left, Green saw the commotion down the alley. "I said, 'Eric, it looks like a fight down there. Let's go break it up.' "

The officers jogged down the alley, and the group beating the man slowed down as Green and Lee moved closer. "I heard one guy say, 'Chill out, man. Here come the police,' " Green said. "I heard one of the guys say, 'Fuck the police. Man. This guy was pissing in my yard.' " The officer told the assailants to leave Logan alone. "I said, 'It's not that serious, a guy pissing in your yard,' " Green recalled.

By the time he got to court to testify on this day, Green had described the shooting of his partner many times. His testimony was consistent with all of his previous statements and depositions, never departing from his original account. But sitting up there on the stand, in front of a packed room, he recounted that night as if for the first time, his voice shaking, his eyes watering. He recalled hearing Officer Barner yell, "He's got a gun, he's got a gun!" and then saw Aloysius holding the revolver in his left hand. Green said he tried to pull out his own gun as everyone scattered. He ducked by the garage and looked down the gangway. "I saw Aloysius Oliver standing there with a gun pointed at us and he fired. He fired a gun at us."

Green said he fell to the ground and tried to take cover. He heard two more shots and then saw the other officers wrestling with Aloysius and handcuffing him. When it was over, he saw his partner in a pool of blood. Green stopped testifying for a moment and wept. "I said, 'Please call an ambulance, please call an ambulance.' I was over trying to comfort Eric, trying to see if he can respond to me." Green put his head down and sniffled. Squad cars started arriving at the scene and officers saw that Green was flailing, crying and despondent as he stood over Lee's body. "They were trying to hold me down as I was hollering and I lost it. I was losing it and beating on the cars and everything and losing it, and they was all trying to hold me down to slow me down," he said. "I was saying, 'No, man no, he ain't gonna make it. I seen it. He got a hole in his head, he's bleeding, he ain't gonna make it.' "

Green continued to cry on the stand, his chest was heaving and he was having trouble breathing. He said he barely remembered getting into the ambulance and going to the hospital. "I had to check on him, man." Then he learned his partner was dead. Later, at area headquarters, Green got a glimpse of Aloysius and yelled, "That's the one that shot Eric!" As McKay wrapped up his direct examination, he went back to the prosecution table to retrieve a box containing Officer Lee's clothing, his holster, belt, vest and undershirt, the remnants of a dead man, which had a haunting power and brought him and that night into the courtroom. McKay had Green identify his partner's personal effects to be entered as evidence.

If McKay's job was to present Green as a grieving, sympathetic cop who lost his partner, it was Marijane's job to rip him apart, and the tone shifted immediately when she began her cross-examination. It was already clear that Marijane and Green did not like each other, having sparred during earlier depositions. He looked at her coldly.

"Officer Lee was your friend besides your partner, correct?" Marijane said. "Is there anything you'd like to change before I start asking questions?"

"No."

"You never saw Eric Lee being shot, did you?" Marijane said.

"I saw him point the gun at us, ma'am, and fire."

"Let me ask you this: Did you see Eric Lee fall?"

"I went down and I thought Eric Lee went down because we was caught off guard, ma'am."

Marijane was speaking loudly, a little louder than necessary. She set up a television monitor to show Green a videotape taken in the alley and behind Aloysius's house to replicate the lighting conditions the night of the shooting. The images appeared a little darker than

Green remembered. Marijane asked Green to describe what he saw on the monitor, and he was having trouble making it out. "You can't tell because it's too dark, correct?" Marijane yelled. She pressed on by asking Green to describe more details about the shooting, his position when the gunfire began, what Aloysius was wearing and whether Aloysius could have shot Green and Lee right after he pulled out his gun. "He had his gun out, and you didn't have your gun out, your partner didn't have his gun out and Officer Barner didn't have his gun out, correct?" Marijane said.

"That's correct."

"And Mr. Oliver never attempted to shoot any of you in the alley, correct?"

"At that point, he didn't."

On recross, McKay asked Green who was the first person to pull out a gun that night.

"Aloysius Oliver, sir."

"Why did you pull out your gun?"

"To defend my life and all my fellow officers, sir."

After Green finished, the trial continued with testimony from a number of players who help put together the puzzle—a paramedic, a forensic firearms examiner and the deputy medical examiner, Dr. Kendall Crowns, whose descriptions of Officer Lee's wounds, along with the grisly and clinical postmortem details, prompted Shawn Lee to gasp, burst into tears and hurry out of the courtroom.

The next day, the state continued to assemble the events leading to Lee's death by calling Damon Rogers, one of Aloysius's friends who participated in the beating of "the Hype," Lamar Logan. Rogers testified that he could not tell that the men coming down the alley were police officers until they got closer and he saw a police star around the neck of one of the men. When Assistant State's Attorney Joe Magats asked Rogers whether anyone announced he was police officer, he weakly answered with a noncommittal "Not that I know of." Rogers did say, however, that he remembered Tommie Leach yelling, "Here come the police" and Aloysius responding, "Fuck the police." During the fray, Rogers said he ran for cover and dashed upstairs to his home and saw nothing more. "We grabbed the kids, got on the ground until the gunshots stopped," he said.

On cross-examination, Marijane reminded Rogers that he gave a statement to defense investigator Rich English that didn't match what he just said in court. Rogers agreed that he signed his statement in front of English as "true and correct."

"Now, was he forcing you to say anything?" Marijane asked.

"No."

"Did you say to Mr. English that, in fact, you never heard anyone say they were police officers?"

"No."

Marijane brought up a copy of the statement and held it in front of Rogers.

"Does it state that Mr. Rogers never heard anyone say they were police officers?"

Rogers shook his head no and answered, "Because I didn't remember."

"He asked you specifically to tell him whether Aloysius Oliver said anything like, 'Fuck the police' or 'I know they're police,' or anything like that, correct?"

"Yes."

"There is nothing in the statement you gave to Mr. English saying that, in fact, Mr. Oliver said anything like you said today in court, correct?"

"Yes."

"You wouldn't lie, would you?" Marijane said, raising her voice. "You never said you heard anyone say they were the police." She got louder still, asking again if Rogers remembered telling English that Aloysius knew he was shooting at police. "Read the statement!" she said. Rogers shook his head. He did not recall saying anything like that. Marijane wanted to suggest to jurors that Rogers felt pressured by detectives to provide answers that were more incriminating toward Aloysius. Rogers admitted that when the police came to talk with him, he felt intimidated. The detectives took him to the station and questioned him there. English simply visited Rogers at his apartment and never pressured him, telling Rogers that he didn't have to answer any questions and was free to ask the investigator to leave his home at any time.

"Which part of what you told the ladies and gentlemen today is true?" Marijane said.

"All of it is true."

"So in other words, what you told Rich English was true?"

"Yes."

"And what you told the state's attorney was true?"

"Yes."

"Well, let me ask you this: which is it?"

"It took the tape to refresh my memory."

"So Mr. Magats, Mr. McKay and Mr. O'Connor refreshed your memory, correct?"

"Yes."

"They refreshed your memory by playing the tape, going over your testimony in practice today, correct?"

"Yes."

"You told Mr. English, when he asked you whether Aloysius Oliver said anything, you told him he never said anything, correct?" Marijane continued.

"Yes," Rogers said flatly.

"Well, let me ask you this," Marijane said. "Did Mr. English ask you to lie?"

"No."

Marijane finished and walked back to the defense table with a self-satisfied look.

After a short break, the state called Officer Vincent Barner. Like Green, Barner was African American, a big, beefy and muscular man who filled out his well-cut suit. Magats asked Barner to take the jurors through the events of that night. Barner carefully repeated the story about the fight he saw in the alley, about how he was wearing his badge clipped on the collar of his shirt and was wearing his gun on a belt that was visible outside his pants when he approached the group, making it clear he was a cop. He told Magats that as Officer Green approached the fight in the alley, he yelled, "Stop, police!"

"Why is it important to you as a Chicago police officer that you have your badge out and announce police?" Magats asked.

"It is important, it is really important because you always want to let the people around you know that you are the police and not just someone walking up," Barner said.

Magats asked Barner to describe the shooting. Barner said he was watching Aloysius standing with his hands in his pockets of his sweat-shirt. "I asked the defendant to take his hands out of his pocket." Aloysius did not respond. Barner repeated the order. "His right hand came straight out of his pocket, but his left hand didn't come straight out. He pulled and then tugged on his jacket and then he pulled again and that's when I seen a gun in his hand." Barner screamed out so his fellow officers could hear. "He's got a gun!"

Barner began to well up with tears and his voice broke as he recounted how he ran for cover behind a parked car after Aloysius raised his gun. He heard a woman screaming in the backyard. Barner then ran down a dark gangway on the side of the house and heard two shots behind him. He tripped and fell, dropping his gun. He got back up and continued down the gangway, but was stopped by a locked gate. On the other side, he saw Tommie Leach running and yelled for him to stop. "And he turned around and he had a gun in his hand and pointed it in my direction," Barner said. "I fired for fear of my life that he was going to shoot at me." The shot missed, and Leach disappeared into the night. Then Barner turned around and found himself face to face with Aloysius in the gangway and a gun pointed at his chest. "When I saw that gun pointed at me I pulled my gun, leveled my gun up and I said I was the police. He said, 'You the police?' and he raised the gun from here and he said, 'You're the police,' and he had it like to my face and I tried to fire, but my gun wouldn't fire and I grabbed his, and I grabbed it . . ." Barner began crying, put his head down and had to stop to compose himself. "I was so scared. I was scared, man. I grabbed that gun. My gun didn't fire, and I just grabbed, held on to one end and I wasn't going to let it go," Barner said, sniffling. "If I let that gun go, I wouldn't be here right now."

Hearing Barner's screams for help, the other officers ran down the gangway. Barner said that he continued to struggle with Aloysius for the gun, trying to knock him up against the wall. Barner dropped his own gun and grabbed Aloysius's, which fired as he snatched it, though neither man was hit by the shot. Officer Jones tackled Aloysius as he broke free from Barner and tried to run. Barner walked back to where the scuffle began. "That's when I realized it was Eric laying in the alley." He again had to stop testifying to compose himself, and Shawn Lee began weeping in the gallery, triggering other officers to cry, as well. A woman sitting on a bench on the other side of the courtroom in a black hat and dark glasses was holding a Bible on her lap and moving back and forth, chanting, "Liar. Liar."

Now it was Marijane's turn with the witness. Officer Barner's eyes narrowed and he leaned forward, as if ready to defend himself from attack as she stood up and moved toward the stand. His expression changed from grief to steely. Marijane brought him back to the scene of the crime and asked, from where he was standing, whether he could identify who was beating up Lamar Logan in the alley. Barner admitted he could not see their faces, but knew afterward who they were. She pressed him on remembering his exact location within the backyard during the chase. Back and forth she asked about where he ran, where he stood, where he was looking, what he did. The tension between them was building. She asked questions with her back turned to Barner, looking up and out at the gallery, her voice projecting away from the witness, but loud enough for him to hear her.

Marijane then asked about Barner's confrontation with Aloysius in the gangway when, she suggested, Aloysius first realized he was being chased by an officer. "Mr. Oliver was about five feet away from you, correct?"

"Yes."

"And he said, 'You the police?' didn't he?" she said.

"Yes, as he raised that gun toward my face."

"Did he fire it?"

"I didn't give him the chance."

"When you say you didn't give him the chance, did he at all fire? Did you hear it click? Did you hear it cock?"

"My gun clicked. I drew my gun."

"Did you hear Mr. Oliver click his gun?"

"No, I didn't."

"You fired at Mr. Oliver first, correct."

"I tried."

"Well, let me ask you this: Did Mr. Oliver fire when your gun jammed?"

"I didn't give him the chance."

Marijane wanted to talk about what Aloysius was wearing that night. Barner earlier said that Aloysius had on a "hoody," a sweatshirt with a hood and a pouch where he could stuff his hands. Marijane pointed out that in the Chicago Police Department photo of Aloysius taken right after his arrest, he wasn't wearing a hoody, but rather a different kind of sweatshirt. Barner admitted he apparently misidentified the garment. Marijane sounded annoyed with Barner. "Sir, you never saw Mr. Oliver shoot Eric Lee, did you?" she said.

"No, I didn't."

"You don't know except what you've been told by your brother officers that Aloysius Oliver shot Eric Lee, correct?"

"Excuse me?"

"You don't know except what you've been told that Aloysius Oliver shot Eric Lee, correct?"

"That's correct."

"Thank you. That's all, judge."

Magats came back with the sweatshirt, and asked Barner to identify it as the one that Aloysius was wearing that night. The sweatshirt had pockets, but no hood. Barner said that was the one.

Marijane came back angry. "Do you remember when I asked you to describe the hoody that Mr. Oliver was wearing?"

"No, not really."

"You don't remember not more than five minutes ago when I asked you to describe the hoody, what it looked like?"

"Yes, I do."

She reminded him that he said it had a pouch. "You said 'pouch' and I said 'pouch' and you said 'yes,' right?"

"Yes, I answered yes."

"Show us the pouch on there, not the pockets—the pouch."

Barner shrugged. He couldn't, because there was no pouch.

"Show us the hood." Marijane said.

"There is no hood."

"This isn't a hoody in neighborhood slang, is it, no matter how much you or the state would like to say it is, is it? It's a warm-up jacket, right?"

"It's a warm-up jacket, it's a sweater, it's a—"

"Hoody."

"You can call it many things."

"You examined this in the state attorney's office, didn't you? You saw this."

"I saw it. I didn't touch it."

"And you know Officer Green described in fact what Mr. Oliver was wearing as a gray hoody and you were trying to back up your brother officer's testimony by describing for the ladies and gentlemen of the jury a hoody, weren't you?"

O'Connor objected.

Marijane pressed on and asked Barner when the last time he saw the jacket was. He said the day before inside the state attorney's office.

"Do you know what a hood is?" she said.

"Yes, I know what a hood is."

"Do you remember me directly asking you whether or not Mr. Oliver's jacket had a hood?"

"I'm sure you did at this point."

"And do you remember your answer being yes, it had a hood?"

"Yes, I guess I said it had a hood," he sighed. "You said hoody, and I said yes, it had a hood."

"No, sir, let's not try and confuse."

McKay objected.

"Sir, isn't it correct that this incident took place so quick that you don't know what happened?"

"That's incorrect."

Marijane ended on an insult, suggesting that despite Barner's

preparation for the trial, his testimony was inconsistent. "Isn't it correct that you read reports, you read incidents, you saw evidence?"

"That's correct."

"And you *still* can't get it right, can you?"

"Objection," yelled McKay.

"Sustained. Jury disregard," Moran said.

"That's all, judge," Marijane said.

Barner appeared exhausted. But it wouldn't be the last time he
and Marijane would go at it during this trial.

CHAPTER FOURTEEN

A Shot in the Dark

MARIJANE PLACEK WALKED INTO THE COURTROOM the next morning wearing a luminous two-piece pink jacket and matching skirt with black trim that was accented with a black-and-white polka-dotted scarf. A woman sitting in the gallery remarked, "She looks like a bottle of Pepto Bismol." Marijane did not hear the comment, but would not have cared. She was aware of the attention her outfit drew because that's why she wore clothing like that. She was buoyant today. "Oh, I'm having fun now," Marijane said to me as she carried her files to the defense table. "A lot of people talk about this kind of thing being sad or depressing. I love it. I've got the state on the run, and I'm loving this." Marijane's exuberance was deliberate, a signal to her opponents that she was not afraid, that her confidence was unflagging. Yet her public displays of levity, coupled with her sometimes cold demeanor to the other side, were insulting to the widow and parents of Officer Lee, who shook their heads when they saw her walk in. Marijane rarely disguised her feelings or censored herself during a trial or afterwards.

Sandy Chavez, a counselor who worked for the state's attorney's victim witness assistance program, had been sitting with the Lee family throughout the trial, guiding them through the process, explaining the legal complexities and offering emotional support when they needed it. Chavez had a warm, inviting and sympathetic face, and was the kind of person who freely gave hugs and would tell you that everything was going to work out all right. She had been observing public defenders at Twenty-sixth Street for seventeen years, and got along with most, though she was not fond of Marijane. "Some public defenders are nice, but it seems she's never been nice to anyone," Chavez told me during an interview later. "It makes me cringe when I hear Marijane is representing someone in a case. To me, that means there's going to be a circus."

Chavez came to her job with firsthand experience as both a victim and witness to violent crime, and knew well the absurdities and frustrations of the legal system. When she was a girl in the city's Pilsen neighborhood, she watched terrified from a window of her home as a gang member shot a family friend in the back of the head execution-style. In gang-controlled turf where witnesses closed curtains and shut their eyes when they heard gunfire, Chavez was brave enough to not only identify the shooter for police, but also to testify against him in court. That decision prompted retaliation by gang members who shot and wounded two of Chavez's brothers. One of the shooters was acquitted, and the other was never arrested. Afterward, Chavez's home was set on fire by arsonists who she believed continued the retaliation. Years later, her brother-in-law was killed by a stray bullet in a drive-by shooting, and no one was ever charged. Her experience with the legal system was utter failure and disappointment. Incensed at the violence in her community, Chavez spoke publicly at rallies about the need for greater police presence in her neighborhood and the need for more respect for its residents. Richard M. Daley, who was state's attorney at the time, invited Chavez to join a new unit he created for victims and witnesses of crimes. "I said to the mayor that I never wanted another family to experience the pain that I felt," Chavez told me. "Our family never got justice. Absolutely never. I want others to feel that they can, that they can close that chapter of their life and move on. We walk the path with them, and we take them by the hand. I never had that."

So when Chavez sat with the grieving family of Eric Lee and watched Marijane icily charge past them, she felt offended. "I can't understand it, and I never will," Chavez said. "There are some public defenders who are good. I've seen some come up and offer their condolences to the families, saying that it's nothing personal." And that was just it. To Marijane, it *was* nothing personal, which meant there was no reason for her to say anything. "If you start thinking about how the victim's family feels, and how you would feel, you couldn't do it," Marijane explained. "When I'm on trial, and we're in a truly adversarial proceeding, I hate the mother of the victim, I hate the father of the victim, I hate the children of the victim. I hate every part of it. It's actually a terrible thing, but I can literally hate them when I'm fighting. I have to."

To hate and to be hated was part of the job. Marijane knew that parents, spouses, children and friends of murder victims despised her. She felt they *should* despise her. Marijane told me a story about one murder trial during which she had to teach the father of the victim to hate her because that's the way it was supposed to be. She represented a client who was accused of tossing a Molotov cocktail into the man's home, an apparent act of retaliation over street drug sales. Three children and their grandmother died in the fire, but the father was not home at the time. One of the girls who escaped the burning house without her siblings was called to testify during the trial, and Marijane was unrelenting as she cross-examined the child, bringing the girl to tears. During a break, the girl's father began walking toward Marijane full speed, as if he were going to attack. Investigator Richard English saw him coming and stood in front of Marijane to protect her. The father urgently wanted to talk to Marijane. He yelled out, "You're one of the best goddamn lawyers I've ever seen. I want to take your card." Marijane couldn't believe what she heard. "He was a known drug dealer and had a case coming up. And he wanted *me* to represent him." Marijane was enraged. "I said, 'Get out of here. Get out of my way, you fucking bastard.' I had such contempt for that man. He broke my boundary. You cannot come up to the person who represented the man who killed your daughter and say, "Will you be my lawyer?' Not in my ethic, not in my soul, not in my nationality. You should want me dead." Marijane would have understood if the man had yelled or cursed or tried to attack her. "I would have respected him, and I wouldn't have reported him for hitting me, or trying to hit me or trying to get in my face and call me a bitch or whatever," she said. "You don't praise me and say I'm good. Don't do it. That was the most appalling thing I've ever seen in the courtroom." Marijane stopped to underline her point. She was not in court to make friends. She was there to hate. "I am that hard. I am that cruel. Get that right," she insisted. "I know what I am doing. This is not any kind of soft thing. I signed on, and I am doing it."

As she sat down ready for the Oliver trial to resume, Marijane returned to her trial face, hard and cruel. Before beginning to call more witnesses, Assistant State's Attorney O'Connor announced that he had a last-minute piece of evidence to turn over to the defense. It was a report written by a police captain that had not been included in the original discovery documents. Marijane seized on this late development as patently unfair. After a quick reading of the report, she said it might contain information at odds with testimony from the officers who were present during the shooting. She immediately asked Judge Moran for a mistrial, arguing that not having access to those documents before the trial put the defense at a disadvantage. Moran said he would not make a decision until he had time to review the report and hear arguments. The trial would continue. Moran summoned the jurors into the courtroom.

The state resumed by calling Johanna Harris, Aloysius's girlfriend at the time of the shooting. She was now sixteen, and in high school. She was petite, dressed in a cream-colored sweater, and spoke in a soft, girlish voice. As O'Connor began asking questions, Harris took glances at Aloysius and quickly returned her gaze forward. Aloysius smiled. But if he thought his girlfriend was going to help his case, he was mistaken. Harris told O'Connor that since Aloysius's arrest, she had been communicating with him through letters. O'Connor mentioned one letter in which Aloysius requested a special favor. "In that letter, what did he ask you to do?"

"He told me that if anybody came out to talk to me not to talk to them."

"What else?" O'Connor said.

"He said that if they asked me who shot first, say the police shot first."

Harris gave her version of the shooting. She described how Aloysius instructed her to get his cousin after he saw "the junkie man" urinating in the yard. She watched as they beat the man in the alley and clearly heard Tommie Leach say, "Here come the police." Harris testified she heard Aloysius respond, "Fuck the police." As Aloysius ran and fired shots, Harris said she ran into the garage, closed the door and began screaming. O'Connor showed her Aloysius's gun and asked if she recognized it.

"Yes," she said. "I was right behind him."

Marijane stood up and got unfriendly right away. "You told a completely different story when the state's attorney of Cook County put you on the stand before the grand jury, correct?"

"Correct," Harris said meekly.

"So you lied to the police?" Marijane asked, her voice increasing in volume.

"Yes."

Harris explained that it wasn't until she met with investigators a month earlier did she sort out the story of how events unfolded that night. "And that's the first time you told anyone what you told the jury, correct?" Marijane said.

"Yes."

"I'm going to ask you something right now, and I don't mean to embarrass you, please believe me," Marijane said. "Do you have any children?"

"Yes."

"Is Aloysius Oliver the father?"

"No."

Marijane asked this question because she wanted jurors to see that Harris wasn't some innocent schoolgirl taken advantage of by her client, but rather a sexually active teenager. Marijane continued on to pick apart Harris's grand jury testimony, and pointed to her conflicting stories. Did Harris tell the grand jury that she saw a badge or heard an officer identify himself or not? "I'm not sure," Harris said.

"You don't remember telling police that Aloysius Oliver said, 'Fuck the police' "

"I don't remember."

"Nothing further."

The prosecution had been saving one of its most important pieces of evidence until now: Aloysius's videotaped confession. To explain how the tape was made, prosecutors called Assistant State's Attorney Darren O'Brien, supervisor of the felony review unit. O'Brien explained that he was summoned to the police station to assist detectives in taping the confession. When he walked into the interrogation room, O'Brien said he noticed the three bandages on Aloysius's face. But Aloysius seemed otherwise fine and made no allegations that he had been beaten or abused. He did not complain of any pain or discomfort and said the detectives had treated him well.

O'Connor and McKay rolled out a video monitor to show the jury Aloysius's confession. The screen faced the jurors, which meant that Aloysius could only hear the audio of himself. Marijane and Ruth McBeth moved over to the right side of the courtroom to get a better view. "I saw a person down there taking a leak by my garbage can," Aloysius said on the tape as he began recounting his version of events that night. "I was really upset that he was in our backyard . . . and I grabbed my gun." He described the shooting and, after the television screen went black, Aloysius's face came on again and jurors heard his postconfession apology. "I know it's not going to bring him back, but I'm sorry," Aloysius said. Lee's family, and the cops who sat on the left side of the courtroom, shook their heads and snorted at the apology. They were not impressed.

Ruth handled the cross-examination of O'Brien, attempting to discredit the methods used to obtain the confession. She implied to O'Brien that he asked Aloysius leading questions during the confession, rather than letting Aloysius tell the story on his own. "Why not ask him, 'Tell me what happened?' and then let him go on?" Ruth said.

"There are many ways to find out what happened," O'Brien responded. "I chose to ask him question by question."

When O'Brien finished testifying, Judge Moran informed the jury they would have a three-day weekend. Monday was the Martin Luther King Jr. holiday. He reminded them to stay away from newspapers and television accounts of the trial, and not to discuss it with anyone. Marijane and Ruth would have a few extra days to absorb the trial so far and refine their defense strategies.

* * *

The following Tuesday afternoon James McKay called Detective
Tom Kelly, the same detective who Marijane had prodded unrelent-
ingly during the hearing to throw out Aloysius's confession. McKay
wanted the jury to know that Kelly handled the confession properly,
and certainly did not beat it out of Aloysius. Kelly explained to the
jury how he first he met with Aloysius in an interview room of the
police station at Fifty-first Street and Wentworth Avenue, and noticed that Aloysius had three "abrasions" on his face but otherwise
seemed fine. Kelly said that he conducted the interrogation and confession by the rules, and he read Aloysius his Miranda warnings from
a Fraternal Order of Police handbook. "I asked him if he wanted to
talk to me or make a statement to me," Kelly said. "At first, he said
he had no knowledge of any shootings." Kelly then offered bandages
to Aloysius, made sure he was fed and talked to him again about 4:45
a.m. "I told Mr. Oliver I didn't believe him," Kelly said. "Mr. Oliver
said, 'Okay, I was lying. Now I'll tell you the truth.' " Aloysius gave
his account, and Kelly called the state attorney's office to have someone come to the station to "memorialize" the confession on tape.

Now it was Marijane's turn with Kelly. They were ready for each
other. If he was anxious or annoyed, Kelly did not show it. Slowly,
deliberately and in meticulous detail, Marijane asked Kelly to recount his involvement in the investigation the night of the shooting,
from the time he arrived at the scene to taking Aloysius's confession.
Marijane picked away, attempting to get Kelly to account for nearly
every minute of his time, a near impossibility. The unflappable Kelly
appeared more defensive as the questioning continued. He crossed
his arms and occasionally covered his mouth with his left hand as he
spoke. Shawn and Anna Lee shook their heads at Marijane, looking
exasperated at her barrage of questions.

Marijane asked Kelly about the interrogation methods he used in
getting Aloysius's confession.

"Did you ask him any leading questions?" Marijane asked Kelly.

"No."

"Who was the first person to inform him that, in fact, a Chicago
police officer had died?"

"I was."

"And he was surprised, correct?"

"I have no idea if he was surprised or not."

"Do you remember what he said?"

"At what point?"

"When you told him Lee was dead."

Marijane's voice rose, her tone more accusatory as she continued, "You didn't tell the jury everything, did you?"

"Not every single word, no, ma'am."

"You not only had to tell him that Eric Lee was dead," Marijane said, now yelling as she walked across the room. "You said, 'You shot a Chicago police officer.' He was surprised, wasn't he?"

"I have no idea."

She continued with the questions and now had her back to Kelly, walking away as she spoke. The exchange got heated as the questions piled up. "I'm completely lost, ma'am," Kelly said at one point.

Marijane wanted to know whether there were discrepancies between what Aloysius told Kelly before his videotaped confession and the actual confession. Didn't Aloysius say he fired a shot because he was afraid, that he didn't know he was shooting at police officers?

"No," Kelly said.

"You would remember that, correct?"

"I hope so."

"You would have remembered that if you were at the video, correct?

"I'm telling you I don't recall him saying that."

"That would have been self-defense, correct?"

McKay yelled, "Objection!"

"Well, let me ask you this: You, of course, wouldn't just remember things useful to convict Mr. Oliver while forgetting things that might be useful to him, would you?"

"Objection," McKay said.

"This witness may answer," Judge Moran said.

"Are you asking me if I have selective memory?" Kelly asked Marijane.

"Yes, that's what I'm asking you, officer," she replied.

"I don't have selective memory, then."

"Mr. Oliver told you he was frightened. He told you he thought he would be shot. He told you he fired in self-defense."

"Objection!" McKay yelled again.

"Do you ever remember Mr. Oliver apologizing?" Marijane continued.

"Yes."

"I can't hear you! Remove your hand from your mouth."

Marijane got what she wanted from the detective and let him go.

The next day, Officer Barner returned to explain apparent differences between his earlier testimony and what was contained in the recently obtained police reports the defense had not seen until now, including one report from a Captain James Paoletti. Marijane wanted to know why the early summary reports of the shooting made no mention of Barner announcing he was a police officer. Marijane jumped right in, loud and strong.

"Is there anything about those facts you wish to change for the ladies and gentlemen of the jury?"

"None whatsoever," Barner answered.

Marijane sounded like a parent lecturing a child as she addressed the officer. People shifted in their seats. She asked Barner whether he remembered speaking to a deputy superintendent after the shooting. "I don't remember talking to a deputy superintendent at all, ma'am." Marijane had the reports on the table in front of her and tried to make issue that Barner was never quoted in them as announcing he was a police officer before Aloysius fired his gun. Reading from a report, she asked if he remembered ever telling anyone he heard a gunshot. "Ma'am, I have no idea what you're reading, but I never said that to a superintendent."

"Did you ever have a conversation with Captain Paoletti?"

"I never told Captain Paoletti anything of that sort."

Marijane, with her usual asperity, continued her questions about Captain Paoletti, on and on, wearing down Barner's patience. He leaned forward, looking angry, worried and concerned. Then she asked if he remembered ever talking to an Officer Zipolski. He said he did not. She asked again. "Ma'am, I never had a conversation with Officer Zipolski!"

"Do you know what a weapon discharge report is?" Marijane asked.

"I don't remember signing a report."

"Well," Marijane said, showing him a piece of paper. "Is this your signature?"

"Just because my signature is on it, doesn't mean I wrote it."

"Would you sign a report without reading it?"

She walked up to Barner and stood before him face to face. "Did you sign it because it was true and correct at the time?"

"I signed it, ma'am."

Barner said he did not type it himself and did not remember making the report. "Are you saying you would sign a report that contained lies?" Marijane said.

"No!" Barner came back. "That's just a scenario of what happened."

Marijane slammed the report on the witness stand, the sound amplified by the microphone. "Did you sign that report as true and correct?"

Yes, Barner said, he signed it.

But the report, Marijane pointed out, never said anything about Barner announcing he was a police officer during the melee. He acknowledged that it did not. Again, she asked whether he signed it as true and correct. Barner said he did.

"Why did you sign it?" Marijane asked.

"Ma'am, at this point, I don't know."

"Did you read those documents before you signed it?"

"I doubt it."

Even though he signed this document for which Marijane seemed to be placing great weight, Barner tried to diminish the importance of the report, characterizing it as a supplement among a long list of reports on the incident. "It's just a brief scenario of what took place," he said.

Marijane wouldn't let it go. "Well, let me ask you this, sir: Isn't it correct that the first time you told what you told to the ladies and gentlemen last week was in this courtroom? You told a superinten-dent something different, you told your captain something different, you told your lieutenant something different, you told your sergeant something different, and in fact you told the discharge report which you signed yourself something different than you told the ladies and gentlemen last week?"

"Could you repeat that question, ma'am?"

She asked again. "Correct?"

"No, ma'am."

"Is there any reason the Chicago Police Department would lie about you?"

"Objection," McKay yelled.

"Well, let me ask you this: Is there any reason Captain Paoletti would lie?"

"Objection." McKay was angry.

"That's all, judge." Marijane walked back to the defense table.

Assistant State's Attorney Magats tried to clarify the confusion. Magats had Barner explain that supplemental reports included sum-maries of the incident, not contents of the entire investigation. "They are not step by step. What you told the jury was correct," Magats said to Barner.

"Yes."

Magats made the point to jurors that during the trauma and con-fusion after the shooting, Barner may have forgotten signing papers and telling people things because he was upset and disoriented. "When you were at the scene, what was your emotional state?" he asked Barner.

"It's hard to explain when you see somebody you just got finished talking to, somebody I can say I love him because we care about each other, sitting there in an alley bleeding from the head and not mov-ing . . . I cannot explain to no one in here how I felt." Barner paused, covered his face with his hands and looked down. "I didn't know if he was alive or dead . . . I was confused, just hurt, scared. There is no way to explain it. I just kept thinking of his wife and child."

Marijane objected loudly, and Judge Moran told the jury to disre-gard the remarks.

Marijane's aggressive performance upset Lee's family. After Barner's testimony, Shawn Lee was crying out in the hallway. Sandy Chavez walked over to embrace her.

Officer Andre Green came back to the stand briefly and then, after five days of testimony, the state rested its case late that afternoon. Judge Moran asked Marijane and Ruth whether they wanted to begin the next morning. Marijane said they wanted to continue rather than leave for the day.

The defense team decided to begin its attack by picking apart the multiple police reports generated from the shooting, to point out discrepancies from one another and to challenge which was more credible. Marijane's first witness was Thomas Folliard, a deputy superintendent with the Chicago Police Department who wrote a summary of the incident after walking through the crime scene and speaking to the officers who were there. Marijane wanted to press him on the initial police reports to find contradictions or missing pieces. She wanted to know what Barner said to him that night. Folliard admitted that he didn't take notes because in his mind, his report was an overall summation, not an investigative document. Someone would take more formal statements from the officers later because they were too upset and needed time to calm down. Barner especially was in no condition to speak. "He was so excited, I had trouble telling him what was mandated and required from him. He was distraught to the point of almost being incoherent. And there were officers at the scene who were more incoherent than Officer Barner," Folliard said.

Marijane asked him to describe what he meant in more detail. "They would be hyperventilating and having trouble articulating what they just observed. And shaking. There were officers crying. There were officers that appeared to be somehow accepting fault of the incident. There was just a lot of raw emotion going on."

Captain James Paoletti was next. He was the watch commander on the night of the shooting and prepared a summary report, as well as injury and weapons discharge reports. The captain's reports did not include detailed or complete statements from officers Green and

Barner. "Let me ask you this: Would it be correct in saying that the Chicago Police Department encourages officers to sign untrue reports?" Marijane said.

"Absolutely not."

McKay objected, but the judge let it stand.

"Would it be correct in your experience as a watch commander and a Chicago police officer that, in fact, the reason officers sign reports is they verify it's true and correct?"

McKay objected again, but Moran let it go.

"Yes, ma'am."

Marijane cited various reports and asked whether officers signed them to indicate they were true and correct. "Have you ever made an attempt to correct your report?" Marijane asked.

"I have not."

Under cross-examination by McKay, Paoletti repeated Folliard's explanation that it was impossible to get accurate and reliable statements from the officers so soon after the shooting. "It's not an investigative report, is it?" McKay asked. "The investigation of a crime is conducted by different police officers, correct?"

"That's correct."

Marijane came back with an insult. "So in other words," she said loudly, "you know nothing about investigations?"

"Not correct."

She asked Paoletti how long he had been with the department. He said thirty-four years. "And you know nothing about investigating crimes, right?"

"I didn't say that, ma'am."

"Well . . . do you know something about investigating crimes?"

"I would like to think so."

Marijane moved on to the night Aloysius was taken to the police station after his arrest. "When you took custody of him, he had no injuries," she said.

"You have made a statement," Paoletti responded. "You have not asked me a question."

"I'm asking you, did he have any injuries on his face?"

"I do not recall."

Paoletti's failure to recall this point was significant. Jurors had seen Aloysius with bandages on his face during his videotaped confession, which was taken at the police station. Marijane was trying to imply that Aloysius was roughed up sometime before he confessed. She read from a deposition in which Paoletti said Aloysius did not appear hurt or in need of bandages when he was taken into custody. "You saw no cuts, bruises or abrasions or bleeding or anything like that at that time, right?"

"Not that I can remember, no."

Jurors would have to draw their own conclusions about whether Aloysius took a beating after arriving at the police station.

John Nixon came to Chicago from his home in Bippus, Indiana, to serve as the defense team's star witness. The quirky British forensics and ballistics expert was called to demonstrate that Aloysius could not have deliberately shot Eric Lee and raise the possibility, remote as it was, that the shot could have originated elsewhere, maybe from one of the other officers' own guns. Nixon, who had a beard now, was dressed in a gray suit when he came to testify the next day. He took the stand and immediately commanded the attention of the gallery with his refined English diction and polite manner. Marijane asked Nixon to recite his credentials to the court so that he could be qualified as an expert witness. He went over his long list of employers, at times being vague and deepening the mystery about his background. Nixon said that his career included a stint with the British Defence Department during the collapse of the communism in Eastern Europe. He explained his work in reverse engineering, the process of deconstructing weapons to learn how they were made, and he spoke of how he analyzed foreign weapons technology. Marijane asked Nixon whether he'd ever published any professional papers related to his work. He said he had but could not reveal their titles because they were classified, commissioned by NATO and the British government. To jurors, he must have sounded like a character from a James Bond film. McKay looked as if he wanted to groan.

McKay was not going to let the judge qualify Nixon as an expert witness without a fight. As he questioned him, McKay had a mocking sort of contempt in his voice. "You work mostly out of your house, right?" he said.

"No, I have an outbuilding which I use as a lab and test facility," Nixon replied.

"That's like a shed or garage next to your house?"

"It is a brick building which is probably about two and a half thousand square feet."

McKay asked whether Nixon operated an accredited crime lab, whether he was a member of an accredited firearms or tool mark examiner's organization. Nixon said no to both questions. "And part of your work while you were working at the ministry of defense in England was animal testing, right?" McKay said.

"I didn't specifically shoot the animals, but I reviewed the reports."

"You shot animals?" McKay said.

Marijane objected. McKay tried again to bring up Nixon's work analyzing wounds on animals. Moran, seeing where this was going, asked him to move on. McKay asked Nixon about his experience as an expert witness in this country. Nixon said that since he had been living in the United States, he'd testified only for defense lawyers and never for prosecutors or law enforcement. Marijane stood up for another round. She wanted to make one thing clear about the suggestion Nixon was an animal hater.

"Who is Major Doberman?" she asked.

"He is a dog that I have who is a Doberman and he is a trained guard dog and he protects the facility that I have," Nixon said.

"Is he a member of your staff?"

"I count him as such, yes."

She asked Nixon to clarify the animal-shooting reference. He said he reviewed tests on animals other people shot to analyze wounds, "primarily pigs, some goats."

McKay still wouldn't let go. "You say you never shot pigs?"

"Judge!" Marijane said.

Moran was angry. "Enough of that, okay? Something else, please."

The judge qualified Nixon as an expert witness and allowed Marijane to begin her questioning. "Well, Mr. Nixon," she said, "let's talk now about the real facts of this case."

Nixon told the jury that he visited the crime scene and shot video during the day and at night to re-create the lighting conditions. He used a special digital camera that adjusted to lighting conditions and took light measurements in the places where the key players stood. As prelude to his discussion on how difficult it was to fire accurate successive shots from a .357 Magnum pistol, Nixon demonstrated to the jury how Aloysius's revolver worked. He explained it was a double-action gun, which meant that "when you pull the trigger, this hammer at the back here will come back and then you pull the trigger a little further the hammer falls. It both raises and drops the hammer." A double-action gun was more difficult to shoot unless the hammer was already cocked back, he explained.

Marijane then played the video Nixon shot of the crime scene. At times, the picture was so dark that it was difficult to distinguish anything. Nixon shot video footage from both the shooter's point of view and Lee's point of view. Nixon contended that the lighting conditions were similar to that on the night of the shooting, making it very difficult to aim a gun at a target. "I came to a number of opinions, and one of them was that it wouldn't be possible to see the sights on the gun given the lighting conditions," Nixon said. He demonstrated using the sights of the gun and said without enough light, you could not line up the gap with the front fin.

In anticipation of the state's cross-examination, Marijane had Nixon explain to the jury that he was being paid $380 an hour for his time in court. "Is your opinion ever influenced by the amount of money you make?" Marijane asked. "No," he said. "Occasionally, I will render an opinion they don't like," he said. Nixon finished up by reiterating his opinion that Aloysius's shot was unlikely aimed at Officer Lee. "It is my opinion that given the quick time that this happened in the lighting conditions, the fact that the target was moving, it probably couldn't have been an aimed shot."

McKay looked as if he couldn't wait to get up. "How much do you get paid to sit around and wait?" he said. Nixon told him $380.

"Do you know how much these jurors get paid to sit around and wait?" McKay responded.

"Objection!" Marijane was furious. The judge called a sidebar and told the jury to disregard that exchange. McKay came back to the issue of aiming the gun. "Aiming a gun, sir, is not pointing a gun in the general direction of somebody, is it?"

"No, not by my definition," Nixon said.

McKay picked up the revolver from the table and placed the barrel of Aloysius's gun on his own temple. "I am not aiming the gun at my head, am I?" he said.

"No," Nixon said, "you are pointing the gun at your head."

McKay, adding to the theatrics, asked Nixon to pick up the gun and point it at him. Nixon stood up, holding the gun at chest level and pointed toward McKay. "You're not aiming at me, are you?" McKay said. "You are pointing a gun at me?"

"That's correct. Yes."

McKay pointed out to the jury that based on the lighting conditions, Aloysius would have had a better view of Lee than Lee of Aloysius. "Would you agree, Mr. Nixon, that aiming a gun in the technical sense has nothing to do with shooting a human being?"

"You wouldn't need to aim it," Nixon said. "If someone was standing in the path of the bullet, then they're going to get hit with it."

Marijane got another chance to question Nixon. "You were told to, in fact, believe the police version as to what happened, correct?" Marijane's voice was at yelling volume.

"Yes, I specifically asked the defense team what evidence I should consider, and they told me the police statements were the ones to go by."

Marijane began her next question, her voice rising. "Miss Placek, quit yelling," O'Connor said.

"I'm sorry, I don't mean to offend their sensibilities," she said.

She continued, pointing out one key piece of information she hoped would raise some doubt. "There is no forensic evidence that in fact Mr. Oliver's gun shot Officer Lee, correct?"

"No, there isn't," Nixon said.

"Based on your expert opinion, is Mr. Aloysius Oliver the only one who could have fired that gun?"

"No."

"Is it your opinion based on looking strictly at the police's version of the events that Aloysius Oliver intended to shoot Officer Lee?"

"Objection!" McKay said.

"That's all, judge," Marijane said, and she walked back to the table. She said the defense would rest its case. Moran said closing arguments would begin tomorrow.

The next morning a mix of lawyers, cops, courthouse employees and press people arrived early to get seats. As on the opening day of the trial, there was not enough room for everyone, and groups of people were forced to stand in the corridor. Judge Moran would not allow anyone to stand inside the courtroom. When everyone was seated, he asked the defense to begin.

Marijane, wearing a brown and burgundy checked coat, black shirt and tie, got up, strode toward the jury box and began to build her case piece by piece. She reminded jurors at the outset that Aloysius was still presumed innocent. "As he sits here," she said, "he has done nothing." Her closing strategy was to create a scenario of self-defense in which Aloysius, in fear for his life, carried a gun when he thought someone was breaking into his backyard and ended up, unintentionally, shooting toward someone he didn't realize was a police officer. Borrowing themes from her opening argument, she painted a picture of a dangerous neighborhood where Aloysius sometimes feared for his own safety, where on the night Eric Lee was shot, Aloysius didn't know who was coming down that alley. "Mr. Oliver was ready to, in fact, take care of people who wished to rob his home. The problem is, he didn't know that when he was running for his life that those people were the Chicago police," Marijane said. "No one involved in this event really knows what happened."

She pointed out that there was no physical evidence linking Aloysius to the crime, just as Mr. Nixon pointed out. The bullets that killed the officer were never found. There weren't even any casings recovered at the scene. "We do not truly know who shot Officer Lee," she said. "The Chicago Police Department still doesn't. This is a tragedy. This is a terrible tragedy. A police officer did not deserve to die . . . This is not an instance of justice. This should not be vengeance."

Aloysius's confession, Marijane implied once more, came only after he was beaten, an assertion that prompted an objection from McKay. The judge said that the jury heard the evidence and could decide for itself. Marijane picked up Aloysius's revolver and clicked twice, and said he could have blamed others for firing the gun that night, but he did not. He told the truth, that he shot because he was in fear for his life. "You heard a true expression of somebody who thought he was going to get shot." Marijane suggested the jury consider second-degree murder. "Something happened different out there, and it doesn't warrant first-degree murder," she said. "This is more than a tragedy. Officer Lee was more than a fine police officer. This tragedy becomes compounded if Aloysius Oliver is convicted."

She lowered her voice. "You stand as gods now, in judgment of another human being," she concluded. "Render him a just decision."

David O'Connor, in a pressed, clean navy suit, appeared incensed at it all. He told the jury that Aloysius Oliver was a man who never wanted to take responsibility for his actions. "Responsible twenty-six-year-olds are not responsible if they're pulling out .357s from a couch or beating up people, or telling their girlfriends to go get some help," he said. "Responsible twenty-six-year-olds aren't going to say, 'Fuck the police,' run, take a gun and shoot."

His argument gained momentum. "What we just heard was a bottomless bag of excuses for his conduct. When do those excuses end? We're asking for those excuses to end today. Does anybody believe he didn't know it was the police? Consider how ludicrous that claim actually is. Oliver kept saying, 'Fuck the police.' I apologize for using those words. The fact that he says those words gives him the knowledge. For Aloysius Oliver to say he didn't know they were the police is absolute nonsense. Damon Rogers had one eye and he knew they were the police." Then, with a line he must have devised earlier, O'Connor delivered this zinger: "It sounds a helluva lot

more like an Oliver Stone production than an Aloysius Oliver production. He directed it. He was the actor. He's the one who acted
with brutality and viciousness. He's the one who produced death."

What, O'Connor wondered aloud, was the point of Nixon's testimony? People who point guns at other people don't necessarily have
to aim to strike them. "I'm not sure to what extent she's arguing self-
defense or he didn't do it." He threw up his arms. "I'm here to say
I'm confused. Did Aloysius Oliver shoot the gun in self-defense or is
there another shooter out there? Which is it?" O'Connor finished
by pulling out a photo of Eric Lee and showing it to the jury. "The
victim was a young, heroic, vibrant police officer named Eric Lee,"
he said. "Eric Lee died protecting the least among us. In this case
you got to see Eric Lee serve and protect for the last time."

He lowered his voice to a whisper. "Do justice. Do justice."

After O'Connor finished, Marijane asked the judge, based on her
litany of previous complaints and objections, for a mistrial, which
Moran quickly denied. He instructed the jury on the laws that applied to the case and sent them back to begin deliberations. It was
nearly dark outside now, and the courthouse was going to close in
about a half hour. The jury would stay until they reached a verdict,
or, if it got too late, would be sequestered at a nearby hotel.

Aloysius was taken to the holding pen behind the courtroom. Marijane and Ruth went back to their offices, and then drove to Bacchanalia Ristorante, an Italian place about a mile away from the
courthouse, to grab a bite and wait for the jury's verdict. They supplied their cell phone numbers to the judge's clerk so they could be
summoned if there were a verdict while they were having dinner.
Julie Norman and her husband, John, along with Andrew Northrup
and Marijane's friend and fellow public defender, Peg Solomon,
joined the group at the restaurant. I was allowed to join them. It was
a Friday night, and the back dining room at Bacchanalia was packed
with people. When Marijane walked in, a group of lawyers and
judges sitting at a long table in the back called out to her and she said
her hellos. "I've got a jury out," she said. "Murder case." She explained no more and went to the table to sit with the others. Mari-

jane ordered a mixed salad and hot tea. "The judge said no drink-ing," she explained, forgoing her usual double bourbon. There was little talk at the table, mostly quiet anticipation. "I don't know how the family can go through this, the waiting," Ruth told me. "Both families."

A half hour after they sat down, Northrup's cell phone rang. Everyone stopped to listen. He nodded his head and said, "Yes, uh, huh. Okay." He hung up the phone. "The jury has a question," Northrup announced. Marijane decided to have the restaurant box their orders to go. No one seemed comfortable waiting there, any-way. Back at the courthouse, the building was now empty except for a few cleaning staff, sheriff's deputies and those associated with the Oliver case. Upstairs on the sixth floor, police officers lingered in the hall along with members of Lee's family. The attorneys were in and out of the courtroom. Aloysius's sister and mother sat talking on a bench in the courtroom.

Around 9:00 p.m., a police officer in the hallway yelled out. "There's a verdict!" Bodies rushed toward the courtroom, people flipped open their cells phones, cops spoke into their radios and the room quickly filled. As they had during every proceeding through-out the case, Lee's family sat to the judge's right, and Aloysius's fam-ily sat on his left. Lillian Oliver sat two rows back, silent, her body moving back and forth, her face taut and pained. Ruth walked over to talk with her, and suggested that if sitting through the verdict might be too difficult, Lillian should leave, and Ruth would inform her of the results privately. Lillian decided it was a good idea to leave. She might get too emotional. Aloysius's sisters remained.

About 9:10 p.m., O'Connor, McKay and Magats walked into the courtroom and took their places, nodding toward Lee's parents and widow. Marijane, Ruth and Northrup stood up with Aloysius before the jury came in. Aloysius looked toward the jury door as jurors walked in and took their seats across the room from him. The judge asked if they had reached a verdict, and the foreman said yes, they had.

The next moment hung there. The foreman read the charges, and then said the word "guilty."

Shawn Lee cried out. Bodies shuffled and shifted in their seats amid murmuring and gasps. Shawn got up and was led by friends from the courtroom, unsteady on her legs. Aloysius remained with his head down. "Go make sure my mom is okay," he said to Ruth. She and Northrup bolted up from their chairs and rushed downstairs to get to Lillian before she heard the news from someone else. Cops and friends spilled into the hallway; many were crying. Officer Green, tears in his eyes, hugged other officers and stepped aside to tell reporters poised with notebooks that he was relieved. "It's like a bad nightmare right now," he said. "I'm sad. I don't get my partner back."

After a few minutes, Marijane walked out to the hallway knowing the press would want her to comment. True to form, she would not concede a loss. After the verdict, she filed another motion for a mistrial, which the judge would hear at a later date before sentencing. "We don't expect this verdict to hold. We believe in our motion for a new trial that other things will be revealed. We still have quite a few things to show," Marijane said, her back to a group of police officers just a few feet away. "Although we were disappointed, the six hours they spent shows there's more to it. If they discussed this for six hours, there must be some reasonable doubt. This jury was under a tremendous amount of pressure." Police behind her continued hugging and kissing and congratulating each other. "You might be surprised at what you find out at the next hearing," Marijane said.

Downstairs in the main lobby, news crews set up television cameras and created a press area to interview the prosecutors and Lee's family. Cook County State's Attorney Richard Devine was the first to speak. "The jury sent out a strong and clear message," Devine said, as Lee's family stood behind him. "They did a terrific job." Prosecutor David O'Connor seemed reserved, slightly nervous. His comments were restrained, and he was reluctant to gloat. "Eric Lee served and protected the people of this community. He died a hero," O'Connor said. "We were very pleased a jury saw how he died in the line of duty. Eric is looking down on us."

Shawn Lee walked past the throng, preferring not to take part in the press conference. There was little for her to be happy about. She was still grieving and not ready to speak publicly. Eric Lee's father

Bobby, a gentle, gray-haired man with wire-rimmed glasses, spoke for the family. He offered his thanks to the jury and to prosecutors and urged that Eric's work as a police officer not be forgotten. "I'm so proud of my son doing his job serving and protecting. I think my son made a difference." He paused and cast his eyes upward. "Thank you, Eric, I love you very much!" he said. "I have been praying for this day. Thank you, Lord, for answering my prayers." And then he walked out, down the courthouse steps and into the cold night.

Marijane and Ruth decided to go for a long car ride to decompress, heading toward Lake Michigan and then along Lakeshore Drive. Coming down from a trial, win or lose, took time. So much buildup and then it was over. They needed to come back to earth slowly, to take a deep breath. They felt like astronauts stepping on land with wobbly legs after coming back from space. Ruth got on her cell phone to call Lillian Oliver later to make sure she was all right, and told her to keep the faith. They were not finished.

Publicly, Marijane had put on her game face, refusing to let the verdict dampen her spirits and making it clear to the press and her opponents that she was not about to give up the fight. But losing still hurt. "If I lose, I'm devastated because it means I'm not good enough to win," she later told me. "I win for me. My ego is on the line. My whole existence is on the line. When I lose, I'm no good. Winning is delicious. But you don't glory in your wins. That's because you get so frightened of losing. I don't remember my wins. I remember my losses."

CHAPTER FIFTEEN

Downs and Ups

IN THE MONTHS FOLLOWING Aloysius Oliver's guilty verdict, Marijane Placek's life seemed to fall into a downward spiral. On Valentine's Day 2003, while walking in the parking lot of a supermarket to pick up a carrot cake for a party, she was struck by a car driven by an elderly woman. The driver was going just a few miles per hour when the front bumper hit Marijane's legs, knocking her to the pavement and leaving her briefly unconscious. When Marijane shook herself alert, she told the gathering witnesses not to call an ambulance or police. She would be fine. She called her friend, JD, and asked him to get over there to pick her up and take her to the hospital. Marijane felt sorry for the old woman driver, who was terrified at what happened, and didn't file a police report. There was no real harm done. Marijane's head was slightly bumped and scraped, which required some bandages and ice. No head X-rays or MRIs or anything ridiculous like that. She was rattled but fine.

About a month later, the host of the Valentine's party rescheduled for Marijane's benefit, and the celebration went late into the night. After the party ended, Marijane dropped off her friend Peg Solomon and arrived at her brick bungalow home about two in the morning. When she got out of her car, Marijane sniffed the air. Something didn't smell right. She detected a charred odor around the house. She went to the back to open the door, but the key did not work. She walked around the side of the house and felt small pieces of glass crunch beneath her feet. "What the fuck?" she said to herself.

Marijane walked to the front of the house. Her first thought was that she had been burglarized. On the front door, she saw a padlock. She pounded on the door, but didn't hear the dogs barking. They always stirred up when she got home. She felt sick to her stomach. Her babies Gus and Spartacus were gone. (Her other dog, Caesar, had since died.) The next-door neighbors saw that Marijane had come home and called out to her. "The dogs are okay! They're at the vet." The neighbors came out into the chilly night and told Marijane that her house caught fire earlier in the evening. They called the fire department at the first sign of smoke and told the firefighters who arrived first that there were two dogs inside. The firefighters broke in, rescued the dogs and were able to extinguish the blaze quickly. One of the firefighters put an oxygen mask over Gus's mouth and nose to help him breathe. No one knew where Marijane was that night or how to reach her when the fire department came. The fire appeared to have started by a malfunction in the refrigerator.

Marijane called police and asked that an officer come over to open the padlock and let her in the house. Once she got inside, Marijane saw the hardwood floors were covered with water, the rugs were soggy and the acrid smell of smoke permeated everything. Her precious wardrobe, taking up an entire second bedroom, appeared ruined with a coating of soot and water. Much of her book collection—volumes about horses, theater and out-of-print classics—was soaked and smoke stained. The loss of those books, more than anything else, brought her to tears. They were irreplaceable, each evoking memories of the time and place she read them. "It reminded me of the burning of the library in Alexandria," Marijane told me in that way she ascribed grandness to everything in her life and also displayed her education. She was referring to the ancient Greek library, thought to have been destroyed during an invasion by Julius Caesar's army. Marijane used a neighbor's phone to call Solomon, who by now was in a deep sleep. "My house burned down," Marijane said. "Get over here."

The next afternoon, Marijane and Solomon went shopping. Marijane needed everything from a toothbrush and underwear to makeup and clothing. She had to be in court the next day and wasn't going to let this stop her. Having a court date was the best thing that could have happened because it would force her to concentrate on her case and not be distracted by the fire. Marijane and Solomon returned to the house and collected some jewelry from boxes in the bedroom and closet so that Marijane would have some accessories with her new clothes. Marijane picked up the dogs from the vet and took them up to Solomon's house where they would have temporary residence. Marijane's insurance company agreed to rent her another home nearby during the cleanup and repair. She insisted that it have a yard for Gus and Spartacus.

Amid Marijane's personal chaos, there was much work ahead in the Oliver case. Ruth McBeth, Marijane and Northrup prepared a motion asking Judge Moran to grant a new trial, arguing that the trial was unfair from jury selection to the judge's decision to prevent the defense from using the disciplinary records of officers who were there the night of the shooting. They also claimed that Moran erred in not allowing John Nixon to present an animated re-creation of the shooting, and said it was unfair for Lee's family and friends to wear buttons with his photo in the courtroom because it was prejudicial to the jury. Moran set a hearing on May 25, 2004. Shawn Lee, along with Officer Lee's parents, returned to court, frustrated that the defense would not let it go. Ruth told Moran that his decision to exclude some evidence and the prosecution's failure to turn over material in a timely manner "caused Mr. Oliver irreparable prejudice because of the grave nature and seriousness of this case." The defense, she told the judge, had knowledge of more than three hundred pages of disciplinary blemishes against police officers listed as witnesses or potential witnesses in the case. The jury never got to hear that information, which might have had bearing as they weighed the police account of the shooting. Assistant State's Attorney O'Connor countered that the state did its best to turn over what it had in a timely manner. "At every turn we disclosed information, even when we didn't have to," he said. O'Connor felt a personal attack at the implication he purposely withheld information. "We have taken great measures to provide this defendant with a fair trial."

Moran didn't take long. After O'Connor finished, the judge denied the motion for a new trial. In the hallway, after the judge's ruling, Marijane drew reporters over to offer some comments and began a rather loud speech. "We're disappointed the judge didn't grant our motion for what we thought were fundamental errors, and, uh . . ." She suddenly stopped talking. Officer Lee's widow and parents were walking close by, within earshot. Marijane whispered: "I don't want to cause them any more pain. If anyone was defending someone who killed someone I loved, I wouldn't want to hear this. We don't want to add to their pain." The lawyer who during the trial summoned hate for everyone on the other side could still show respect for them outside the courtroom. After the Lee family got into the elevator, Marijane resumed. The defense intended to press on with its challenge for a new trial, but also had to prepare for Aloysius's sentencing hearing and try to save his life. "We're not quite done yet," she said.

The Oliver case would simmer for a few more months before his sentencing hearing, and other cases piled up on Marijane's desk. One of her newest clients was a man who fired his public defender and had been trying to represent himself, rather ineffectively. Not getting anywhere, causing endless delays to his case and frustration to the judge, he finally relented and agreed to take a public defender again. His name was Elvis Buford, a small studious-looking man with black plastic-frame glasses and a quiet, meek-sounding voice. He was charged four years earlier with beating a man to death, cutting him up in pieces and discarding the remains in various locations on a road trip through Southern Illinois. "The problem with Elvis was that he thought he could be his own lawyer," Marijane said to me, rolling her eyes. "He's kind of a borderline case, if you know what I mean." In Marijane's opinion, Elvis had a good chance of escaping a first-degree murder conviction, but his handwritten motions and amateur legal maneuvers only muddled things up. "He had a pretty good self-defense case, even though he beat the guy to death," Marijane explained. "But the dismemberment is a problem. People don't like dismemberment. I ran it by my pretend jury of friends, and they didn't like it, though it didn't bother me."

Police said that Buford killed Raphael Rush, twenty, over an unpaid debt. In an effort to conceal the crime, Buford cut up the body with a circular saw. Rush's hands were found in a river and other sections of his body were found in a septic tank at a gas station downstate. Buford had gone to great lengths to cover up what he did. But Marijane thought she could get him a good deal because, like the Joan Tribblet case, what he did with the body, though gruesome and deliberate, did not explain the killing itself. Marijane figured she could get him a fair sentence in exchange for a guilty plea and dispose of the case quickly. Marijane asked Buford, who was forty-seven, what he thought about making a deal rather than continuing to fight. Even though she loved to fight, this one, she knew, was a loser, and paramount to her job was to do what was in the best interest of her clients. She could only advise. They made the ultimate call. After spending so much fruitless time trying to be his own lawyer, Buford decided it was time to let go. He had been making progress through mental health counseling at the jail and was ready to take some responsibility. He would admit to killing Rush. Buford's story was that he beat Rush with a sledgehammer because he thought Rush was making a move on his girlfriend. Buford also would admit that he cut up the corpse with an electric saw, put the parts in a plastic container and threw them away during his drive out of Chicago. As they prepared to go to court to finalize the deal, everything seemed to be in order.

On the day of his formal plea, Buford sat with Marijane and Ruth at the defense table and told Judge Kenneth Wadas that he understood the possible consequences of his admission of guilt and that he pled guilty voluntarily. Wadas asked Buford if he had anything to say before sentencing. Buford in a low, respectful voice, said he did, and began to apologize to Rush's family, who sat on the other side of a glass partition in the courtroom. As Buford said he was sorry, Reginald Rush, the brother of the victim, leapt from his courtroom seat, swung open the glass door separating the gallery from the courtroom and ran toward Buford to attack him, taking a swing, but missing. Marijane and Ruth jumped from their seats and tried to push him out of the way. Assistant State's Attorney Mike Hood grabbed Rush from behind and wrestled him to a table and pinned him. Courtroom deputies quickly restrained Rush and removed him.

After the ruckus settled, the judge asked that Rush be brought back to court to stand before him. The judge said he understood the emotional outburst, but said the attack was out of line and an assault on the court. He sentenced Rush to six months in jail for contempt. Buford came back before the judge to finish his statement and asked Wadas to show mercy on Rush. "If you could find it in your heart to let that young man go home to his mother, I would be eternally grateful," Buford said. Judge Wadas said he would consider lifting the contempt charge, and then sentenced Buford to twenty-two years in prison. All in all, it was a pretty good deal for Buford. "If it weren't for cutting up the body, it wouldn't be such a bad case," Marijane said afterward. "This is a clue for future murderers: Don't cut up the body!"

Just before leaving for lunch on May 19, while I happened to be in her office, Marijane got a surprise call from her old friend and colleague Allan Sincox, a former member of the Murder Task Force who was now with the State Appellate Defender's Office. Sincox had big news about a former client he and Marijane represented ten years earlier. Elizabeth "Betsy" Ehlert, who was convicted of murdering her newborn baby and throwing it in a creek, was getting out of prison. The Illinois Supreme Court reversed her conviction.

"No shit?" Marijane said. "That's wonderful. That fucker . . . God bless him. We won, huh? That's pretty cool." She listened for another moment. "You glory hog! You didn't mention my name to the law bulletin? Call them back. Good job, Allan. Thank you."

When the call was over, Marijane leaned back in her chair with a satisfied look. She always believed she and Sincox should have won that case. "Now I really feel vindicated," Marijane told me. "But Betsy lost her kids. She lost everything in the world and she's broke." Betsy had another more serious problem. She was dying of cancer. Marijane would do something she rarely did, which was to meet her old client and get more personally involved in her life.

No one was really sure what happened early on the morning of August 21, 1990, when Betsy gave birth at home to a fetus she claimed was already dead inside her. Betsy told many lies before that night, which made her story suspicious. Four months before Betsy gave birth, her fiancé, Steven King, noticed she was gaining weight around her belly. He asked her about it, and she concocted a story that she had a cyst and had seen a doctor about having it removed. A few weeks later, Betsy told King she was bleeding and was going to schedule surgery to take care of the cyst. She never got around to it, and told King another story. This time, she said she had ovarian cancer. Later that month, she told him she got a second opinion from another doctor who said the tumor was not cancerous. She canceled her appointments to have the tumor removed.

On August 17, Betsy called King at work to tell him that tests showed she was six to eight weeks pregnant, but the fetus was dead. She told King the doctor gave her a shot to induce an abortion within forty-eight hours. Four days later, about 3:00 a.m., Betsy woke up King and said she was in labor. She screamed in pain. Rather than remain with her to witness the impending miscarriage, King would later testify that he decided to leave the bedroom. He did not call for help, saying he was hysterical, crying and frightened. King began pacing around the house through the hallway, living room and kitchen as Betsy moaned and wriggled alone in the bedroom. About thirty minutes later, he told Betsy he was going to call paramedics. Betsy yelled out for him to hang on, that the labor was almost over, and asked him to get a plastic bag. He got a bag from under the kitchen sink and was fifteen to twenty steps from the bedroom when, he testified, he heard a single cry that lasted about two seconds. He stepped closer and asked Betsy about the noise. She said he must have heard the family dog yelping. He handed Betsy the bag through the doorway.

King went into the living room to wait. He heard no other noise, no cries, whimpers or baby sounds. A few minutes later, Betsy emerged from the bedroom in her robe and went into the bathroom. King kept asking whether she was all right and she told him to calm down, everything was fine. He said he heard something rustling as she picked up the bag, but that it did not sound like cries or a baby's gasps for breath. Betsy walked back to the kitchen and King heard the door slam. When she returned a few minutes later, he asked what she had done with the bag. She said she threw it in the creek behind the house. Betsy went back into the bedroom, and King heard her writhing and screaming in pain again. He walked in to see she was delivering the afterbirth, and he helped clean up the bed.

The next morning, King felt panicked. He was distraught, going over in his mind whether he heard a baby cry. He told his mother about the incident and later asked Betsy again about the cry. She insisted it was a dog or that he probably imagined the noise. Two days later employees of the local park district found the fetus in a lake near a golf course. It turned out that a creek right behind Betsy's house fed into the lake, and police eventually linked her to the dead baby through DNA. On September 6, 1990, King was questioned at the police station and relayed the story about hearing what he thought was a cry in the bedroom. He had convinced himself he imagined the sound.

Police questioned Betsy. She told them she had miscarried a fifteen-week-old fetus and flushed it down the toilet. When police told her that they spoke with King, Betsy changed her story, saying she threw the fetus in the garbage. Then she said King tossed it in the garbage. When officers said King told a different story, Betsy said she did not remember what happened, but that King wouldn't lie. Her stories became pathetic. She said her water broke while trying to retrieve her son's toy from a tree in the yard. She said she left the fetus in a bag near the tree. Police asked if she threw the bag in the creek and she said, "No, unless you want me to say I did it, then I did it." In another interview, she told her police that her ex-husband, not King, was the father of the baby. She admitted frequent sex with her ex the previous year. Betsy was clearly a deeply confused and disturbed woman. A few days later, she called police to say she could not live with herself and wanted to tell the truth. She asked detectives to assure her that King would take care of her children if she went to jail. Her new story was that after she delivered a dead fetus, she went to the bathroom, and King went into the bedroom, picked up the remains and threw them out. Police decided her various stories just didn't add up. She was charged with murder and assigned a public defender.

"When we first started, I really thought she was pretty nuts," Allan Sincox, who was first appointed to defend Betsy, told me during an interview. "She was not particularly easy to deal with, very demanding, very insistent. But after a while we got over that, and I realized that was her way. She sort of calmed down over a period of time." Even so, defending Betsy was going to be tough. "She said she had no recollection of what happened that night," Sincox explained. "Whatever recollections she had were all over the ballpark and were kind of inconsistent. She never remembered the birth of the baby at all."

What made the case even stranger was that Betsy's mother was murdered two years earlier. The case was never solved, and police were always suspicious that Betsy was somehow involved. Betsy's mother was Joan Schanmier, fifty-seven, an executive secretary at WGN Radio in Chicago. She was found fatally stabbed more than fifteen times in the living room of the family's home in suburban Palatine in September 1988. Betsy and her two children were inside the house at the time of Schanmier's slaying, but Betsy maintained in interviews with Palatine police that she slept through her mother's attack, had no idea what happened or who might have wanted to kill her.

Sincox knew the key to this case was whether proof existed beyond a reasonable doubt that the baby was born alive. If it was alive, was there proof that Betsy had done something to cause the death? And if so, did she have the mental capacity for it to be murder? He raised those issues at trial and thought he had a pretty good case. Still, a jury believed the prosecution's explanation that it was simply murder. Two years later, the Illinois Appellate Court overturned the verdict, in part, because the prosecution presented irrelevant and highly prejudicial evidence at the trial including the fact that Betsy had two previous abortions. Sincox again represented her at the second trial, and asked Marijane to join the defense team. They decided to focus on Betsy's mental health, attempting to offer a better explanation of why she was telling all these inconsistent stories and lies— that she was pregnant, that she wasn't pregnant, that she had cancerous tumors. "It was almost to the point where some of this stuff sounded almost delusional and very strange. It just didn't make a whole lot of sense," Sincox said. Sincox and Marijane theorized that Betsy's mental problems at the time were connected to her pregnancy and to the grieving over the death of her mother.

They arranged to have her evaluated by psychiatrists. "Initially, I didn't want to raise an insanity defense because I don't think they ever work. And as soon as you raise insanity, the judge or the jury assumes the person is guilty," Sincox said. He tried to introduce as evidence a psychiatrist's testimony to explain Betsy's behavior, but the judge would not allow it unless they raised an insanity defense. In preparation for the possibility of a guilty verdict and sentencing, they hired mitigator Julie Norman whose skills as a therapist and counselor might help draw Betsy out and bring some manner of sympathy to her case. Julie delved into Betsy's childhood and spent many hours with her at the jail extracting her story. Betsy's tale of childhood trauma had familiar tones. She told Julie she was sexually abused by her father as a child. The abuse led to a pregnancy at age fourteen, which she aborted. That early trauma, her lawyers contended, was one of the reasons she detached herself from her most recent pregnancy.

The second trial was held before Cook County Circuit Judge Karen Thompson Tobin without a jury. During the trial Dr. Mitra Kalelkar, assistant chief medical examiner of Cook County, testified that she could not determine with a reasonable degree of medical certainty that the baby had been born alive. She said she found no unusual cause of death, but her "suspicion was that the baby drowned." Two pathologists testifying for the defense agreed that the cause of death was uncertain, and that the fetus could have died during birth from loss of blood or obstruction of the airway or asphyxiation. Even if it were alive at birth, the baby could have quickly died from failure to clear its airway, blood loss or infection. One of the pathologists found evidence to suggest the baby was alive when labor began, but did not survive. It was possible that respiratory distress would cause a baby to give a feeble cry then die.

Judge Thompson Tobin was not persuaded that the baby was born dead. She found Betsy guilty of first-degree murder and sentenced her to thirty years in prison. Following Betsy's conviction, the state terminated her parental rights and took away her two young sons, who were later adopted by other families. The boys eventually stopped contacting their birth mother. Betsy was crushed.

"When Betsy lost," Julie Norman told me, "it was like getting stabbed in the stomach." While Betsy served her time in prison, Julie kept in touch with her and developed a close bond. Julie sent Betsy clothes, books and money and visited from time to time. Betsy told Julie that she was the only woman she allowed to hug her. "We had spent hours with her trying to reconstruct what happened that night and she just couldn't," Julie said. "I think she really was psychotic then."

Marijane and Sincox believed that the case was a good candidate for appeal. Sincox volunteered to do some research in his spare time and begin the appeals process. "I was starting to get a strong feeling about this whole business of the cause of death," he said. "I really wanted that raised. I really thought she was wronged and I really felt the judge was wrong. It seemed to me that we should have won." Sincox also was troubled by King's account of the miscarriage. What did he really see and hear? "I certainly don't think he ever heard any cries," he said.

Sincox got his chance to argue the case before the Illinois Supreme Court, raising those very issues. A few months later, he got the news that the court overturned Betsy's conviction. Justice Charles Freeman wrote the majority opinion, asserting that proof of a crime required proof that a crime occurred. He pointed out that a defendant could not be convicted of murdering a person who already had died. The court believed the state failed to prove Betsy's baby was born alive, that the expert testimony affirmed that their findings could not prove a live birth to a reasonable degree of medical certainty. Even though there was evidence that Betsy did not want the baby and lied about the pregnancy, there simply was no evidence she killed it. Even if it were born alive, the evidence was insufficient to show the death was a result of Betsy's actions. The dissenting opinion was bitter. Justice Robert Thomas wrote: "For all practical purposes, it is now legal in Illinois for a parent to murder his or her newborn infant," he wrote. "Suffocate an infant and throw its body in the water, or simply throw it in the water without killing it first, deny guilt, and you are home free."

Betsy had been imprisoned for more than thirteen years, labeled as a murderer. Even though she had suffered from mental health problems before her conviction, she got no counseling inside. She survived prison by educating herself and acting as friend and confidante to younger inmates. She took college-level courses, earned a two-year associate's degree and got a certificate to be a paralegal. "I was with Betsy for a long time and saw a lot of changes within her," Sincox said. Now forty-five years old, Betsy faced the prospect of freedom with no money, no home and no family to embrace her when she was released. Her father had died while she was in prison. Her sons, who were now sixteen and twenty-one, had no contact with their mother for ten years after she lost custody. Betsy did not know how to reach them. She also had inoperable lung cancer and required further treatment, which had begun while she was still incarcerated. Her newfound freedom was on a ticking clock, and no one knew how long she had to taste life on the outside. Betsy asked Sincox and Julie to pick her up from prison because there was no one else to do it. "Our plan for her was to get her out, beat this cancer and get her a job," Julie said.

Before leaving to pick up Betsy, Julie had arranged to find temporary shelter at place that offered housing to the poor and homeless who were seriously ill. She also made some calls to get Betsy on public aid and eligible to continue cancer treatment at the county hospital. Marijane took on a role she was perfectly suited to handle. She would go clothes shopping for Betsy. Marijane wanted to do something to help boost Betsy's confidence and help her look sharp. Betsy needed more than just clothing to make her feel like a woman again. She needed a wig. Chemotherapy and radiation treatment had taken her hair. Marijane drove to her favorite wig shop and found something perfect. She gave it to Julie to bring with her when they picked up Betsy from prison. Sincox and Julie drove about four hours south of Chicago to the Lincoln Correctional Center. They were escorted to a visiting area where Betsy had been waiting. Betsy got up to greet them, but was embarrassed to be seen without hair. Julie gave her the wig, and Betsy ducked into a washroom to put it on. She came out and they all cried and embraced once more. On the ride home, Betsy said that one of her only wishes was to see the two sons she left behind.

A week later Marijane, Sincox and Julie organized a coming-home celebration party at Bacchanalia restaurant on the Friday before the Independence Day weekend. The staff pushed two tables together in the back dining room, which was dimly lit and adorned with rustic-style wallpaper and tiny white electric lights strung over plants. Betsy arrived wearing a gray business suit, black pumps and her new strawberry-blond wig. Her skin was pale and her face looked tired, but her eyes had the life and the joy of someone savoring her freedom.

"Doesn't she look great?" Julie said to everyone at the table.

"You actually look better than I do in my stupid shirt," said Marijane, who was wearing a red, white and blue blouse. Betsy looked well assembled but frail. Her voice was raspy and her breath was short.

Sincox arrived carrying a cooler with bottles of champagne on ice. Joining the table was myself and one of Betsy's friends from prison, a dark-haired woman named Jenny. Stefano Esposito, the courts reporter for the *Chicago Sun-Times*, also stopped by to get an interview with Betsy. The group sat at a long table nibbling crusty bread and foccacia with tomato sauce and mozzarella. Betsy studied the menu, pondering the choices, the pastas, fish and veal dishes she had not tasted for years. "All these decisions. What do I wear, what do I drink?" She ordered an Absolut vodka on the rocks with olives, and then reached into a bag and pulled out two plastic, shiny gold trophies, like those sold in novelty shops. "These are for my number-one lawyers," she announced. "These are for the best lawyers in the bar association."

Betsy lit a cigarette, and inhaled deeply into her cancerous lungs. No one said anything. They all knew it didn't matter. "I didn't believe it would happen until I got out," she said. "I've had Allan and Marijane and Julie with me the whole time."

The mood shifted when Betsy said she wanted to locate her sons. "I don't know how much time I have left," she said with tears in her eyes. "I don't know what they've been told about me, what they think about me. It was one thing to be convicted of murder, but when they took away my children, they took away my heart." Marijane put her hand on Betsy's arm. "You're going to get your family back. We're going to have a wonderful time," Marijane said. Her eyes were watery, as well. "Your children will know you and will want to see you and will love you."

Betsy was amused and confused at her table setting. "Oh, I have two forks. I'm used to a plastic fork and a plastic spoon," she said. "And I'm used to eating chicken thighs in prison." She told her lawyers that on the inside, she used to place leftover food inside foil potato chip bags and put them on top of bare lightbulbs to heat when the guards weren't around. When someone in prison had a birthday, they celebrated with homemade nachos. Marijane urged Betsy to order the New York strip steak, one of her favorites. Betsy ordered it cooked medium rare. They sipped drinks and laughed and the staff brought out appetizers of fried calamari, antipasto, melon and prosciutto. Marijane had a few double bourbons. Julie ordered an Absolut on ice.

"All my lawyers are lushes!" Betsy joked as she looked at the table full of drinks. She raised her glass. "This is my little family. I've known them for fourteen years."

Sincox uncorked a bottle of champagne and poured glasses for everyone. "To the state of Illinois," he said. "May they always lose gracefully."

The waitress brought Betsy's steak, which covered three quarters of her plate. Betsy looked at the hunk of meat, and then around the table as others were being served their dishes. "Is this what it's like to be normal?" she blurted out, holding up a large, wood-handled knife. "I mean, look at this steak knife." She sliced a thick chunk of meat, guided it into her mouth and chewed slowly. "This is the best steak I've ever had."

Marijane leaned over and whispered to Betsy that if she wanted somewhere to go for Thanksgiving, she was invited to her home.

Then Marijane sat back and yelled out. "Excuuuse me." She wanted everyone's attention to make her toast. "Betsy," she said, "you've given me enthusiasm to continue my career."

"You've been my backbone," Betsy said. "You guys believed in me when no one else did. It's great to sit here today knowing we were right all along."

Beneath the festive mood was a sadness that everyone seemed to know but did not speak of. As much as this was a celebration, it was the culmination of several tragedies—a woman who suffered from an abusive childhood, the death of a newborn, years of life wasted in prison and now the cancer eating away at Betsy's insides. The sun disappeared behind the buildings along Oakley Avenue by the time lunch was over and everyone had finished their last drinks. It was time to go. Outside in the warm night, Marijane and Betsy embraced. Marijane would go home to her dogs with a bag of leftovers and move on to her next case. Betsy would go to a shelter with her bag of leftovers and wonder about a future in which she knew not how long she had and whether she would ever see her sons again.

CHAPTER SIXTEEN

Always Afraid

"I can't remember a time when I wasn't afraid," Aloysius Oliver told Julie Norman during one of her visits with him at the county jail.

Aloysius had begun to feel more comfortable with Julie, and more willing to reveal his vulnerable side. Julie had been coming to the jail more frequently and with a greater sense of urgency during the summer of 2004 in preparation for Aloysius's upcoming sentencing hearing. They met in the windowless, empty, subterranean library of the jail's maximum security unit and sat in plastic chairs under fluorescent lights to talk. A guard was posted a few yards away at the door, presumably out of earshot. Aloysius looked forward to Julie's visits. She was always upbeat when she came to see him, warm, respectful and never judgmental. Julie needed Aloysius to be even more forthcoming about himself, to dig deeper into his own past to help her construct the story of his life, the good and the bad, uncensored and honestly. She drew on her background as a social worker and counselor to encourage Aloysius to open up, to recall his childhood, to share his dreams, fears, mistakes and regrets. When Julie heard Aloysius say he was always afraid, she knew she had found a theme for his sentencing hearing. Julie's plan was to portray Aloysius to the judge as a kid who grew up in fear, raised in a world of violence, without a father, a life borne amid poverty and shaped by bad influences on the streets from which he came. "I never felt Aloysius was an animal or a monster," Julie told me. "I don't think he ever had a chance."

Trying to explain criminal behavior that way was risky. Judges and prosecutors had heard it all before, and the counterarguments inevitably pointed to people who made it out of the ghetto with clean criminal records, jobs and families. The old "he was a victim of his environment" argument was derided by prosecutors as a predictable tactic used by liberals who refused to accept the notion that adults were responsible for their own behavior and committed crimes knowing the difference between right and wrong. Julie was aware she had a reputation as a classic bleeding-heart softie who liked all her clients no matter how revolting or violent their crimes. She embraced the label. "You know what, that's just about true," she told me. "Because if you can't find the good or the valuable or the kind or the spiritual in people, then why are you a therapist or a counselor or a social worker?" Julie wanted to understand what went wrong for Aloysius Oliver, to seek an explanation of how he developed from a boy to a man and what brought him to that fatal August night in the alley behind Carpenter Street with a .357 revolver.

Aloysius Oliver was born in Indianola, Mississippi, a city of about twelve hundred, nestled in a fertile crescent of cotton, soybean, rice and catfish farms in the Delta. Indianola was about 73 percent black and mostly poor, in the heart of rural Sunflower County where 40 percent of the residents lived below the federal poverty line. Cotton was once the main industry in town, but catfish farming and processing were now driving the local economy. Indianola was about seven hundred miles south of Chicago, and was among the southern cities from which thousands of blacks—descendents of slaves and share-croppers—left for the north during the great migration in search of economic opportunity and hopes of racial tolerance. Indianola also prided itself as the birthplace of blues legend B.B. King, who got his start at Club Ebony on Hanna Street, and recorded an album paying honor to his hometown called *Indianola Mississippi Seeds*. Aloysius began life amid the kind of poverty described in B.B. King's own tales of the blues. The newborn Aloysius was brought home to an already crowded three-room house with ten other relatives and siblings. His mother, Lillian, was seventeen when she had him, and he was her second child. Her firstborn, Angela, came when she was fifteen. Lillian briefly dropped out of high school after Angela was born, but returned to finish and graduate. Aloysius's father was also a teenager. According to Lillian, he was not involved in his son's life and never provided child support. Not long after Aloysius was born, his dad hit the road and had nothing to do with his boy again.

Aloysius was a sickly newborn. At three months old, he nearly died from an asthma attack and was admitted to the South Sunflower County Hospital in Indianola. That incident was the beginning of a series of hospitalizations throughout his childhood. During one stay, he had to remain in the hospital for days under an oxygen tent. The skinny little boy carried an inhaler wherever he went. While he was still a toddler, many of Aloysius's relatives moved to Chicago, their promised land, where they got jobs, found apartments and started new lives. Lillian moved there as well to be with her family in 1977. She and the kids stayed with one of her sisters at first, but Lillian wanted to get a place of their own. When Aloysius was three, Lillian moved the family to the ABLA Public Housing Projects, a sprawling complex of buildings that included more than 3,500 apartments on the city's South Side. They lived on West Hastings Street in one of seven high-rise buildings that stood next to one another, buildings where the elevators rarely worked and street gangs and drug peddlers roamed the surrounding turf. At the time, ABLA was considered among the city's most dangerous projects. Even though some of Lillian's siblings lived there, she intended the move to ABLA to be temporary. "I wanted to move us out of there because it was bad," Lillian told me when I went to visit her to talk about her son after his conviction. "It was crazy. There was always fighting, there was always somebody shooting someone." She got Aloysius into Head Start, a government-subsidized preschool program, and then enrolled him at Gladstone Elementary. Her boy was going to get an education, and she encouraged him to do well. Aloysius was a small, skinny child, and because of his asthma, he couldn't play sports, go swimming or engage in the kinds of strenuous activities that other children his age did. He often stayed inside the apartment, listened to music and began reading books on his own. He studied the Bible as a teenager and could quote scripture well enough to impress his relatives. He was mostly docile and stayed out of trouble as a boy, his mother said. She was a strict disciplinarian, however, who hit her son with "whatever came to hand." That meant a couple of whoopings here and there but never, ever, according to Lillian, violent beatings.

Even though his mother's intentions may have been good, Aloysius never got to stay at one school very long. He attended three different elementary schools, all of them crowded, in high-crime areas and choked with gang members. If there was refuge, it was on Sundays. Aloysius's family regularly attended a Baptist church. According to one aunt, Aloysius knew the Bible so well that he got into lengthy discussions with an uncle who was an assistant pastor. When Aloysius wanted to earn some spending money, he went to local supermarkets and helped people load their groceries into their cars for tips. He took the "El" train for more than an hour to O'Hare International Airport where he gathered trolleys to help people wheel their baggage.

Life at home was tense at times. Lillian had several live-in boyfriends while her son was growing up, and some of them were mean, drunk and nasty. But she could be tough. When they raised a hand to her, she hit back, never allowing any of them to push her around. She moved the family three times before Aloysius began attending Dunbar High School. He did well in school, and excelled in math. Reading and studying came easy, but looking out into the neighborhood made his mind wander. Living in the city's poorest neighborhoods meant living among gangs. Teenage boys like Aloysius found it difficult, if not impossible, to resist the allure of belonging and being protected. At age thirteen, Aloysius began hanging out with the Gangster Disciples, one of Chicago's most violent and notorious gangs. Rather than hitting the books, he spent time on the streets with thugs, started smoking marijuana and got into trouble. During his early teens, Aloysius was arrested for burglary, criminal damage to property and trespassing. He credited a public defender for beating the charges and said he felt she really cared about him. Compared to his friends on the street, Aloysius was a good kid. He studied hard enough to graduate high school, and even got a scholarship to Chicago State University, where he planned to major in accounting. But his college career lasted less than a semester. The lure of the streets was greater than his desire for an education. "He blew it," Aloysius's mother told me with frustration in her voice. "I said, 'What are you doing out the streets? You can do better than that.' "

Aloysius liked getting high and hanging out. He told an investigator with the State's Attorney's Office that he drank a six-pack of 32-ounce beers five days a week and smoked about a quarter ounce of marijuana every other day. He wasn't into anything heavier than that, however, and never participated in any kind of drug treatment program. But Aloysius did more than get high. By 1991, he began to build his adult arrest record. The first arrest was for battery and possession of a firearm, though the charges were dropped. In 1993, he got his first felony conviction for sale and delivery of cocaine and was sentenced to one year of probation. Later that same year, he was charged with aggravated battery and strong-arm robbery and sentenced to three years in prison. He was back on the street in a year. Shortly after he got out, Aloysius was arrested on charges of beating up his sister, Angela. The charges were dropped after brother and sister told authorities that it was a misunderstanding. Aloysius stayed out of jail until 1996 when he was charged with criminal trespass to a vehicle and got five days for time served. In 1998, he was charged with simple assault on his mom. Lillian said she was angry with her boyfriend and got a gun to threaten him. She and Aloysius began to argue about it, and she told him to move out. Lillian called the police and told officers that her son said, "I'm gonna whip your ass." The case was dropped. Then, in 2000, Aloysius was convicted in Milwaukee, ninety miles north of Chicago, for possession of a firearm and cocaine and sentenced to eighteen months in prison. He was out in about nine months. When Aloysius came back to Chicago, he got the one and only full-time job he ever had in his adult life. He was hired as a line inspector in a furniture factory for $5.25 an hour. But it did not last long. Eight months later, he was laid off. A month after that, Aloysius was arrested and convicted of domestic battery against a girlfriend, and got one year of probation. By the end of the following summer, he was charged with the most serious crime of them all: first-degree murder in the death of Officer Eric Lee.

* * *

Julie Norman began to compile all these markers of Aloysius's life as she prepared for his sentencing hearing. Julie had worked with defendants who had thicker raps sheets, but the problem was that Aloysius's arrests included crimes with guns and violence against other people. To be sure, the state's attorney's office was going to play this up, and portray Aloysius as a career criminal with a violent past, not some poor kid who was a victim of poverty and circumstance. Each time she visited Aloysius at the county jail, Julie tried to extract a little more, searching for something that would help her strengthen his case. She tried to bond with him, to make him feel more comfortable about revealing himself. Julie would sit at a table across from Aloysius and look directly into his eyes. She never felt threatened by him. She believed she saw pain, longing and vulnerability in his face. Julie eventually felt comfortable enough to sit by Aloysius's side, rather than across from him as she did with other inmates, but was always careful to keep boundaries about touching arms or hands. Julie asked Aloysius whether he could remember his first exposure to violence. He recalled an incident in which an elderly man in his neighborhood was beaten by some teenagers who used a car jack to batter him. Aloysius could not understand why no one tried to stop the attack or would come to the old man's aid. He told Julie that violence was a "normal, regular, usual" form of behavior in his own family. His mother fought with boyfriends, his mother fought with him and fought with his siblings, Aloysius said.

She wanted to explore this further, so Julie went to visit Lillian Oliver to ask more about the family background. Lillian was uncomfortable with all these personal questions. She became defensive and stopped answering Julie. Lillian didn't want family secrets coming out, stories about these so-called beatings or abuses, especially in an open courtroom. She was angry at Julie for getting so nosy and said she wanted to be left alone. "You're going to look at my family and say I was a bad person, that I was a bad mom and that's why this happened," Lillian said to Julie. "I don't like people, and I don't trust people." Julie was hurt. She was trying to save this woman's son from execution and expected understanding from Lillian, not hostility. As

Julie got up to leave the apartment teary-eyed, she moved toward Lillian to embrace her, then kissed her on the cheek and whispered in her ear. "But I like *you*." When she got to her car, Julie burst into tears. "I do have feelings for that family, and I do have feelings for Aloysius," Julie later told me. "My sense was that Mom did use physical discipline on the kids and maybe sometimes crossed the line, but this was not a home in which the mother was the primary beater. When the boyfriends hit her, she would hit back. She never let the boyfriends hit the kids."

Based on her interviews, Julie concluded that Aloysius followed his family's pattern of domestic violence and suffered because he never had a positive male role model. She wrote in one of her initial reports: "Aloysius Oliver seems to expect little from life, having grown up in an emotionally barren, impoverished, and unstable family. He experiences a damaged sense of himself . . . Relationships with family members, particularly mother, are troubled." As part of the mitigation, Julie began to prepare a report for the judge that would show that Aloysius met many of the criteria for the U.S. Department of Justice Model of Risk Factors for Violence in the Community. It was a bureaucratic way of documenting the kinds of experiences that destabilize young lives and put them at risk for committing violence. This, at least, would explain how Aloysius grew into the man he was and, Julie hoped, would trigger some compassion from the judge. She concluded that from age six through adolescence, Aloysius met twelve of the fourteen risk factors. "His family suffered extreme economic deprivation and lived in disorganized communities," she wrote. "There was easy availability to firearms and illegal drugs. Media portrayals of his community and culture were negative. He was exposed to violence and racial prejudice. Family conflict and management problems were ongoing. Academic achievement was not emphasized within the family, and alienation from the larger society existed. Mr. Oliver's peers and relatives participated in delinquent behavior, and by the abuse of alcohol by adults in the family, attitudes toward substance abuse were favorable. His role models were alcoholic, drug-using uncles, those were the adult males. Men who abused his mother and sold drugs, men who abused him and his sisters, violence when he left the house."

Lillian Oliver could see where Julie was going, and didn't like it. "They wanted the judge to think he had a bad upbringing, but he didn't," she told me. "I know for a fact that my life wasn't that bad."

With the help of her husband, John Peterson, Julie searched out more family and friends, school records, criminal records, anything they could find to document Aloysius's life. Many of the family members she interviewed told Julie that they did not believe Aloysius killed Officer Lee. There was a feeling in the community that the cops involved were dirty and that Lee was killed by another cop. Rumors like that spread around in neighborhoods where the police and the residents lived in distrust.

Julie saw Aloysius's fear grow as his sentencing date neared. He feared the death penalty and he feared life in prison. Prison would be a slower, more painful death. "He said, 'Look at me. I'm a little guy. Do you think I'll ever get out? How many years do you think I'll live? What's it going to be for me? How long do you think I'm going to last in there?' " He began to cry. That was the first time Julie reached over and touched his arm. She sensed that Aloysius was growing more despondent and hopeless. He felt like a failure. He was alone. He had never developed close emotional bonds to people or had long-lasting relationships with women. He was thin, and frail and weak. He was, Julie said, a very sad man. On another visit, Aloysius told Julie he didn't care anymore about what she was doing. He saw no point in this mitigation exercise. "Why do you have to bring up all this stuff about my family?" he said. "What does any of this matter?" He did not say it angrily, but rather softly, as if he were fading away. He seemed listless and deeply troubled. Julie asked whether he had thoughts about suicide. "I wouldn't do that," he said.

"Is it against your religion?" Julie asked.

"Well, not like in the Catholic religion, but it's wrong."

She asked what he meant by that, and Aloysius told her about his recent spiritual and religious studies through a ministry called the Yahweh's Assembly in Messiah. Aloysius first heard of the group while he was doing prison time in Wisconsin. He had found a pamphlet describing Yahweh, a religious movement whose followers believed both the Old and New Testaments. "Our goal is to follow the teachings of Scripture and pattern our lives accordingly," according to the literature. Yahweh, its followers said, was the correct name of the Heavenly Father. "We have found that much modern-day belief and teaching has deviated from the original truth of the Scripture. So we make every effort to root out error and return to pure worship. We believe in obedience to the commandments set down by the Heavenly Father." It all sounded interesting at the time. When Aloysius was released from prison in Wisconsin, however, he lost interest in Yahweh. Now, he needed it more than ever. Aloysius told Julie that his long stay in jail prompted him to begin asking spiritual questions. He was seeking understanding and redemption for the mistakes of his life. In Yahweh, Aloysius found a place to focus his energy and begin to try to make some sense of the world and his place in it.

As part of his spiritual quest, Aloysius had begun writing letters to the Elder George Garner, who presided at the Yahweh's Assembly in Messiah, Rocheport, Missouri. The assembly offered correspondence courses, as well as audiocassettes and DVDs to its followers, and kindly appreciated donations. Aloysius wrote regularly to Elder Garner, celebrating his rediscovered faith and posing religious questions. In one letter, Aloysius proclaimed that he felt the assembly was the true church, that everything in his life finally has fallen into place, that he had no doubts "that with you is where I need to be, the TRUE assembly. Halleluyah and Halleluyah for being so gracious unto me and leading me to YAIM. Halleluyah!" He wrote of his prayers, and asked whether there were deacons or elders around Chicago who might visit him in jail. He asked for advice on praying, and mentioned that he had quit smoking but started up again. "I've handed my situation over to Yahweh."

Julie thought Aloysius's spiritual quest might be valuable in seeking mercy for him at sentencing. But talking about religious awakening could prove tricky because judges have seen more than enough inmates find God in jail, a god who seemed to dwell exclusively in prison cells but was notably absent from the inmates' lives on the outside. She encouraged Aloysius to continue his Bible correspondence course with the assembly, and would discuss this religious conversion with Marijane Placek and Ruth McBeth to see where they might go with it. In the meantime, Julie tried to think of other strategies. She asked her husband to try to track down some of Aloysius's school-teachers who might be able talk about how school was his refuge in a dangerous environment, how he was a decent, smart boy who tried to stay out of trouble. Some of Aloysius's teachers were by now retired, some old, some dead. Peterson got a copy of the Dunbar High School yearbook and photocopied pages of students and teachers. Julie brought the pages to Aloysius to jog his memory and asked him to suggest teachers they could call. Aloysius cried while paging through the book, seeing his old self, his teachers and his friends. Peterson contacted about twenty teachers in all. Those who were able to recall Aloysius offered vague comments such as he was a "friendly," "nonaggressive" and "a respectful student." It wasn't much, but five of them indicated a willingness to give statements and possibly testify on Aloysius's behalf. John also found that some of the teachers he located already had spoken with someone at the State's Attorney's Office and were skittish about cooperating.

Julie wrote down a list of potential witnesses and how each person might help. She and Aloysius went over the list and crossed off those who could cause more harm than good. They concluded that Aloysius's mother and sister Angela were still too angry to testify, and could be volatile and unpredictable on the stand. "You can prep them, but you don't know what they'll say or do," Julie said. The best way to provide the judge with Aloysius's family history was for Julie to do it through her own testimony. Julie's only concern was that Lillian might become angered hearing her talk about how the Oliver family grew up in impoverished, drug-infested, gang-ridden neighborhoods within a sometimes violent household. "But these are the facts," Julie said. "That's the way it was."

Lillian Oliver told me that she was getting more worried. She knew that people wanted her son dead. "Let me tell you something," she said when I visited her for another interview. "If you don't know my son, don't judge him. Don't judge him if you don't know him. My son told me many times 'I didn't do it.' And I believed him."

CHAPTER SEVENTEEN

Arguing for Life

"DOING A DEATH CASE," Assistant Public Defender Woody Jordan told me, "is like reliving the worst time of your life."

Woody and his colleagues in the Murder Task Force were burdened with an immense responsibility. When clients were found guilty of capital murder, they had to try to save their lives and had to live with the consequences of failing. A death case required a focus and emotional investment that taxed some of these lawyers to their limits. As Aloysius Oliver's sentencing hearing drew near, I wanted to know what it felt like to be a guilty man's only hope of life, and what it took to fight against prosecutors who would summon everything in their power to try to kill your client. So I asked some of the Murder Task Force Members both current and retired, to share stories with me about what it meant to argue for life, what it meant to win and how it felt to lose.

Woody told me the story of a client named Thomas Melka. When he got Melka's case file and saw the crime scene photos for the first time, Woody remembered thinking to himself, I'm fucked.

The images made Woody feel sick to his stomach, the twist in his gut triggered not by the gruesomeness he viewed, but by the realization that his client would surely get the death penalty for this. He looked over the pictures again, seeing a young man and a young woman sprawled on the floor next to a Christmas tree surrounded by wrapped presents—a festive holiday party turned into a bloodbath. It happened on Christmas Eve, 1993. Thomas Melka, a part-time college student, was despondent over breaking up with his girlfriend, Cindy Kimberly. He went to visit her at the party, hoping to convince her that he really loved her and that he wanted to marry her. While the party was in full swing, Melka ducked into a bathroom, looked in the mirror and held a semiautomatic pistol to his head, debating whether he should kill himself right there. Instead, he walked out of the bathroom and started firing.

Woody narrated the scene to me from there. "He came in there as they were taking the ham out of the oven. He said, 'Merry Christmas to everybody!' and then he started shooting," he said. Woody stood up, pointing his right index finger like a weapon. "Boom. Boom. Boom," he said, jerking his hand back each time to simulate the recoil of the gun. Woody walked around his office re-creating the shooting from room to room. "Boom. Boom. Boom." In all, Melka pulled the trigger nine times. Party guests finally wrestled him to the ground before he could shoot again. Dead on the floor were Colleen Kimberly, the sister of Melka's ex-girlfriend, and Rob Boss, twenty-five, his ex-girlfriend's new boyfriend. Three other people were wounded. Among the crime scene photos was an image of a table next to the Christmas tree that was decorated with plastic reindeer and a Santa Claus figure, the dead bodies off in the background. The scene could not have been more heartbreaking, packing the kind of emotional punch that a jury would certainly consider when weighing whether to kill Melka for his crime.

This wasn't a case about whether Melka shot them or not. There were plenty of witnesses, forensic evidence and his own admission to prove he did it without any doubt. So how was Woody going to save this guy's life? Woody had to muster up an argument that would explain his client's actions that night and find something redeeming about him. He had to argue that his client did not deserve to die.

Years before current Murder Task Force members such as Woody began working on death cases, their predecessors had to learn how to save lives on the job after the Illinois reinstated the death penalty in 1977. The law separated trials into phases: to decide guilt or innocence, to determine eligibility for the death penalty and then a separate sentencing hearing. A person was eligible for the death penalty, for example, if the crime was considered cold, calculated and premeditated, or if the victim was killed during the course of a felony such as robbery or rape, or if the victim was a police officer. During

the sentencing hearing, prosecutors would argue aggravating circumstances, bring in a defendant's criminal history and use whatever
they could to portray that person as unworthy of continuing life.
The defense tried, as Woody would try, to answer with mitigation,
perhaps explaining how the client got to the flash point but still deserved a chance at redemption and forgiveness. A mitigating factor
might be that the person acted out of fear, that the murder occurred
while the defendant was under extreme emotional or mental stress.
The sentencing required extensive preparation and challenged the
task force lawyers to develop arguments they had not been called
upon to make before.

"You can never be prepared for something like when you're forced
to sit next to a client who the state wants to kill," Todd Musburger,
one of the original task force members who was on the job when the
state brought back capital punishment, told me. "We're lawyers, not
doctors. I don't think we were put in court with the skills to save a
life. Of all the things I've ever had to do in court, that was the most
gut-wrenching." Musburger got a headline-grabbing death penalty
case that tested his legal skills, emotional strength and commitment
to the job like never before. He led a team that included three other
lawyers to represent Hernando Williams, a black man who in 1978
was charged with kidnapping, raping and shooting Linda Goldstone, who was white and the wife of a prominent Chicago obstetrician. It was the kind of crime that horrified and enraged the
community. Goldstone, twenty-nine, had been on her way to teach a
Lamaze childbirth class at Prentice Women's Hospital downtown.
Williams, twenty-three, surprised Goldstone as she walked into a
parking lot stairwell, forced her into his car and for the next thirty-
six hours raped and beat her. During the ordeal, he locked her in the
trunk of the car, then took her to a hotel room to rape her some
more. He finally ended the terrorized woman's life by shooting her
as she screamed for mercy. Her body was found in an empty, litter-
strewn garage on the city's far South Side. Williams was linked to
the murder after someone who heard screaming from inside his car
trunk called police and provided the license plate number. Police

found Williams cleaning out the trunk of his car when they tracked him down. When they ran his name through police records, they learned that Williams had been out on bond while awaiting trial on charges of raping and kidnapping another woman a year earlier.

At the police station that night, Williams confessed and offered a chilling account of Goldstone's kidnapping and torture. Twice during her captivity, Williams allowed her to call her husband to say she was all right and would be home soon. He stopped at a bar for drinks while she was locked in the trunk and kept her there as he drove to court for a brief appearance on his pending rape charge. He told police that Goldstone might have lived had she listened to him. He had decided to free her and provide bus fare if she promised not to call police. When Williams saw her walk up to a home seeking help, he grabbed her away. "She was hysterical and I got hysterical," Williams said in his confession. "And before I knew it, I just turned around and shot her."

To prosecutors, this was clearly a death case—a rapist who mocked the judicial system by going out and raping again, torturing his victim and then, as she begged for her life, killed her. "With this victim—as a caregiver, a life giver, a childbirth instructor—we had a no-win situation," Musburger recalled. Williams decided to plead guilty just as his trial was to begin, hoping that by taking responsibility he would demonstrate his willingness and ability to become rehabilitated. Assistant State's Attorney Robert Boharic, who was prepared to go to trial, said Williams's plea was just a defense ploy to avoid the death penalty. But avoiding the death penalty was far from guaranteed. Williams had a lot against him. "The character of the victim controlled the case," Musburger said. "I am not blaming the victim. There is no question that she was a positive force for everybody she came in touch with. But when you look at the contrast, what is a jury to do? One of our heathens has removed one of our shining lights."

Still, Musburger came to see Williams as a person, not a monster, during their many visits at the jail and through interviews with his client's friends and family. That's what happened in cases like this. Defenders sat in a room with their clients and they heard their voices, felt them breathing, saw their fear and vulnerability. It was hard to imagine them committing the brutal acts for which they were charged. Musburger found that Williams was a smart but deeply troubled man. He grew up with opportunity and relative privilege, and made no claims of abuse or abandonment or being lured to violence by street gangs, as many defendants did. Williams admired his father, who was a minister, and told Musburger he once considered becoming a minister himself. He did well in high school, but dropped out and fathered his first child at fourteen. He fathered three more after that. His own siblings were victims of urban violence. Williams told Musburger he blamed himself after his brother was killed in an accidental shooting because he should have been visiting with him that night. He blamed himself when his sister was raped because he was supposed to meet her at the train after she got off work to escort her home. Before he committed rape and murder, Williams tried to do something with his life. He went to school to learn to be a security guard, spent time in the National Guard (though he got a dishonorable discharge), worked at a discount store and was briefly married, but he strayed and got divorced. At the time of the Goldstone killing, Williams had been working at his father's canvas goods supply company. His life, in many ways, was ordinary, which made his crime all the more difficult to understand. Musburger would draw on all of this as he created a biography of his client for the jury, a biography to make Williams a real but deeply flawed person who deserved mercy. That's how mitigation was supposed to work.

The sentencing hearing lasted for eight emotional and contentious weeks. At one point, the defense team walked out of court, frustrated that Judge James Strunck was thwarting their efforts by refusing to allow testimony of their expert witnesses, including one who would have described what an electrocution did to a human being, and a university professor who would have testified that the death penalty did not work as a deterrent. But the judge's message was clear: his courtroom was not going to become a forum to debate the merits or fairness of the death penalty.

The prosecution brought in dozens of witnesses to document the crime from beginning to end, and in brutal detail. I reviewed the transcripts, as well as newspaper articles, to try to get a feel of what the hearing was like, and it was wrenching. Family and friends of the victim gave tearful testimony about Linda Goldstone's short, wonderful life, how her death left such a hole in their hearts and in the world. Musburger took the risky, but in his mind, necessary step of having Williams testify for his own life, and during two days on the stand, Williams recounted his childhood, his hopes, dreams and disappointments. He admitted that a year before attacking Goldstone, he had raped and kidnapped a young women on his way to a job interview at a chemical plant. Musburger asked him to describe the night he raped and killed Goldstone. "At that time in your life, Hernando, were you close to anyone that you loved so much that they could prevent this darker side of you to come out that night?"

"I don't think so."

Williams dispassionately recounted the crime from beginning to end. "Do you think you were the same Hernando that you are in front of us today that you were when you abducted Mrs. Goldstone?" Musburger asked.

"I think at the time, I may have been not only the Hernando that you see today, I was also another Hernando."

"What do you mean?"

"I have always lived somewhat an image or portrayed an image that other people expect of me," Williams said. "At the same time I was totally different. I was brutal or cruel."

"Were you always the same Hernando I am seeing in the court today when you were with Mrs. Goldstone?"

"No."

"What kind of Hernando were you?"

"The only thing I could say, I was a monster or I was very vicious."

Williams said he did not understand his own motives. "I know that there is nothing that I could say that would even justify what I did, but through professional help since I've been here I've been able to do something that as long as I can remember, I was never able to do, and that was to be not what someone expected me to be, and I am able to accept that I did those things, although I don't know the reason—even throughout these whole procedures, there's a lot of things I don't remember, and some of them had to be ugly monstrous-types of images that I did not project during that time."

Prosecutor Robert Boharic attacked Williams's testimony and questioned his so-called contrition, pointing out the many lies that Williams told during the investigation, implying that he decided to confess not because he wanted to tell the truth and unburden himself, but because it became clear the police had overwhelming evidence against him. Borharic asked Williams again to recount the rape in detail for the jury to hear, to show what he believed was the real Hernando. "You knew that she was married when you were raping her?"

"Yes," Williams said.

"And you didn't care about that, did you?"

"At the time, no."

"It doesn't matter to you how she felt, did it?"

"I can't say what mattered at the time."

"Did you enjoy that feeling of power, Mr. Williams, that you had over that woman for that period of time, did you enjoy it?"

"I don't . . . I can't say that I enjoyed it."

"Did you have any mercy on her, Mr. Williams, when you raped her the first time?"

"No."

"Did you have any mercy on her when you raped her the second time?"

"No."

"You didn't have any mercy on Linda Goldstone, right?"

"No, I didn't."

"You didn't have any mercy on Linda Goldstone's family, did you?"

"No."

It was as if Williams was sealing his own fate. For how could he ask for mercy when he showed none to his victim?

The night before Musburger made his closing argument he was up rehearsing, writing and rewriting. He was frightened, unsure that he would be able to get up before the jury and be persuasive enough to elicit sympathy and understanding for his client. If only they could understand, if only they could see the worth of this man's life. "I don't know that I slept at all," Musburger said. "That closing argument was an overwhelming process to me."

Before a packed courtroom on a Saturday morning, Assistant State's Attorney Joseph Locallo made the first closing statement, pointing out the contrast between Williams and Goldstone, just as Musburger predicted. "Think about Jim and Linda Goldstone, obstetrician and the teacher of Lamaze, dedicated to the proposition of giving life, love, and—the irony is so damned apparent—the criminal bent on taking life away. Here are their tools, the forceps, assisting in bringing a child into a mother's arms, and his tool, a gun, which has now taken that same child away from her mother's arms." Williams, Locallo said, simply was arrogant and contemptuous of society. "I still can't look at him. I am tired of looking at him. I have had it up to here looking at him for these long weeks," Locallo said. The choice was theirs, he told the jury, allow Williams to spit in the face of justice "or you can tell the criminal, ladies and gentlemen, you just have had enough."

Musburger stood up and summoned all that he was. His opening lines spoke not only of his own feelings, but for the many defense lawyers who had the task of trying to persuade a judge or jury that life was worth saving, no matter whose life. "Before I can say anything to you, I have to speak of the fear that I have right now, a fear that I have never felt before, the fear that my words will be inadequate, that I will not say what I should say or say something I shouldn't. I am afraid of the expectation on me as being able to say something great, yet I know there is nothing great about me. And I am afraid that because of my inadequacy, you will kill my client," Musburger began. "I am also afraid of the extraordinary power that you now possess, and I wonder if you are afraid with me."

Musburger spoke as if he were fighting back tears. The room was silent as he continued. He looked at the jury—eight men and four women—and told them that they could be sympathetic to the victim, but that ordering another death would not undo the tragedy.

"They are asking you to continue the chain of violence that has been brought before you," he said. "They do not want you to know or feel about him. You need not understand the thing that you are being asked to destroy. There can be no justification or excuse. There can, however, be some understanding." Williams, Musburger continued, had a growing sickness within him. "Will you accept the easy solution that the state is offering," he said. "Mr. Boharic accused Mr. Williams of playing God with his victims. Shortly, Mr. Boharic will ask you to play God. They will cover up with euphemisms what they're asking you to do. They will speak of capital punishment. They will speak of the death penalty. They will not speak to you of the two thousand volts of electricity that they propose to put through Hernando Williams's body. They will not tell you how his brain will fry, his blood will boil, his eyes will pop out."

Hernando Williams's mother, who was sitting in the second row of the spectator gallery of the courtroom, wept as Musburger went on, pleading to jurors to save his client's life. "How will you justify the use of your power to take his blood? Yes, the prosecutors seek his blood. They want the big trophy. They were denied the conviction that they wanted by a man who at last was able to at least recognize the monster within him. By his plea of guilty, he recognized this. He did not come before you to confess and avoid responsibility," Musburger said. "When you return to your homes and reunite yourself with your loved ones and prepare for Christmas or Chanukah, will you draw your loved ones to you and say, 'Today, I sent a man to death'? When you look back on 1979, will you remember it as the year that you sent someone to death? Ladies and gentlemen, the sacred trust and responsibility of this man's life, I now give to you." Musburger walked back to the defense table with tears in his eyes. He had given the greatest and most emotionally draining speech of his life.

The jury reached a unanimous decision in less than an hour, casting just a single ballot to tally their votes. "Such a short time. Such a short time," Musburger recalled as we spoke about the case in his office twenty-five years later. Hernando Williams, the jurors decided, should be killed. "It was devastating," Musburger said. His eyes filled with tears as he recalled that day. He had trouble continuing our conversation. Twenty-five years have not diminished his hurt.

After the jury recommended death, Musburger walked back to the holding pen behind the courtroom with the other lawyers to talk with Williams. "Strangely, Hernando showed more courage than the rest of us," Musburger said. "He thanked us graciously and seemed to know how hard we tried and how much his case had come to mean to us." Then, with nothing more they could do for their client, Musburger and the rest of the defense team left the courthouse and went to Greek Town for a dinner. "It was a wake of course, only this time we were drowning our sorrows in drink for someone who was still alive," Musburger said. "I remember telling my wife, Betty, that we would never forget what we had been through. How often that has been proven correct.

"I do believe that if Hernando had been charged with raping and killing a black, homeless prostitute, he would still be alive," Musburger said. "In the end, I feel what juries do is look at the victim of the crime. They don't look at the perpetrator unless we have some extraordinary circumstance on his life. I believe that juries in death cases decide life or death based on the status, the character and the suffering of the victim and the victim's family."

Woody Jordan's client, Thomas Melka, had a much different background than Williams, but the state wanted to kill him just the same. He was white, grew up with relative privilege and had no history of violence. His victims also were white and shared a similar middle-class status. But Melka killed two people and nearly killed three others on Christmas Eve. And there were those photos to remind the jurors. At first, Woody thought he'd try an insanity defense to explain Melka's homicidal outburst. However, psychologists who examined Melka reported that he was mentally fit to stand trial and was legally sane at the time of the killings. That didn't mean Melka was free from mental illness. Forensic psychologist Larry Heinrich, whom Woody hired to evaluate Melka, concluded that just before the shooting, Melka expressed "major depressive reaction with some possible paranoid delusional thinking." Heinrich told Woody that

Melka showed signs of clinical depression, but it was not clear whether his violent actions were a result of his psychotic state. Melka claimed to have had a complete loss of memory during the shooting, and his condition after the incident seemed to deteriorate. While in jail awaiting trial, Melka suffered from major depression, was suicidal and treated with antidepressant and antipsychotic drugs, according to Woody. At one time, Melka had to be placed in leather restraints so that he couldn't harm himself. When Woody interviewed Melka's mother, she told him she long suspected something was wrong with her son. He had been upset and depressed for weeks before the shooting.

Woody developed his strategy: he would portray Melka as a vulnerable and sick young man who had a good life before he lost his mind. This was not a case of contrasts, as in the Williams case. Woody would tell jurors that Thomas Melka could have been any one of us. He would build on the idea that a seemingly healthy, decent, educated person could snap. "What a person has done in their life should count for something," Woody told me. "This was a good, middle-class white boy. He was on the track team. He was a student at the University of Illinois. He lived a very good middle-class life and he suffered from depression. That's it."

Melka was born in Czechoslovakia, and his parents divorced when he was still a toddler. His mother, Katarina Vancova, brought Melka to the United States and settled in Chicago. She got a job as a librarian at the University of Chicago, and they lived in Hyde Park near the campus. His mom taught Melka to read and write, though was very protective of him and kept the boy close to home. He was the center of her life, but at times he felt his mom smothered him. After graduating high school, Melka went to the University of Illinois to study engineering and history but could not continue because, his mother said, he had emotional and financial difficulties. He worked summers as a lifeguard and was very shy around girls until he met Kimberly, his first love. "He was very possessive of her," Woody said. "After he broke up with her, his depression got worse and worse. He was within a hair of being insane." That's when he came over with a gun on that Christmas Eve in 1993. Woody went behind a metal file cabinet in his office and pulled out a poster board on which yellow and orange ribbons were mounted. They were awards for track and field. "This was his mitigation," Woody said. "He was your typical, middle-class American kid." On the board were ribbons for the 800-meter relay, the 40-meter dash, the medley relay.

During the sentencing hearing Melka's mother testified tearfully, pleading for her son's life. The psychologists testified and agreed on Melka's fragile mental state. But Woody never got too cocky. When he thought he was doing well, he remembered what he was up against. "I'd just look at that picture." He also had to counter the emotional statements and letters from the parents and siblings of the murder victims. "I have endured much pain in my life. This by far is the deepest," wrote Maureen Miksis, mother of Rob Boss. "My life will never be the same. The zest is gone." And this, from the parents, who spoke of their daughter, an honor student who volunteered with the teen club Christmas pageant, drama club, gymnastics club, the girl who went around with a scraggly half-stuffed toy lion named Hoobie. "We don't know if we'll ever be able to recover. But we know that Thomas Melka can never be allowed to be free to inflict this kind of heartbreak on anyone else."

Prosecutor Thomas Bilyk reminded the jury that not only did Melka kill two people, but he tried to kill three others, and committed the crimes in a cold, calculated and premeditated manner—all aggravating factors. These were young people with their entire lives ahead of them, lives of promise. "I ask you to consider that there is no place on this planet, there is no place in our community for the likes of Thomas Melka. I ask you to sentence the defendant to the only sentence that will stop and close the floodgates of pain and suffering that Thomas Melka has opened in this case," he said. "I ask you to impose the only sentence that will close the wounds opened by Thomas Melka in this case . . . I ask that you return a sentence of death."

Woody got up to make his case. Life in prison, he told the jury, would be punishment enough. Melka would die behind bars an old man. He would eat prison food, sleep on a hard bed in a small cell.

"Look at him, folks. Look at him. What do you think is going to happen to him? He's a small guy," Woody said. "Isn't it sufficient punishment to never see another woman again for the rest of your life? Isn't it sufficient punishment to be behind a set of bars for the rest of your life until the day you die? To never be able to touch your mother again, to never be able to shake hands with one of your friends again?" Melka suffered from an emotional disturbance so profound that he thought he would marry his ex-girlfriend after the shooting. "Now if that doesn't show you somebody who is mentally disturbed, I don't know what does. Is that a rational, normal method for somebody to get to marry somebody?" Woody said. "This illness has affected him. It has changed him. It has warped him. He is sick. Mental illness is a disease. It's just like heart disease. You can't make it go away.

"If you really stop and think about Thomas Melka, before he was sick, he was sort of the American dream. The immigrant that came to this country at a young age with his mother, no father. Whose mother worked hard all her life to provide him a home, who insisted on two things in her home: work and education. Work and education . . . He almost made it. He was halfway through college. He almost made the American dream. He was a person that any one of us would be proud to know, who would be happy to have a conversation with. Then he got sick, and he changed. He changed. I'm not offering that as an excuse. I'm not offering any of these mitigating factors as an excuse. They are not an excuse. But a person who has lived from the day they were born, the rest of their life in that way, should not be killed, should not have their life taken away from them.

"What he has done in his prior life is worth something. His life is worth something. His life is worth something now, albeit he'll be in prison for the rest of his life," Woody said. "This isn't a thug on the corner. This isn't a dope dealer, a burglar. He's sick. Just one of you has to realize that his life is worth something, that his life has value, that his life should be preserved. Just one of you. This isn't pretty. We never said it was. And he should be punished. Please consider his mental illness. Please consider the way that he has lived his life. Please consider how he's been good to his fellow man before this Christmas Eve, and please save his life."

After he finished his closing statement, Woody felt he nailed it. He didn't think the jury would vote to kill his client. "That was the best fucking closing argument I ever made," he told me. The jury deliberated for hours, which was a good sign. Woody knew that asking regular people to decide whether another human being should live or die was a profound and scary responsibility. "It's as hard for them to give death as it is for us to get a not guilty." Jurors finally came back. They recommended Thomas Melka be sentenced to life in prison. Woody wanted to cry right there in court, but held himself until he walked out of the building and down the street. "It was just like in high school where you never want to let them see you cry," he said. "That life sentence was better than sex. It don't get better than that. That was the only case I ever won where I cried."

Murder Task Force lawyers had other death cases in which their clients lived their entire lives as if they were destined for a brutal end, clients whose sad stories were so hard to fathom that death might even come as a relief. If a judge or jury were liberal-minded enough, they might earn pity and compassion rather than wrath. Former Task Force member Robert Queeney had one of those cases, and it exposed him to one of the saddest, most pathetic and tragic lives he had ever seen. And like Woody, a crime scene photograph showed Queeney just what he faced: a murdered six-year-old boy, nearly decapitated by the killer who sliced into his throat. "I saw the photograph and I almost vomited," he recalled. "This kid has his neck cut all the way back, almost to the cartilage."

The man accused of this horrific act was George Del Vecchio, a truck driver and ex-convict who was on parole from a murder conviction when he was sixteen. According to police, on the night of December 22, 1977, Del Vecchio got high on PCP and went to the home of Karen Canzoneri at about 5:00 a.m. She awoke to find him standing over her bed holding a knife, and he raped her. After the assault, Canzoneri escaped through a window and called police. When officers arrived, they found Canzoneri's six-year-old son, Tony, dead, his throat slashed from ear to ear. Police found Del Vecchio hiding on the roof and arrested him. Detectives believed that Del

Vecchio had killed the boy first to silence him before sexually assaulting his mother. "I got the file, looked at it and couldn't handle it," Queeney recalled. "I had a son the same age. That photograph. I couldn't fucking take it."

But he had to. "So I met George and got to know him real well," Queeney said. "I found him likable. He was very courteous and his story was quite compelling." What Queeney found was a man whose childhood was tortured —born out of wedlock to a white mother and Hispanic father, relentlessly teased by a relative who was a Ku Klux Klansman. "The guy called the kid a spic since the day he was born. George was a kid consumed with rage. He was just shit on his whole life." That rage built into his teen years when he started taking drugs. Then, in February 1965, at age sixteen, Del Vecchio and two young companions went on a two-day crime spree. On the second day they encountered Fred Christiansen, an elderly man, whom they decided to murder and rob. Del Vecchio shot Mr. Christiansen five times as his accomplices kicked the dying man to silence his cries for help. The boys snatched eleven dollars from Christiansen's wallet. After police arrested Del Vecchio, he claimed that he was looking for drug money when he killed Christiansen. Del Vecchio provided the prosecutors with a written confession. His lawyer sought to have Del Vecchio convicted and sentenced before his seventeenth birthday. That way, Del Vecchio would be sent to a youth correctional facility until his twenty-first birthday and then be given an adult sentence and transferred to an adult prison.

During his stay at the youth facility, Del Vecchio achieved a sterling record and the judge took that into consideration when he turned twenty-one. He sentenced Del Vecchio to the statutory minimum of fourteen years in an adult prison. Del Vecchio was credited with time served and he continued to be a model inmate. He was paroled in April 1973. "He was a paradoxical figure. He wanted to go to law school. He was really smart. George had an IQ of 165," Queeney told me. "So he drives a truck, delivered fish, he was a great employee. Then he met a girl and got into PCP."

Four years later, Del Vecchio was charged with murdering the boy and raping his mother. "He was very sincere, earnest, intense, remorseful. And he was scared of himself," Queeney said. "I honestly thought we could win it." Del Vecchio's version of events was that he was having consensual sex with Canzoneri, though she happened to be his best friend's wife. "He was high on PCP and not in his right mind." Queeny said. "The phone rang, he freaked out and cut the boy's throat to stop him from screaming." Queeney had a dilemma: he wanted to put on an insanity defense, but Judge Louis Garippo indicated that if Queeney chose that strategy, the judge might allow prosecutors to tell jurors about Del Vecchio's first murder. Queeney believed such a revelation would be too prejudicial against his client and increase the likelihood that he'd get death. Queeney opted out of the insanity defense and argued that his client was too high to know what he was doing that night. It didn't work, and Del Vecchio was found guilty. Worse, the judge allowed the jury to hear about the first murder anyway during the sentencing phase, saying they had a right to know his criminal history while deciding whether Del Vecchio should live or die.

As he pleaded for his client's life, Queeney tried to create a portrait of a young man who knew nothing other than violence and rage. His mother, who had been married four times since she was fourteen and suffered years of domestic violence, got on the stand and talked about beating Del Vecchio with a broom handle when he was little. "I didn't know very much about being a mother," she testified. "I didn't know how to nurture and care for him. Children weren't people to me. They were things you have a responsibility for. You clothed and you fed them."

Queeney had never heard a story so heartbreaking. "If you listened to the story of his childhood, I mean, it was incredible. He was filled with homicidal rage since he was six or seven years old," Queeney said. I could hear the frustration and sadness in Queeney's voice as he talked about Del Vecchio. "I felt for George. He was a kid who had the shit beat out of him. I didn't give up. If you beat a dog every day of his life, he bites back. You can't blame the dog. I didn't think you could blame him. It's not to say that what George did wasn't horrific. But if anybody deserved a chance, I thought it was him."

Del Vecchio got on the stand before his sentencing and told the jury he was not even sure whether he wanted to live or die anymore. "I've reached a point in my life where I'm fairly disgusted with myself," he said. "Quite frankly, I think it would be much easier to die. But there is a part of me that clings to life. I'd like to attain some success as a man, as a human being . . . instead of dying with a feeling of shame, like a coward." Queeney was near tears and shaky as he gave his closing argument, telling the jury that his client came from a lifetime of abuse and hurt, and that the murder occurred while he was on drugs. "He was, in essence, a Jekyll and Hyde," Queeney said. "George Del Vecchio did not ask to be what he is. He does not like what he is. He is a man filled with rage and hate.

"I got up there and I sort of cried," Queeney recalled. "I told his whole life story up there, and I thought I told it pretty well. He was a very, very sensitive guy and he was very smart, very idealistic. Even the guards testified that he was all right." Queeney said that Del Vecchio was not to blame for the man he became. "I mean, he had parents who put out cigarettes on his body. He had the rug taken out from under him."

The jurors were not moved and sentenced Del Vecchio to death. After he was shipped off to death row, Del Vecchio continued to correspond with his public defender. "We became very close," Queeney said. "He wrote me a letter and said, 'I just want you to know you're the greatest lawyer in the world, and I thank you from the bottom of my heart.' " In November 1995, Del Vecchio made one last plea to spare his life at a clemency hearing, saying he had taken great amounts of drugs and drink, including various pills, cocaine, pot, hashish, LSD and PCP before killing Tony Canzoneri. "This tragic death was an act of insanity, not premeditated murder," he said in a taped message before the prison review board. "I never intended to hurt that child or anyone." Tony's mother brought the little boy's shoes and a scrapbook to the hearing. "This is what I have left of my son," she said. "Please put this man to death. Please get him off the earth because he is a dangerous, vicious animal." Governor Jim Edgar refused to lift the execution. On November 21, 1995, Del Vecchio ate his last meal. He asked for filet mignon with mushrooms, shellfish, baked potato with sour cream, Brussels sprouts, corn on the cob, salad with Italian dressing, cannoli and pistachio ice cream. Early the next morning, Del Vecchio was put to death by injection. "He told me not to feel bad," Queeney said. "He had concern for others. Eventually, I felt that not only had I done a good job, I just tried so fucking hard. You have to accept those things. I don't know how I would feel if I had not turned over every stone."

"With a jury, you have to touch their wounds," Marijane told me when I asked how she connects with jurors in death penalty cases. "That will save a guy's life. You put the jury in the client's position. But you need more than one juror. Nobody is secure being the only one. You need a friend. A single juror is not enough. The others will beat them down."

When Marijane lost her first death case, she was sad, sad not as much for her client as she was for herself. The man she defended, Frank Redd, was in her eyes "a piece of shit" and represented one of the worst cases she ever encountered. Redd was the client convicted of raping and killing the two little girls. "My mother was alive and she saw that I was upset. I had never done a death penalty case before, and I did the closing arguments," Marijane recalled. "I did the usual, 'Let's not kill him.' But I also said let's save him for science. I said that our society is getting worse, it's terrible, let's study him. When I did Frank Redd, I didn't really know what to say. How do you plead for life in a case like that? We were *supposed* to lose that one. He had a terrible reputation."

Redd's conviction was overturned by the Illinois Supreme Court, which found that prosecutors improperly introduced evidence that the jury should not have heard. Redd got a new trial but made a crucial mistake: this time, he chose to act as his own lawyer and was smashed by the prosecution. After the jury voted to convict, he told jurors that if they wanted to sentence him to death, "so be it." The jury took just twenty minutes to recommend sentencing Redd to death once more. Nine years later while on death row, Redd hanged himself in his prison cell. He was forty-seven.

CHAPTER EIGHTEEN

A Religious Matter

BEFORE THE FINAL DATE WAS SET for Aloysius Oliver's sentencing hearing, Marijane and Ruth sought to have Judge John Moran declare Aloysius ineligible for the death penalty. Marijane was looking mean when she arrived in court, her eyes narrowed, her jaw jutting forward and her mouth in a frown. She was wearing a gray two-piece suit and little makeup, which was surprisingly out of character. McKay and O'Connor turned and said good afternoon, but Marijane passed by without looking at them, and then, after a beat, said good afternoon with her back turned. The prosecutors leaned back and rolled their eyes. There were just a handful of people here today, including Eric Lee's parents and widow and a police union representative. Outside the courthouse the weather was warm, sunny and absent of humidity, making it a perfect July day. People were sitting on the front steps, grabbing a smoke, buying food from the lunch trucks and hanging out in a small plaza across the street. A girl danced and gyrated her hips while talking on her cell phone near the bus stop.

Ruth told Judge Moran that Aloysius should not be eligible for the death penalty because the jury found him guilty of murder, not specifically the murder of a police officer. In addition, the verdict form did not even point out that Eric Lee was a police officer, and one of the factors that made someone eligible for the death penalty was to knowingly kill a police officer. The defense continued to maintain that Aloysius did not know he shot a cop. McKay seemed annoyed with the whole proceeding, as if he had gone over all of this already. When Ruth finished, McKay got up and told the judge that the defense claim was simply without merit, that they were mixing up two separate parts of the trial. "The jury doesn't have to find at

224

the guilt phase whether the defendant is guilty of *capital* murder.
Guilt and eligibility are separate issues," McKay said. Besides, there
was plenty of testimony that Aloysius said "Fuck the police." He
went on to quote witnesses whose statements demonstrated that
Aloysius knew the police were coming. "For him to suggest otherwise," McKay said loudly, "is a mockery of the truth."

Marijane was learning way back in her chair and staring hard at
McKay. When her turn came, she argued that the debate over Aloysius's eligibility for death was a matter of constitutional law. "The
prosecution must, when asking for the highest penalty, do it right,"
she said. "They knew the jury form must fall within the statute. And
Mr. McKay forgets that every one of those witnesses was im-
peached."

Judge Moran denied the motion. Aloysius was eligible for the
death penalty and his hearing was scheduled for September 17,
2004.

Ruth McBeth called a defense team meeting to review their progress
and develop a strategy for the sentencing hearing. Marijane, Ruth,
Andrew Northrup, Julie Norman and her husband, John, met in a
windowless conference room in the public defender's office and sat
around a long table. Marijane seemed preoccupied and sat back a
few inches from the table to listen while the others spoke. Julie began by saying that she and John found several of Aloysius's old
schoolteachers, including a principal who was now retired. "I also
got in touch with an elementary school teacher. He vaguely remem-
bers Oliver, but I think he's willing to talk with us," Julie said.

Marijane leaned back, listening as Julie read from a list of teachers'
names who might cooperate. "Don't care," Marijane said abruptly.
She didn't think a few comments about Aloysius being a nice boy was
going to save his life. Marijane wanted to discuss the deeper, more
philosophical theme of Aloysius's atonement and redemption. Julie
and John said they did some research into Aloysius's religious following, the Yahwehs. They read literature and listened to sermons on
tape, but were still sorting out what it meant. "I've talked a lot to
Aloysius about his conversion. He says his family really doesn't un-

derstand, either," Julie said. "I think it's closer to Judaism than any-thing else." Aloysius had asked Julie whether she could get him a copy of the Pentateuch and haftorahs, the sacred text of the Yahwehs. The book was a Hebrew-English version of the Five Books of Moses, along with selections from the Prophets, called haftorahs. It was a massive book, 1,067 pages long and four inches thick. Julie was hav-ing trouble getting it delivered to Aloysius, however, because the jail would not allow hardcover books, and he would have to receive it with the cover removed. Aloysius said he could not accept a haftorah that was desecrated in such a manner. Marijane said she would call the jail chaplain to see what he could do.

Julie changed the subject and told the team she was trying to lo-cate an ex-girlfriend of Aloysius's who had filed an assault charge against him, an incident the state was planning to bring up at the hearing. Julie wanted to put the woman on the stand to explain what happened. "Otherwise the arrest report says it was domestic vio-lence. If I can get her to come in and say, 'He pushed me, I pushed him,' then we can show it wasn't that big a deal." Julie also told the group she would create a display panel of photographs from Aloy-sius's childhood to show the judge that he was once a vulnerable lit-tle boy just like other little boys. But Julie was afraid that prosecutors were going to come back hard by painting a contrasting picture of the Lee family and the Oliver family, both of which once lived in one of the city's poorest neighborhoods and raised different kinds of men. "Why can one family produce a cop and another a cop killer?" Julie said. "We have to counter that argument."

Marijane looked bored. Ruth suggested they move on to discuss Aloysius's atonement and how it fit into his commitment to Yahweh. "We have to find Aloysius's impact on other people," Ruth said. "That he's able to be compassionate to other people and capable of atonement. John, I'd be interested to know how the Yahwehs talk about atonement."

"In most ways they're more similar to Judaism than Catholicism," he said.

The religious discussion prompted Marijane to bust in. "Was Yahshua a prophet or a son of God or a son of man?" she said. "It strikes me that they are Peterist. Before you become a follower of Christ, you have to go through Judaism and then Catholicism. That's one of the things that split Paul from Peter. Paul was a rabbi. That was one of the debates of the early church. We're still playing to a Catholic judge. We have to find commonality."

Julie interrupted. She said during one of her visits with Aloysius she asked whether his religious studies had prompted him to help others. He told her that he counseled other inmates in the jail and encouraged them to change their ways. She asked about his anger, whether his religion helped him come to terms with what happened. "He told me he felt sorry for the Lee family, sorry that they had a daughter who must grow up without her father," Julie said. "He said 'I made a bad decision,' and he took some responsibility. He said running around a residential neighborhood with a gun was not smart. He said that all his life, he had no dad, no mentor, no one to encourage him."

"This religion is something he turned to try to make sense," Ruth said, beginning to build a theme. "But also because it's about having a father figure."

"His anger is all directed at himself," Julie said. "He said he made bad decisions."

"There's a problem here," Marijane interrupted. "I think the way to save his life is to wrap this up into a religious theme."

"We need to know how this religion parallels with the judge's beliefs or faith, or how it may clash with it," Ruth said.

As the discussion continued, Marijane got on the phone with the jail chaplain. "I've got a real, real death case," she told him. "Yeah. A guy who shot a cop. He needs a haftorah, but he says he can't allow the cover to be torn off. He considers it sacred. He doesn't want it desecrated. What can you do for me?"

After she hung up she said, "There's no way."

"Look," Marijane said, "here is a guy who fucked up every aspect of his life. The state will make that argument. Why didn't he get out of the ghetto like others?"

"His mother got out of the ghetto," Ruth said. "But the state is going to say that he had choices. The mom worked hard and supported the family. He needs instead to make an act of contrition. He's sorry. What were the first words after the verdict? 'Make sure my mother's okay.' "

Julie had been waiting to speak. "I disagree with you, Marijane," she said, her gentle voice rising uncharacteristically. "You said he threw away his life. He didn't. As a kid, he had asthma. I asked him his father's name, and he said you have to ask my mother. He had doubts who his father even was."

Marijane said it would all come down to the tale of two families. "On the one hand, here's a family that stays in the community, teaches in the community, has a police officer in the community, versus the other family that is a problem family of drug addicts, drinkers, et cetera," she said.

Julie was angry. "That family is not a family of losers or drug addicts and dealers; they have jobs," she said.

Ruth tried to calm her. "I know, I know," she said. "We're just anticipating what the state will say."

"Do you think the women know how to parent?" Marijane said.

"Some of them," Julie said. "I know the state will say this is a good family, this is a bad family, and they're both from the ghetto. But it's not the children's fault. The majority of the people in that neighborhood are not scum. They have jobs."

"We still have a problem," Marijane said. "I agree with you, Julie. But this is a typical mitigation. The state is so used to that. We can't use the usual stories. The judge has been hearing this over and over again: 'He's depraved because he's been deprived.' We have to hit on how he can help someone. We need to give a reason to keep him alive. Our target audience is one man: the judge."

"If the judge is going to go with his values and his heart, we are going to have to give him a boatload of support," Ruth said. "We're going to go with this theme of redemption, and that's it. God never shuts the door on that. Forgiveness and redemption are a process. It takes time. God understands that. That's why he gives us our whole life to do it. To live a moral life is a process. It would be unfair to snuff out his life before he learns those lessons, or before he can help others."

"There's your money shot!" Marijane said. "I haven't got death in twelve years." She knocked wood.

"And we have the confession with his apologizing," Ruth said. "That's so powerful. He's sorry."

Marijane and Ruth wanted to test the redemption and forgiveness theme further, and made arrangements to play out a version of the sentencing hearing in front of a focus group. Because they were arguing the case before a judge, and not a jury, they wanted to select a group to represent a similar demographic as Judge Moran, who they knew was religious and socially conservative, a humanist who was fair and open-minded and took his position on the bench seriously. Marijane's friend, Paul Dorcic, who ran a marketing, research and image consulting business, organized the event. Through a database, Dorcic got a list of sixteen participants, most of whom were economically and socially conservative, college-educated professionals, but who did not have an extreme view on the death penalty. He rented a room at a firm called Precision Research Inc., which was in a building next to Interstate 90, just outside O'Hare International Airport. From the parking lot, you could see the shiny bellies of the planes during takeoffs and landings and smell the jet fuel.

Dorcic, who had gray hair and a young-looking face, served as moderator. He escorted the sixteen people into a conference room that had one-way glass through which Marijane and the team could watch in privacy and hear as their audience discussed the lawyers' performance. Dorcic assured the participants that they would remain anonymous. The suite on the other side of the glass was like a private skybox at an athletic stadium with three tiers of cushy high-backed leather chairs that had retractable tables hidden between the chairs on which to place food and drink. On one wall was a large flat-screen television monitor. Behind the suite was a room with trays of sandwiches, salads, soft drinks and coffee.

The lawyers would put on the case in an abbreviated form and gauge how the participants reacted to their strategies. Marijane and Ruth were joined by Andrew Northrup, former law clerk Joseph Runnion, Peg Solomon, Francis Wolfe, Julie Norman, John Peterson and a few other lawyers from the public defender's office who wanted to watch. Northrup played the role of prosecutor and read the charges before the focus group for the opening statement. Marijane then stepped up to deliver one of her favorite lines: "Now, let's hear the rest of the story." And she gave a short version of the defense, pacing across the room, which was cramped and had little space for her to maneuver in her usual way. "He made either the most lucky or unluckiest shot of his life," she said of Aloysius. Marijane played the videotaped confession and told the participants that Aloysius's apology at the end was a true expression of sorrow and regret. She spoke of how smart her client was, that he spread his religious beliefs in the jail. His execution would serve no one. "Instead of relieving the pain of the Lee family, it will only increase it," she said.

"That's a good argument for a jury, but not for a judge," Solomon said while watching from the other side of the mirror. "I'm surprised she used that."

The lawyers took breaks and watched as the participants discussed the performance. One man said he was unmoved by hearing about Aloysius's educational background. Another said, "A lot of prisoners find religion. That's all well and good, but it doesn't change the fact that they committed a crime." Another woman said she wanted to know more about Aloysius's rough childhood. One man said that Marijane did not sound personally connected to the defendant, that she needed to appear more invested in her client, "that she really believes in that kid."

"This is fascinating," Marijane said as she listened to the comments over the speaker.

"He should have known they were cops," one man said. "Did he mean to shoot?" commented another. "Lucky or unlucky? It was a poor choice of words."

Ruth put Julie on the imaginary witness stand. Julie testified how Aloysius never knew his father, grew up in poverty and violence and was always afraid. Julie got up from her chair and put up a three-fold cardboard display that looked like a school science fair project, a sort of collage with childhood photos of Aloysius, the ABLA public housing project and articles about the dangerous neighborhood he lived in as a boy. Julie concluded by telling the group that Aloysius truly felt remorse for what happened.

Changing roles, Marijane came back into the room as the prosecutor this time, aggressive and loud as she cross-examined Julie. "You're not saying everyone who grows up in the projects becomes a murderer, are you?" She brought out that Aloysius had sex with a teenager and that he was arrested on charges of beating his mother. "Isn't it your job," Marijane said to Julie, "to present Aloysius Oliver in the best light?"

At the break, Marijane went to the back for some refreshments and was feeling electric. "This is great. I'm loving this," she said. "You get to try out shit on this jury that you might not try out in court. Like that neighborhood stuff. I love playing the prosecutor."

Solomon seemed unmoved. She wasn't so sure this was a necessary exercise. "The judge has already made up his mind," she said. "He's heard the case." Marijane and Ruth sat back in the big chairs and listened again to the focus group's comments. "When I found out he beat his mother and sister, sheesh, that was it," one man said. Another said that Marijane had blown Julie's testimony apart, while another, more sympathetic woman felt Julie was broadsided. Several criticized Julie's photo display. "I thought that chart was ridiculous," one woman said. "My sixth-grade class could have done something like that." Another said, "I felt sorry for him, that he grew up in the ghetto. But not everyone goes that way. Not everyone in the ghetto becomes a killer."

John Peterson was the next witness in the exercise. He played the role of the Elder George Garner from the Yahweh Assembly, who would testify about Aloysius's newfound religion and commitment to redeem himself. "Why don't they ever find God before they're arrested?" Francis Wolfe asked, repeating a common question. One juror remarked that he didn't think religion should be equated with rehabilitation. "All of a sudden a guy finds religion? I'm skeptical."

Ruth wrapped up by handling the closing argument for the defense, listing reasons why Aloysius should not be killed. Her delivery was quiet, straightforward. "Sorry isn't going to bring back Officer

Lee," she said. "We're not saying that's enough." She told the participants that Aloysius was seeking redemption and understanding, which was why he should be allowed to live. "It is a measure of this man that he struggles with these things," she said. "This is a life worth saving. He will pay the price."

Finally, Joseph Runnion, who had worked as a clerk for Marijane and was going to testify at trial, played the role of Aloysius. In one scenario, he offered no words of apology before being sentenced. In another, he said he was sorry and did not mean to kill the officer. That proved to be among the most valuable parts of the experiment. The apology seemed to connect with the group. One woman said, "I don't think he was a cold-blooded killer. I didn't think he meant to do it." Said another, "I think it was very important that he showed remorse." And finally one woman said, "It's tough for any of us to play god."

In six weeks, Judge Moran would be in that very position.

Lillian Oliver visited her son two days before learning whether he would live or die, and did her best to comfort her frightened child. "He's not doing too good," she told me when I called to ask about Aloysius. "I'm not doing too good." A day later, on the eve of the hearing, Julie went to visit him. "He was totally at peace," Julie told me after the meeting. "He said to me, 'I'm not angry anymore at anyone.' Oliver started out being angry—angry at the police, angry at the state's attorney, angry at the judge, angry at Marijane, angry at everyone." Aloysius, it seemed, had convinced himself that he really didn't kill Officer Eric Lee and that somehow the truth would come out. Yes, he was irresponsible and shot a gun that night, but it may not have been his bullet that killed Officer Lee. If Aloysius decided to include that argument as part of an apology in court that could deflate his attempt at contrition and put into question the sincerity of his journey toward redemption. He was seeking redemption for making bad decisions but was not taking responsibility for killing Eric Lee. His regrets were for shooting a gun that night, but not for murder. Aloysius held on to the hope that evidence would come out that something else happened, that one of the other cops in the alley that night might have fired a shot—intentionally or accidentally—that could have felled Officer Lee.

The night before the hearing, Julie sat up late reviewing her notes, memorizing the Justice Department Risk Factors for Violence that applied to Aloysius's case. She had a lined piece of notebook paper and wrote down points she thought she would cover. She prepared for the tough cross-examinations by the state's attorneys. "The weird thing about testifying is you never know. There is always something that comes out of left field," she told me. "I'm really nervous. The stakes are high and you know you are going to be torn up in there. They're going to try to make you look bad, and that's hard to take." She was also concerned about Aloysius's family. "They're going to be tense. They tend to use anger as a shield to deeper feelings."

At this point, Julie felt the defense team did the best it could. The next morning, Marijane would make the opening statement and Ruth would make the closing argument. "I never believed in the death penalty," Ruth told me. "I don't think it brings closure to the victim's family. It is not a deterrent. I have a problem arguing to people who are open to it. You have to think of a reason to save someone's life. Who are we saving this man for? With Aloysius, there are the facts of the crime to consider. Would he be able to do this again? No. It was an unintentional shot. Did he mean it? I still have to wonder. I really can't accept that's how it happened."

Shawn Lee did not wonder how it happened. She knew Aloysius Oliver killed her husband, and she wanted Aloysius to die for it. It was the only punishment she saw fit for the man who made her a widow and left their daughter fatherless. Shawn would come to Aloysius's sentencing hearing hoping that Judge Moran would agree there was no place on this earth for such a man. Yet until the day Eric was killed, Shawn had been against the death penalty, believing that it was simply wrong to kill, that murder had no justification in any circumstance. It was a theoretical concept back then. Now things were different. Her feelings about capital punishment were visceral, not philosophical. Eric was her first love, her true love, such a good man, such a wonderful dad, such an important part of her life and her community. "Before Eric's death, I felt that I had compassion for everyone and everything," she told me during an interview. "I felt that every man and woman had something good inside of them." Her husband had an abundance of good inside him, and it barely had time to flourish before Aloysius took it away in an instant.

This was the other part of the story, the other life that Judge Moran would consider in his deliberations. The defense team was right. This was a tale of two very different families. Eric Dwayne Lee was the first of four children born to Bobby Lee and Anna Bates-Lee on October 11, 1963, in Chicago. Bobby, who was born and raised in Arkansas, drove a bus for the Chicago Transit Authority. Anna, a lifelong Chicagoan, worked in accounting and technology for a bank. The Lees raised their family in a blue-collar neighborhood just blocks from where the Olivers had once lived. Eric was a good kid and a good student, earning honors from grammar school throughout high school. He played basketball, usually as a forward, and ran track, excelling as a hurdler. After graduating Leo High School, he went to the University of Illinois at Chicago, but two years later decided to join the United States Marine Corps. Eric went off to basic training in San Diego, and for the next four years traveled around the world, assigned to bases in Japan and South Korea. He specialized as a rifleman and sharpshooter, and had earned the rank of corporal at the time of his honorable discharge. Eric came back to Chicago in 1989 stronger, more focused and with a heftier, more muscular physique. He had talked about becoming a cop and took a job as a contract security guard in a downtown office building while going through the police application process. Shawn worked in an office building nearby for the collections department of Encyclopaedia Brittanica. She and her coworkers used to go to the same bar after work on Fridays to unwind, and that's where she first saw Eric with his friends. She and Eric would wave from across the room to each other, but Eric seemed too shy to come over and say hello. Shawn would drive home, blushing the whole way, thinking about this man. "After six months of waving, he finally asked for my phone number," she recalled. They went on their first date on

August 10, 1990. It wasn't very romantic. Eric took her to a furniture store. He was searching for a bedroom set for his apartment and wanted to consult with her. "The idea that this man wanted my opinion impressed me, but as our date went along, I realized my then boyfriend was quite shy and I thought he was a little boring," she told me. "But I guess all of that improved because we were together almost every day from that date."

Shawn knew by their third date that he was the one she would marry. She got a sense that he was one of the most caring and giving men she would ever meet. Eric didn't have much to say at first. "But after a few months, I saw another side of him. He was humorous and charming," she said. Shawn remembered one date during which they went for a boat ride along the Chicago River. It was the night the Chicago Bulls won the first of six NBA titles and turned out to be a raucous and exciting night for both of them. Eric told Shawn that his goal was to become a Chicago police officer, that it was something he always wanted to do. Shawn was proud, but a little uneasy because she had cops in her family, some of whom were killed in the line of duty. Her great-grandfather was killed in 1968 and her great-uncle was killed on the job in 1973. She also had cousins still on the force and often heard their stories of what it was like to be working the streets.

On September 11, 1993, Eric and Shawn were married at the Salem Baptist Church, Shawn in a traditional white gown and Eric in a white jacket and black pants. A year later, their daughter, Erica, was born, and the thrill of fatherhood showed in Eric's face every day. He took great joy in being a dad. He taught Erica to ride a bike and to climb trees. When Erica took tap dancing and ballet lessons, her dad drove her, picked her up and attended all her recitals. When his little girl began playing soccer, he coached her team. He was the kind of dad that many kids from the neighborhood dreamed of having. When Eric was on the job with the Chicago Police Department, Shawn always spoke with him during his shift, needing the reassurance that he was okay. One New Year's night, Shawn heard on the television news about gunfire at some housing projects and that people were shooting at police officers. When Eric got home, she had a talk with him. "You've got to leave," she said. Instead, Eric suggested he could get off street patrol by becoming a plainclothes officer, perhaps joining the Englewood Rangers, a special undercover squad. Shawn knew the work was still dangerous, but perhaps less chancy because the Rangers were highly trained and prepared when they conducted raids and drug busts. They didn't drive around the streets all night or take random calls that could put them in danger. And the Rangers didn't wear the standard blue uniforms, which would make them instantly identifiable as police officers and easier targets for those who dared take shots at them.

Eric got the transfer to Englewood in 2000 and liked the change. His new assignment allowed him to be part of a more focused and concentrated effort at arresting criminals such as drug dealers, prostitutes and gangbangers. He told Shawn that he was happy to be back in Englewood where they both grew up and where he could make a difference. Eric's partner on the squad, Andre Green, could see that he was exhilarated with his new beat. "Englewood was a good learning district. It's where all the action was," Green told me. "We enjoyed the job. We all had war stories out there. We were in a few dangerous situations together, and there were guns. You look back and you realize how close we had come."

As happy as Eric was working in Englewood, he also was hoping to move up the ranks of the police department and took steps to ensure a better future for his family. He went to night school to earn a bachelor's degree in criminal justice from Chicago State University, the same school from which Aloysius Oliver dropped out after only a few weeks. In May 2000, Eric graduated summa cum laude. He talked with Shawn about some day leaving police work to become a financial planner.

Bobby and Anna Lee knew that every night Eric went to work, there was the possibility that he could get hurt or killed. As the parents lay in bed at night, they sometimes heard sirens, wondering each time whether Eric was zooming to a crime or being transported in an ambulance. Bobby Lee knew firsthand the risks of working in the city late at night. During his thirty-four years as a bus driver, he navigated some of the city's most dangerous neighborhoods, often during late shifts. He drove through the smoldering remains of the West Side after rioters burned and looted the neighborhood following the assassination of Dr. Martin Luther King Jr. Like his son, he drove by the Robert Taylor public housing buildings on New Year's as the sound of gunfire cracked from alleys, windows and rooftops, and remembered crouching and ducking when he heard the pops of pistols. "All those years, nothing ever happened to me," Bobby Lee told me. "I was truly blessed." But every night he worried about his son being out there. "I always wanted him to be as careful as possible. In a job like that, there were times it was scary. I know he had a lot of adventures out there."

On that August night, Shawn was chatting on the phone with one of Eric's friends, who also was a cop. He stopped talking and told Shawn to hold on a minute; there was some commotion over the police radio. An officer had been shot. Shawn hung up and dialed Eric's cell phone. Someone answered, but it wasn't Eric. It was an officer who told her Eric had been hit. Bobby Lee had heard on the television news that an officer had been shot, and his first thought was that it was Eric. "My wife and I just knew something happened that night," Bobby Lee told me as we sat in his living room where he heard the awful news. A few minutes later, he got the call that his son had been wounded. He drove to the hospital hoping Eric would be okay and that they would be talking to each other soon. Shawn, in a daze, raced over there as well. When Shawn arrived, she could tell by the expressions on the officers' faces what she was about to learn. She was escorted into a room where Eric lay on a table with bandages over his head. His body was still warm to her touch.

"On August 19, 2001, my joy, happiness, and peace were taken away from me. Eric went to work that evening and never returned home." That was the beginning of a letter that Shawn wrote to Judge Moran as part of the presentencing process. "I will never forget the pain I felt that night as I stood there in disbelief. I will never forget anything about this fatal night. I will never forget the days that followed, having to tell our six-year-old daughter that her daddy wasn't coming home again . . . I will never forget the steps I had to take such as selecting a funeral home, a church, a casket, and cemetery.

"I will never forget thinking, What am I going to do without Eric . . . my best friend. Judge Moran, I will never forget the hundreds and hundreds of cards and phone calls I received that didn't take away my hurt, my pain, my agony! I will never forget the many months I couldn't eat, couldn't sleep and couldn't think clearly because my life had changed overnight. I will never forget the hurt in my daughter's eyes, the nightmares and sleepless nights."

The judge received eleven such letters—victim impact statements, they were called—from other family members. These, too, he would consider in deciding whether to send Aloysius to the death chamber. They were letters of anger, desperation and heartbreaking sadness. They told the judge of the struggles to accept such a sudden, senseless loss. Bobby Lee wrote how unfair it was for a man who cared so much about life and serving others to be killed by one who did not care. "To the defendant, I can only say you caused an endless chain of pain to all of us, taking my son from my wife and I, taking a husband from Shawn and a father from Erica," he wrote. "I am still struggling and will be for the rest of my life with the loss of Eric. Not only was he my son, he was a great friend of mine. I loved him very much."

Eric's mother, Anna, whose pain of losing her firstborn child was inconsolable, wrote her letter as if she were addressing her son: "I wish I could have protected you the way I did when you were a child. You are in good hands now, in God's hands, no more sorrow and no more pain. I don't have to cringe every time I hear a police siren; I just pray that God will watch over the other officers out there. There is so much violence, evil and hatred in the world today, I pray that things will change soon. Please let justice take place for Eric."

Shawn helped Erica, who was six years old when her father was killed, prepare a letter for the judge, which was typed and placed in Moran's file. "The man who killed my daddy is a terrible man," Erica wrote. "My life has changed because of what this man did in many ways. My mom and I are really frustrated and sad. This man really hurt my feelings by taking my daddy away from me. My heart is broken and so is my mom's because we miss my daddy very much. This man has really hurt my family."

Shawn later told me about the struggle and pain she felt by shifting her view of capital punishment and going to court wanting Aloysius to die. She never wanted to feel the hate that she felt toward Aloysius. It hurt to realize how she had changed. "I was totally against the death penalty, but now, going through the course of the trial, it's changed my heart. That's the sickening part," she said. "I honestly hurt saying this, but I feel so very different. I feel like I could walk into a room with Oliver on the other side and pull the lever and walk away feeling nothing. That's how much Eric's murder has affected me. I don't like feeling the way that I do, but I have to be honest with myself and pray for strength to be a compassionate person again." Her rage against those who murder the innocent was complete. "I feel they are no longer worthy of breathing, eating, sleeping, visiting the loved ones they still have. They don't deserve any of this after the deep-rooted pain you feel and the changes made to your very being," she said. "There is a pain and hurt that runs very deep and anger, an entire range of emotions that will be with me for the rest of my life. I am still a God-fearing woman who prays for forgiveness for my enemy and for myself."

CHAPTER NINETEEN

Judgment Day

EARLY ON THE MORNING of September 17, 2004, deputies escorted Aloysius Oliver from the jail to the holding pen behind courtroom 606 to learn whether he would live or die. Outside it was a bright blue day, the warmth of summer still in the air. Down the street from the courthouse, mothers held their children's hands as they walked to school. Upstairs in the Murder Task Force office, Woody Jordan was at his computer playing a military battle game. "The judge ain't gonna kill him," Woody predicted as he shot at helicopters and tanks. "He's a good Catholic man. I don't see it happening."

Marijane Placek arrived in an unusually happy mood. "I'm not nervous," she declared. "I feel great." Ruth McBeth, too, told me she felt good, but she could not hide that she appeared a little jittery. "I want to get down there now. If the room is full of cops, I want to take it in, absorb it and breathe it and feed off that energy." That energy was there. When she exited the elevator, Ruth saw the hallway already was crowded with cops, lawyers, television and newspaper reporters. Shawn Lee, along with Lee's parents, was speaking to the prosecutors in a hallway off the main corridor.

Julie Norman took a seat in the back of the courtroom. She already had been busy that morning trying to reassure Aloysius's former teachers that their upcoming testimony was going to be fine, and she had sat down with Elder George Garner to explain how the hearing was going to work. Julie also was trying to calm herself, feeling the enormity of the moment, the obligation and the pressure to do a good job as a witness. She did deep-breathing exercises as she sat on the bench looking straight ahead. Julie took three deep breaths, held the last one and then exhaled slowly. She repeated the pattern and began to focus on what she planned to say. She'd reviewed all the notes, went over everything in her head and decided she was as ready as she'd ever be. Marijane's friends Michael Huskey and David Bow were able to squeeze into the courtroom to watch the hearing, and were looking resplendent. Michael was in a sage suit with a pink tie and David was in a cream-colored suit. Ruth came over to the bench and hugged Julie to wish her good luck. Julie watched as Lillian Oliver and her daughters came in and looked for seats. "I feel affection for that family," Julie whispered to me. "And I do feel positive about Aloysius." Lillian Oliver sat near the end of a bench in the second row. She was wearing a black, gold and gray print dress, her arms and shoulders exposed, revealing a tattoo memorializing her late nephew Tommie Leach. Her hair was braided in cornrows and she was wearing dark sunglasses. Aloysius's sisters Angela and Ashiyenetta sat in the front row. Aloysius, dressed in the same gray suit he had worn throughout the trial, sat back in his chair. He looked over at his family from time to time, but his face showed no expression.

The room now filled and the doors closed, David O'Connor made his brief opening statement for the prosecution. He looked alive, confident and poised, speaking in a voice that sounded incensed, a tone that he had carried throughout the trial. Aloysius, he told Judge Moran, lived his entire adult life breaking the law, violating and brutalizing other people and deserved the ultimate punishment. "Your honor, we respectfully stand before you and indicate that we will be asking for a sentence of death for his crime," O'Connor said.

Marijane, wearing a deep purple dress for the occasion, stood up to answer. To take Aloysius's life, she began, would only compound a tragedy. "His background is both paradoxical and typical," she said. Her client had witnessed violence his whole life, inside his home and on the streets of his neighborhood, which had a profound effect on his being. But Marijane told the judge that Aloysius had since moved forward. "You will hear how that religion has changed Mr. Oliver, how he almost became an apostle for that religion within the jail, teaching and showing other men," she said. "He will stand as an example of 'Do as I'm now doing, not as I did in the past because I, although now trying to take advantage of my potential, wasted so much before.' "

Assistant State's Attorney James McKay laid the foundation for the prosecution's death argument by offering their version of Aloysius's life story, a story highlighted by a litany of arrests and charges filed against him during the past thirteen years. He told the judge that Aloysius's adult criminal history began with an arrest for battery on Christmas Day, 1991, when he was accused of punching two men in the mouth. He went on to accumulate arrests for shooting a gun, selling crack cocaine, peddling marijuana, committing robbery, aggravated battery and assault. His rap sheet was his life's résumé. O'Connor called up a police officer to testify that Aloysius was arrested in November 2000 on charges of beating a pregnant woman who had sought help in a hospital emergency room. The officer was in the ER when she found the woman in a fetal position on the floor, bleeding from the nose, and Aloysius standing nearby. The officer asked if he had harmed her, and she said yes. Aloysius bolted from the hospital but was quickly caught by another cop. He later pleaded guilty and got a year's probation. The woman told the officer that Aloysius hit her because her pregnancy did not coincide with the time they had been dating. She had been afraid to seek help from police because she was afraid of him, and he knew where she lived.

Another detective took the stand to tell the judge she investigated Aloysius on a sexual assault charge after a thirteen-year-old girl showed up at a hospital with her legal guardian in May 2001. The guardian brought her there after the girl said she had been at a neighbor's house for the past three days having sex. The girl was Johanna Harris, the same girl who was with Aloysius the night he shot Officer Lee. Aloysius told police he thought she was fifteen, and denied having intercourse with her. He agreed to give a DNA sample, which later proved a match to semen taken from the girl. No charges were ever filed. In addition, the prosecution called jail guards who testified that Aloysius got fourteen days in the hole for beating and robbing another inmate, and got another four because he tried to hit a female guard when he refused an order to take his hands out of his pants. When the prosecutors finished, they had painted a picture of a longtime small-time criminal capable and sometimes willing to get violent.

The defense had to divert the judge's attention from Aloysius's criminal past to a past in which he was a just a kid, and then a young man, who was trying to navigate life in a dangerous neighborhood and violent household. They began by reaching back to his school days. The first defense witness was Ira Jean Weaver, a retired teacher from Dunbar Vocational Career Academy. Under questioning by Andrew Northrup, Weaver said she remembered Aloysius from a keyboarding class because his first name was so unusual. "In my class, he was a good student," she said. "He gave me no problems. He was very mannered, very respectful. I never had any problems out of him at all." The teacher's comments were brief and safe, not glowing or as effusive as the lawyers might have hoped, but they were something.

McKay came back on cross-examination, reminding the teacher that it had been more than ten years since she last saw him. "He was smart enough to know right from wrong, right?" McKay said.

"Yes."

Frank Sedlek, another retired teacher from Dunbar who taught social studies and United States history used words like "quiet," "respectful" and "nice" in describing Aloysius. "He was a good student and got along with his peers," he said.

McKay came back with a zinger. "Do you think murdering a police officer is respectful?"

Marijane loudly objected, and the judge sustained it. The teacher left the stand.

Julie Norman had been mentally rehearsing and doing her breathing exercises as the teachers testified. Now it was her turn, and she was called to the witness stand. Her job was to weave Aloysius's life together in a way that would help the judge understand how the boy developed into the man he became. Julie carried a stack of notes and reports about Aloysius, and took her seat. Ruth handled the questioning, leaving most of the taking to Julie, who was prepared to give a narrative when prompted. Ruth asked Julie to talk about Aloysius's early years and family history. Julie spoke of his impoverished beginnings, the absence of a father, his witnessing of violence inside and outside the home and his life in a dangerous public housing project. She told the judge of her visits with Aloysius in the jail. "I asked him, 'What is the first act of violence that you can remember?' And Mr. Oliver said the violence was so usual and so common that he had to stop and think," Julie said. "He told me, 'There's never been a day in my life when I haven't been afraid.'"

Responding to Ruth's open-ended questions, Julie went on to explain how the young Aloysius saw his mother living with various boyfriends, how some of them beat her. "Aloysius told me, and his mother corroborated it," she said. "I believe they are a close family, but I think their family has had some problems over the years." Julie said Aloysius was concerned for his younger brother, Andres, worried that he might be headed down the wrong path. Julie stood up and showed the judge two photos of Aloysius, having decided against using the cardboard display she had prepared for the focus group. The first photo showed Aloysius in 1979 during Easter at his aunt's house. In another photo, he was holding a baby niece. Behind those photos was a troubled boy, she said. Then, as she had planned, Julie explained to Moran how Aloysius grew up in an environment that fit the U.S. Department of Justice's measures of risk factors predicting future violence. He grew up amid economic depravation, chaos within the family and alienation from society at large. "He hadn't had access to many of the things that middle-class people take for granted, working-class people," she said. "For instance, Little League, Boy Scouts, regular outings, travel to different cultural events. He didn't have that."

"Have you spoken to Mr. Oliver about this crime, this murder that he's now been convicted of?" Ruth asked Julie.

"Yes."

"What is his attitude?"

"He's very, very sad, very remorseful."

Julie wrapped up by saying she believed that the many years of being exposed to violence and hardship took their toll on Aloysius. "I think he suffers from posttraumatic stress disorder, and has for many years."

Assistant State's Attorney Joe Magats came out hard. "Can you tell Judge Moran the name of one doctor who has diagnosed Aloysius Oliver with posttraumatic stress disorder?" She could not and admitted that he had never been tested for it. Magats asked Julie about the many hours she spent visiting the defendant. "Did you form any kind of special bond with Aloysius Oliver?" he said.

"I have a professional relationship with Mr. Oliver."

"Any feelings of empathy toward him?"

"I feel empathy for him and his family."

"You feel any sympathy toward him?"

"Yes."

"Did you find him to be an intelligent person?"

"I think he's quite bright."

"He knows right from wrong, does he not?"

"Yes."

Magats asked Julie about Aloysius's siblings and their experiences growing up. "Besides Aloysius Oliver, did anyone else in his family grow up to be a cop killer?" he said.

"Objection!" Marijane yelled.

"Was there anyone in the family who has been in trouble with the law to the extent Mr. Oliver has been?" Magats asked.

"No."

Magats finished his cross-examination and Julie stepped down. Marijane pushed back her chair, stood up and called the defense's next and perhaps most important witness: Elder George Garner, pastor and evangelist of the Assemblies of Yahweh and Messiah from Rocheport, Missouri. Garner was tall and stout, with a reddish beard and short hair. He looked Amish and was wearing a gray shirt and tie, but no jacket. Marijane asked him to identify himself and his church.

"Is that a mail order religion?" she asked.

"I don't know what you identify as 'mail order.' We have a mail order section of which I am in charge, but it is a group of small assemblies throughout the United States and other countries," Garner said.

He spoke of his prison ministry, how he visited prisons to conduct Bible studies and promoted the teachings of the scriptures. Marijane asked Garner to explain what his religion was all about. "I believe the easiest way to understand it is we believe in keeping the Old Testament and we believe in keeping the New Testament," he said. "It stands between Christianity and Judaism." Garner told the judge that Aloysius began corresponding with the assembly about three years earlier. "He became kind of a letter writer, which many of them do, and they ask questions galore about the Bible and so we started answering these questions."

"You've heard of what's commonly know as jailhouse conversions, correct?" Marijane asked the elder.

"Yes."

"And just so we're clear on the term, I'm meaning somebody who all of a sudden runs to a religion for the purpose of impressing a judge, correct?"

"Uh huh."

Did the elder believe that Aloysius was just putting on a show for the judge? Garner said he did not. Aloysius had completed a long course of study, and stayed on to complete the program. "That's not a jailhouse conversion," Garner said. "A jailhouse conversion is somebody that picks it up, holds it in his hands for a short period of time, turns his back and walks away from it but still wants to confess with his lips but does nothing to show himself improved by studying."

Marijane asked Garner whether there was anything more he could tell the judge before he decided Aloysius's sentence. "I would say there has been a change in his life. There's no two ways about it," Garner said. "I would only ask that because of the change that he's made that mercy be shown to him. I think that's no more than the Eternal would ask us to do anyway."

The elder stepped down, having made his case for Aloysius's redemption and plea for his life. When McKay finally got his chance, he got up and looked at the elder with dismissive contempt. "Who is Eric Lee?"

"By name I don't recognize," Garner said.

"Does your religion approve of murder?" McKay snapped back.

"Absolutely not."

"Does your religion approve of dealing drugs, illegal drugs?"

"No."

"Were you aware this man sold crack cocaine in 1992?"

"No, I was not aware of it."

"Does your religion approve of robbery?"

"No."

"Were you aware that this man robbed an eighteen-year-old of his bike back in 1993?"

"No, I was not aware of it."

"Does your religion approve of domestic violence?"

"No."

"Were you aware that the defendant, sitting over here, battered his sister back in 1994?"

"No, I was not aware of it."

McKay went on with this flourish. Did the elder's religion approve of stealing cars or lying to police? Did he know that Aloysius beat a pregnant woman or assaulted his mother? "Does your religion approve of having sexual intercourse with thirteen-year-old girls?"

"No, it does not."

McKay made his point. But the elder came back to say that such a history of lawbreaking made Aloysius a prime candidate for redemption. "He would be what we call a sinner and he needs to make a change in his life."

"You would call him a sinner?" McKay asked in mock surprise.

"No doubt in my mind. Wouldn't you?"

McKay blasted back one more time. "Now don't you find it odd, Mr. Garner, that the defendant didn't reach out to you and your assembly until after he murdered a police officer?"

"No, I don't find that odd. The individual doesn't look for salvation until he needs it."

When McKay finished, Marijane returned once more. She asked Garner to elaborate on Aloysius's candidacy for redemption and his commitment to studying the Bible. "Every one of us has fallen underneath the Mosaic teachings," Garner said. "And when you have broken that law, then you become a sinner. And every one of us has done so, and every one of us needs that Redeemer. And that's what Mr. Oliver has sought out—that Redeemer."

"That's all, your honor," Marijane said.

When the elder stepped down, the defense rested. Judge Moran asked Aloysius, as was his right, whether he wanted to make a statement before being sentenced. Aloysius, barely audible, said he did not. Moran reminded him that this was his only chance, and Aloysius again said no. The judge asked if he understood what he was waiving, and made sure he was not coerced or threatened into keeping silent. Ruth had urged Aloysius to say something, but he could not bring it upon himself to apologize, especially now that he was contending that he might not have fired the shot that killed Eric Lee. Moran asked the lawyers to make their summations.

Magats took the first part of the closing. "What the defendant did in this case struck more than just a single victim. It struck at the fiber of our society. Gunning down, shooting twice in the head, a policeman in the performance of his duties is the baddest crime you can get." Aloysius, Magats told the judge, could not blame his upbringing, his poverty or his community for his actions. "He wasn't thinking, Gee, I had a bad background." Aloysius earned his place on death row, Magats said, and the guilt was his alone. "Mercy against the merciless perverts justice."

Ruth had the final word for the defense. Her voice was soft but earnest. She read much of her closing statement from a yellow legal pad and stood back at a lectern as she addressed the judge. "Aloysius Oliver has a family that loves him. Aloysius Oliver has a conscience that troubles him. Aloysius Oliver has a faith in God that is engaging him in the struggle for atonement," she said. "In the blink of an eye, Mr. Oliver made a choice that he can never take back. And he will pay his punishment for that crime for the rest of his life." She took a breath, and continued on, explaining that Aloysius did not act with premeditation, that he truly felt remorse for what occurred.

"He is looking for understanding. He is praying for guidance," Ruth said. "He is looking for how to atone. This is a man who has truly repented. This is a man whose life and current character and struggle and the circumstances of the crime show in mitigation. We urge you to weigh those in the balance, your honor. And we urge you to sentence Mr. Oliver to natural life."

Lillian Oliver, still wearing her dark glasses, was shaking her feet and moving her legs up and down. These last words from Ruth might be all that stood between her son and death.

O'Connor was allowed the final word, and moved the lectern closer to the judge. His voice burst out at high volume, his tone again projecting outrage. "The murder of a police officer is so extraordinary that it justifies an extraordinary punishment," he said. "Those who pierce our safety, attack the innocent with voracity, and kill those who protect us must be legally removed from our society forever. He deserves death because Eric Lee deserved life." O'Connor hit all his marks, listing Aloysius's arrests, listing the aggravation against the mitigation, every drop of blood of his victims, every tear shed because of Aloysius. "We ask that you don't give him what he wants. Give him what he deserves," he said. "Aloysius Maurice Oliver should receive the death penalty." O'Connor reminded the judge one last time, Aloysius's own words. " 'Fuck the police.' That's what he thinks of law enforcement," O'Connor said. "We ask that you serve justice. Serve justice." O'Connor sat down and nodded to the judge that he was finished.

Judge Moran called a twenty-minute recess to ponder his decision. The cops spilled out into the hallway, joined by Lee's family and friends, along with press people and other court watchers. Marijane and Ruth went to the holding area in back to speak with Aloysius during the excruciating final waiting period. They urged him to reconsider his refusal to say something to the judge before being sentenced. A gesture of contrition might help save his life. Aloysius was reluctant to apologize because he still did not want to admit that he intentionally shot Officer Lee. Ruth suggested he read the victim impact statements the Lee family wrote to the judge, the heartbreaking letters from Shawn, Erica and Lee's parents. Aloysius read them, seeing for the first time in detail how Lee's death shattered the officer's family, the emptiness they felt in his absence, the pain of a little girl who would grow up without a dad. Aloysius told his lawyers that he would agree, although reluctantly, to say something to the family when Moran called them back into the courtroom. In the hallway outside, the conversations were muted compared to the usual animated chatter. It was as if everyone felt the gravity of what was about to happen and were reflecting on its meaning, searching their own consciences, wondering how they might handle such an unenviable responsibility as that given to the judge. One man had the power of life or death over another, just as Aloysius had three years ago as he stood and pointed a gun toward Officer Lee. His mother and sisters returned to their seats on the bench saying not a word, helpless in their emotional limbo, not knowing whether they would feel grief or relief in the next moment. Julie said she was more nervous than Aloysius. "Aloysius has a complete and total sense of peace no matter what happens," she told me. "He's coping a lot better than some people."

The judge returned after about a half hour, and he again asked Aloysius whether he wished to say anything. Aloysius told Moran that he had read the victim impact statements and changed his mind. He now wished to say something. Aloysius stood up and looked straight ahead. He appeared gaunt and withdrawn under his oversized suit. His voice was soft and resigned, almost listless. "After reading those statements, I would like to express my condolences to the Lee family," Aloysius said. He turned toward the family, but did not lock eyes with anyone. "I'm sorry that things had to happen the way they did. I'm sorry that . . ." Aloysius seemed lost, unable to figure out where to go next with his apology. "Ain't too much I could say. I mean, things . . . I apologize that things happened to happen . . . happen the way they did." Aloysius cast his eyes down. He could not look any one of the Lee family members straight in the eyes. He struggled to get out his words and looked frustrated at having to say anything at all. "I'm sorry that his wife and his daughter had to lose their husband and father. I'm sorry that his father and brothers had to lose their son and sibling," Aloysius said. And then he stopped. "That's all I've got to say." He sat back down. I heard the sound of sneers from the back of the courtroom.

"Let me just first correct you," Judge Moran snapped back, his voice rising. The judge looked down from his bench at Aloysius and sounded angry. "These things didn't have to happen. It was a choice here. And you made those choices, and you'll have to suffer for the consequences of those choices. The court has reread the victim impact statements, as well, the singular most difficult task this job entails. The court has considered all the evidence and notes, first off, two things about this hearing. First of all, this is not a weighing of two lives. There's no comparison in the life of Eric Lee and the life of the defendant.

"In short, Eric Lee died as a hero," the judge continued. "He was coming to the aid of the police brethren. He did what he was supposed to do as a police officer and as a human being. He did it in the way he was supposed to do it. The second fact and sad truth is whatever is done here today will not bring him back. If it could, the decision would be an easy one. Elder Garner today quoted scripture: 'If we break these laws, we will be punished severely.' For his crime, the defendant will be punished severely."

The judge paused, and the room waited for his next words.

"At this time, the defendant is sentenced to natural life in prison without parole. That will be the order."

Marijane stood up before anyone could react. "We thank the court for its courtesy and patience," she said.

Aloysius's mother, Lillian, then let out a tearful burst. She bent over and buried her hands in her face to cry. Aloysius's sisters Angela and Ashiyenetta cried, and then they all hurried out of the courtroom. Lee's parents hugged and cried. Some of the cops looked angry. Angela, tears in her eyes, said she was relieved. "I want to thank the judge for saving my brother's life," she told me when I stopped her in the hallway. And then she ran off, took the elevator downstairs and left the courthouse.

Outside the courtroom, Shawn Lee stopped to talk to reporters. Her face showed no joy, just disappointment. She believed that Aloysius deserved to die and was incensed at what she saw as his insincere contrition, ridiculing his newfound spirituality and search for redemption. "If he were a Christian man or a man of God, he wouldn't have any problem apologizing," she said. "I think it's all spiel. I think he was advised to do it. It wasn't sincere." Shawn looked tired and ready to go home. "I'm glad that it's over, but I'm not happy with the outcome. After three years of going through this, I've had enough," she said. "I'm happy he will never get out and he'll have to think about the pain and suffering he caused to all of us."

Outside the elevator, Ruth looked tired, too. "It's a sad day," she told me. "What I feel is relief."

"As far as he's concerned, he got the death penalty," Marijane piped in. "Is he happy? No. He didn't want to beg for his life. He's not happy."

The courthouse was mostly empty now. The judges, lawyers and employees of the building had left for the weekend by the time Aloysius's sentencing was handed down. It was a warm September night, and the defense team decided to celebrate the saving of a life by going to Bacchanalia restaurant for drinks and a big meal, and invited me along. When Marijane arrived, she walked into the back dining room proud, offering a jocund greeting to those who had arrived before her. A waitress delivered her usual drink without having to ask: a double bourbon in an iced tea glass. Marijane asked for extra olives, stuffed with bleu cheese, and the waitress brought a wine glass filled with them. Ruth ordered a merlot, her usual, and lit a smoke, inhaling and then exhaling with a long whoosh that sounded like satisfaction and relief. Everyone on the defense team was at the party, as well as Marijane's friends Michael Huskey and David Bow, Peg Solomon and Chris Petersen. Marijane stood up and raised her glass. "A toast for the bravest judge, Judge Moran, who's up for retention this November." Ruth followed by toasting the defense team and thanking everyone for their help.

Marijane ordered the New York strip, rare of course, and by the time it came she had a couple of drinks and was filled with the appetizers that kept coming to the table, farfalle pasta, foccacia, fried calamari. It was a true feast. Marijane was Falstaffian in her exuberance. Early in the Aloysius Oliver case she had insisted that she never got close to clients, but now that the trial was over, Marijane said she felt a little differently about Aloysius. "I actually didn't like him at first. I've had a million clients who have done bad things and he was just another. But he wasn't," she told me. "That's why he's so frustrating. I got to like him. It's not that he's just brighter, the thing that bothers me is that he's intellectually bright. It was harder with him because we tend to see one personality come through with all these defendants. This kid is strong-minded. He's smart. He's the type who you can say could have been something. The majority of my clients haven't finished sixth grade. He realized when he shot that officer what he gave up."

Ruth left the party early, wanting to go home to be with her son and husband and to fall back to earth. She also was planning a long bike ride the next morning that would take her more than one hundred miles, a perfect opportunity for decompression. Marijane, sitting in the corner with her bourbon and her glass full of extra olives made more toasts, happily clinking her glass with the glass of whoever was near. "That's what it's like when we get these little wins," she said. "We sit and we eat and we celebrate. When we win, we feast." And then Marijane broke into a recitation of a few lines from one of her favorite Shakespeare plays, *Henry V.* Her monologue was drawn from a rousing speech King Henry gave to his men on the eve of battle at Agincourt, an inspiring moment as the English were clearly outnumbered by the French. "We few, we happy few, we band of brothers," she said. "For he today that sheds his blood with me shall be my brother . . ." She spoke more of Henry's lines, and then her eyes filled with tears and she stopped. "This is what we do," Marijane said. "We kill and then we feast."

CHAPTER TWENTY

Life's Sentences

DIVISION 9 OF THE COOK COUNTY JAIL was on the far south end of the jail campus near California Avenue and Thirty-first Street, five blocks from the courthouse. Visitors were allowed to meet with inmates by special permission in a large room that was once the jail library. The rows of metal shelves in the room were all empty now. Inmates had to get books from their friends and families or borrow them from each other if they wanted to read. Lawyers frequently met with clients in the vacant room to discuss their cases, though the layout didn't offer much privacy because it was open without walls or dividers. There were no guards posted in the room during visits, but a guard desk was just a few feet from the open door. Five days after his sentencing, on September 22, 2004, Aloysius Oliver agreed to come to the library to talk with me about his case. He was going to be transferred from the county jail to state prison any day.

Aloysius walked into the room in his khaki Department of Corrections uniform, which hung loosely from his body. He shook my hand and sat down in a plastic chair. When he spoke, his voice was soft and he did not sound like a street thug. He enunciated his words clearly, self-assuredly and with an informed vocabulary that was sometimes punctuated with slang such as "know what I'm sayin'," which was a reminder that he came from the streets. He was polite and to the point. He told me that he was not a cop killer, and he was not convinced that he would be in prison for the rest of his days.

Aloysius looked around at the empty bookshelves, which he said were filled when he arrived at the jail more than three years ago. Julie Norman brought him books, and he devoured all genres during his long days in here, novels by John Grisham, Anne Rice, Stephen King, Dean Koontz. "I also like historical nonfiction,

African American history and comparative religion," he told me. "Religion is a beautiful thing. I've studied Islam, Christianity, Buddhism. They all lead back to the same thing." Aloysius explained that he had been on a spiritual quest for a long time, and that quest began in earnest with his incarceration. "Three years ago, I was in turmoil when I got here," Aloysius continued. "When I got here, I left the gang thing. I saw how the gangbangers could turn on their own people, and I knew the so-called brotherhood was not the bond I thought. I always wanted to be part of something. I wanted to be on the winning team." And that was what he found in the Yahweh Assembly, his new team, his new brotherhood. "If I never got here, I would never have found the Assembly," he said. "It's a beautiful thing. Yahweh grabbed me. Everything added up. I used to blame Yahweh for giving me bad choices. But the choices were mine."

Making those bad choices came at critical times during Aloysius's childhood, during his evolution from schoolboy to juvenile delinquent to adult felon. He did not have happy memories of growing up, and barely remembered his birthplace of Indianola, Mississippi, except for the time he went down to visit while in the seventh grade. He remembered the pigs and fruit trees and open spaces where he could run and play. "It was a little old town in the middle of nowhere," he recalled. "It was more fun out there than in the city." Back home was different, living in housing projects and apartments, learning how to stay safe during gunplay outside and knowing how to survive in a world of predators. "I never did the 'kiddie' stuff," he said. "I was a hustler from a young age." His early hustling was the legal kind, helping people with their groceries for tips and carting luggage at the airport. "I caught my first case when I was thirteen." He and five friends were arrested for a series of breaks-ins and charged with burglary, criminal damage to property and trespassing. Aloysius was assigned a public defender. "She was beautiful," he said. "She actually cared, and she beat all the charges." But his experience in the juvenile detention center left him angry. He claimed to have been beaten by the adult staff, treated like an animal rather than a teenage boy. As he grew older, Aloysius spent more time with kids in the neighborhood who didn't waste their efforts earning petty cash by helping people with their groceries. They made their money other ways. "I was introduced to a faster way," he said. "It was quicker money with drugs."

He made the choice to earn easy money by selling drugs. Yet Aloysius was always aware that he was smart enough and had the ability to extract himself from a life of crime if he really set his mind to it. That's why he tried college. It wasn't the intellectual challenges that made him drop out. Studying came easy to him. He was struggling with the lure of thug life against the long road through college and getting a real job. He chose the riskier path. "It was the street life I wanted," he admitted. "I wanted to hustle on the side. I wanted material things. I wanted to look good and impress the ladies. It was a bad decision. I would have done well in school." His religious studies seemed to have made some impact because several times during the conversation, Aloysius repeated certain platitudes about making choices, taking responsibility for his actions and accepting consequences. "I believe as a youth, everything you see affects your character, but I also believe that every individual is accountable for his actions. In life you make choices and you have to deal with that. Some of the choices we are forced to make are unfair," he said. He was not forced to give up college. He did that on his own. "That was one of those bad decisions and I have to live with that."

After Aloysius served his prison time in Milwaukee for possession of cocaine and carrying a firearm, he came home and announced to his family that he wasn't going to live the thug life anymore. He got his job at the furniture factory, but was laid off and went back to hanging out on the street. He didn't even consider reapplying to college. Aloysius and his cousin, Tommie Leach, would halfheartedly fill out job applications when they were in the mood, then come home, play some hoops or video games, sit around and start drinking.

I asked Aloysius to give me his account of the events leading up to the shooting of Officer Eric Lee. On the day of the shooting, Aloysius said that he and Leach had started drinking beers in the afternoon. Later, they wanted to watch a big wrestling match on cable television, but the signal wasn't working, so they drank some more.

Aloysius remembered sitting on the porch of his house, hearing the noise out back and "whooping the guy" in the alley with the help of Leach and Damon Rogers. "We basically beat him away from the gate." Suddenly Leach and Rogers started running when the undercover officers—Aloysius still insisted he did not know they were police officers—came down the alley. "I seen them running and then started shooting," he told me. "It was like seconds. I've racked my brain trying to get a clear picture of what happened."

Aloysius's memory of that night seemed to be better in some details and not others. One of his memories, which the jury never heard but his lawyers implied, was that police beat him up after his arrest. I asked him what happened. He claimed that officers hit him with fists and a flashlight after taking him into custody "until I agreed to say whatever they wanted me to say." I then asked Aloysius whether he had any proof to support his claim, and he had none other than his own account. Marijane and Ruth tried unsuccessfully to argue that his confession was coerced, and Aloysius, looking back, said he thought they could have done a better job making their case. Like so many who got free legal aid from public defenders, Aloysius was critical of his lawyers after the trial. "I still feel my representation could have been a little better," he said. He felt that Marijane wrested charge of the case from Ruth and was close-minded to his thoughts and ideas. "I didn't always agree with her. But I knew she's had a lot of clients and that she knew her stuff. I know she knew the law a lot better than I did," Aloysius said. "We butted heads a lot. There was room for improvement. It was Marijane's show from the beginning."

During his trial, Aloysius said he felt like he was on display, an object of derision and hatred to the police officers who filled the courtroom. The prosecutors dehumanized and mocked him. "It was a big show. It seemed like a comedy to them," he said. "I still don't feel I got a fair trial." He blamed Judge Moran for blocking the defense efforts at every turn. "A lot of their motions had really good merit and should have been granted. He just ignored them. It was like his decision was already made. I think he had his mind made up a long time ago." Aloysius also believed that the judge reacted arrogantly when he at first declined to apologize or say anything about the killing of Officer Lee. Aloysius didn't want to apologize because in his mind, he did not commit intentional murder. When his lawyers urged him to reconsider, Aloysius relented. He figured that it couldn't hurt. But his words were noncommittal. "I said what I said for Ruth's benefit and for the other lawyers. It felt hypocritical for me to get up there and apologize," he said. "I still don't believe I'm the culprit. I don't know what happened. That's why I apologized."

Aloysius told me that he was not frightened at the prospect of going to prison. He'd been there before and knew how it worked. "The penitentiary is better than this place," he said. In the joint, the food was better and it was safer than the county jail because the guards had better control of the gangs. "It will be a lot easier. Here, you've got to worry about gangs who control the TV. They control everything." Aloysius didn't expect to stay there for very long anyway because he believed that his conviction would be reversed. He knew his lawyers were still looking into things, that he would appeal this all the way. He had to believe that because hope was all he could grab on to. The alternative was too frightening.

He got reflective for a moment before heading back to his cell. "We all have faults," he told me. "I'm a lot of things, but I'm definitely not a murderer."

It was a dreary November day that made a bleak neighborhood look even more dismal. The sky was gray and a light rain fell, with a foggy mist shrouding the downtown Chicago skyline as I drove down to the South Side to visit the Englewood police station. The station was about four blocks from the alley where Eric Lee was killed. Every day as he drove to work, Lee's former partner, Officer Andre Green, passed by the spot where Lee was shot. "It's a constant reminder of what happened," he told me.

The Seventh District station was on Racine Avenue and Sixty-first Street, a two story, yellow brick building whose façade was as battered and weathered as the ill-maintained and crumbling buildings in the neighborhood. Within a half block of the station were two liquor stories and two bars, crumbling homes and vacant lots.

Inside the police station on the first floor was a long countertop that served as the front desk. Two chalkboards on the wall listed the shifts and assignments for the day. The lobby was busy with ringing phones, desk sergeants taking reports and a parade of people. The Englewood Rangers worked out of the second floor of the station in an open room filled with metal desks, phones and a few computer terminals. This was where Green and Lee had worked together. Green began his shift in a somber mood on the morning I came to see him. "I used to look forward to coming to work," he told me. "Now, I don't anymore. The job is not the same." He spoke like a man who had the happiness drawn from his insides. Though it had been more than three years since Lee's death, Green continued to feel the void in his life.

On this day, Green was dressed very much in the way he was dressed on the night of the shooting in his plainclothes attire. He wore a knit Chicago Bears cap, a blue, white and yellow trim jersey and baggy carpenter jeans. He looked like he could be a Chicago Bear linebacker himself, but his face was friendly and his manner gentle. Like Lee, Green wanted to stay in Englewood despite its dangers. Remaining there was a way to honor his partner. Green said he went out on the streets each day knowing he could get shot any time, just as Lee did. "If you worry about that every time you go out, you won't be able to work. But deep down, you know the risks." How different it was, he said, being a cop now than when he first considered it as a career. Green remembered when he was a boy, how he and other children looked up to cops. "I remember the Officer Friendly coming into the schools and it inspired me," he said. "The way people feel about police now, it's a whole new way of thinking." Right outside the station, on the streets of Englewood, there were people who hated cops, who distrusted cops, who shot cops.

When Green sat on the witness stand to testify about the night his friend was killed, it took all his strength to relive those moments. "To try to recap the details was hard," he said. "It doesn't seem like it was all that fast, but it was. It was like reliving the whole thing." Being subjected to Marijane's unrelenting questioning was even harder.

"I've run into a lot of public defenders before, but she was the worst," he said. "She just kept asking question after question without letting me finish my answers and she tried to trip me up. She was so aggravating. I guess that's her job. I guess that's her style." Like a lot of cops, Green felt that public defenders were roadblocks to justice whose tactics were sometimes less than honorable. "I have a problem with them. To me, the things they do to try to get people off, the tricks and technicalities, I don't like it. I don't know how they can do it," he said. "You work hard, you put your life on the line and then have these attorneys look for loopholes and try to get them off. And sometimes they win, and you just shake your head." His tirade against defense lawyers did not sound malicious in tone, and he was not mean-spirited in his critique. He clearly understood they had a job to do just as he did. Part of being a cop was having to testify in court and having to deal with defense attorneys like Marijane.

Green's greatest disappointment was that Aloysius was allowed to live. "I thought he should have gotten the death penalty," he said. "Look, from my standpoint, he was trying to shoot us. There was no doubt in my mind about it. The first time I saw him in court, in my head I was thinking that I just want to grab him, but I knew better."

With the holidays approaching, the sadness around the police station was more intense. Green and his fellow officers knew how difficult it would be for Lee's family. They started collecting cash to buy Erica Lee a Christmas gift. The call for donations got such an overwhelming response that there was enough money to start a college fund for her. "Eric was very close to his daughter," Green said. "He did everything with her." His voice cracked and his eyes watered when he remembered his partner. "Eric was probably the most well liked person at the station, and I'm not just saying that because he was my partner. I was proud to be his partner," Green said. "I have nightmares about it. It's going to stay with me for the rest of my life."

During the first year following the death of her husband, Shawn Lee had been overwhelmed by well-wishers. When she went shopping, people would surround her in the supermarket, effusive in their condolences, offering their help, pledging anything she needed. On the street, people walked up to Shawn and Erica and started crying when they spoke to her. She took a year off work to absorb her loss and come to terms living without Eric. She went through the motions of life absent its usual joys. She hurt so much because she loved so much. Her dream of a happy little family was gone.

By the time Aloysius was convicted and sentenced, Shawn had returned to work, taking a job in the credit card services department of the Chicago Patrolmen's Credit Union. Now that the trial was over, the police officers and friends who offered their help didn't come by as much as they used to. If Shawn needed someone to fix something around the house or help run an errand, she leaned on her family instead. She spoke about Eric every day with her daughter. "I try to be open and honest with her because she deserves that much," Shawn told me when I met with her for an interview at an Italian restaurant a few months after Aloysius's sentencing. "Will she be longing for her daddy ten years from now, wondering what life would be like with him as she gets older? I don't know."

Shawn was kind and open with me when I spoke with her. Her face was warm and friendly, but I could still detect the grief behind her eyes, a grief that no doubt would always remain, through perhaps diminish in intensity over time. Every day, sometimes two or three times a day, Shawn visited an Internet website called the Officer Down Memorial Page, which contained a message board dedicated to her husband. There were notes of sympathy from cops everywhere, from Anchorage, Alaska, Boston and Baltimore, Tampa and Toledo, even one from a Royal Canadian Mounted Police officer. She would post her own messages to Eric, telling him about the events in her life, the accomplishments of their daughter. She sent her love and wishes on their anniversary, and shared the pain she still felt. "In the beginning I found a certain peace sitting there just typing to him, reading all the beautiful things friends and strangers have shared, but now I think it's just a part of my being," Shawn told me. "I feel connected to him and I feel like I don't have to say anything and he knows and understands my day. I do feel that sometimes he hears me through my words and it's also a place where I vent, cry and try to digest what has happened. There are days that my life feels so unreal and that I will one day wake up from this nightmare."

Her hatred for Aloysius only grew stronger, especially after listening to his lawyers during the sentencing hearing. "I don't feel sorry for him. I don't feel any compassion for him," she said. "His religious conversion was a joke. To me, they were making a mockery of God. I'm struggling to forgive and continue to have some relationship with God. But my faith has been so shattered." If Aloysius really had given himself to God, she reasoned, he would not have given such a halfhearted apology. "He was so nonchalant about it," she said. "It would have been a relief to know he had some sense of remorse. He came out there and said nothing. It was an insult. It was horrible."

That Aloysius's defense lawyers made issue of his growing up in poverty and surrounded by crime and gangs infuriated Shawn. Both she and Eric grew up amid poverty on Chicago's South Side and in the Englewood community, yet they rose above the despair and hopelessness around them. "Englewood was one of the worst neighborhoods in Chicago, but yet I lived around poor people who cared about their community, about one another and tried to provide the best they could for their families," she said. "There were gangs, drugs, prostitution, school dropouts and numerous other bad things that were right there on every corner, but you had to want more. Aloysius's excuses that his childhood is the cause of his violent behavior and his extensive criminal history are ridiculous. Eric didn't become a gangbanger because that's what he knew. I didn't become a drug addict or a prostitute because that's what was around me. We both strived to want more, our parents strived to move us to a safer neighborhood and ultimately it fell in both of our laps to decide which path we wanted to take. He [Aloysius] made a choice in life. He was lucky enough to have a scholarship and he wasted it. He was not a dumb, illiterate person. It's not your economic status that determines who you will become, it's not how much you have that decides if you will kill, steal or break the law; it's

having morals, values and knowing that we can't always be followers. We must be leaders."

Looking back on the trial, Shawn wondered why Marijane and
Ruth never outwardly showed compassion for her husband. She was
offended that they seemed to cast aside the idea that the trial was
about a victim, a man, not just a cop who got shot. That the lawyers
had to divorce themselves from the victim to do their job was not a
good enough explanation for Shawn. She had hoped, at least, for
some acknowledgment. "He was still a human being," she said. "He
was my husband, he was my friend. What difference does it make to
them to acknowledge that?" The widow Lee knew that she would
never find a man to replace Eric, though someday she might fall in
love with someone else and form the family she always wanted. "For
Erica, I would love for her to have a father figure in her life," she
said. But Shawn had not begun dating. She was too busy. But more
than that, it was about trust, about finding someone special.

Bobby and Anna Lee were both retired and lived in a small brick
house on a quiet street on the far South Side where Eric spent his
teen years. When I went to visit with them, their living room was
decorated with photos and mementos of Eric—a picture of graduation day from the police academy, a studio portrait of Eric, Shawn
and a tiny Erica, plaques from the police department, a ceramic mug
from a police survivors organization. The hurt was still strong, undiminished by time. Just talking about Eric easily triggered tears.
Anna Lee told me she was at peace with the life sentence that Aloysius received. "But I wish they still had dungeons where they torture
people like that," she said. "I guess if he sits in jail for the rest of his
life, that's fine. Sometimes death is too easy." Bobby Lee snickered at
Aloysius's forced apology. "He didn't seem to care at all. It seemed it
was forced upon him," he said. "There is no penalty severe enough
for what he did."

Bobby Lee was angry that someone like Aloysius, a man with a
criminal record, was even out of prison. He should have spent more
time behind bars. He shouldn't have had a gun. The parents lived
heartbroken, in some ways still in disbelief and with anger and dis-

appointment about what could have been. "My son always wanted to help people," Bobby Lee said. "That night, he had no idea he was going up against someone with that kind of record. He had no idea. Eric will always be my hero."

To the north of the Lee home, the house on Carpenter Street where Aloysius and his family lived was long abandoned and boarded up. After the trial, someone placed a padlock on the front door on which two weathered antiviolence posters were taped. The first showed a young black boy with the quote, "Don't Shoot. I want to grow up." The second had three words—"Stop. Killing. People."—and included photos of children killed by handguns. Lillian Oliver was now living in an apartment on the near West Side of Chicago with Angela and Ashiyenetta. She remained at her job as an assistant at the dental school and was still trying to understand how her son could have been convicted of murder when she knew he didn't do it. Lillian believed him when he said he did not know he had fired a gun at a cop. "I told my son, you got in the wrong situation at the wrong time," she told me when I stopped by one evening to talk about the trial. "In the state of Illinois, you cannot get a fair trial. The jury was half asleep. You've got people sleeping, rolling their eyes. I was not surprised at the verdict." She also believed that there was more to come about the two officers who were there that night but did not testify, the same officers who Marijane and Ruth wanted to investigate more fully. "If I was Officer Lee's momma, I would want to know the real truth. Being a mother, I felt for her," she said. Because her son got life instead of death, Lillian believed there was still plenty of time for the truth to come out.

CHAPTER TWENTY-ONE

The Twist

UNITED STATES ATTORNEY PATRICK FITZGERALD had a reputation as America's toughest prosecutor. A thirteen-year veteran of the U.S. Attorney's office, Fitzgerald spent most of his career in New York investigating mobsters and terrorists, including those tied to the first bombing of the World Trade Center, as well as conspirators in U.S. embassy bombings in Africa. In the fall of 2001, just a month after Aloysius Oliver was arrested on charges of killing Officer Eric Lee, President George W. Bush appointed Fitzgerald to take over as the U.S. Attorney for the Northern District of Illinois, which was headquartered in Chicago. The politically independent Fitzgerald came to the city fearing no one, especially not the city's powerful politicians to whom he had no ties or personal connections. Under Fitzgerald's supervision, his office conducted investigations of public corruption that resulted in indictments of aides to Mayor Richard M. Daley and the former governor of Illinois, George Ryan, the same governor lauded for his decision to clear death row and launch reforms of capital punishment. Fitzgerald's office also brought fraud charges against the former publisher of the *Chicago Sun-Times*, David Radler, as well as Conrad Black, the former chief executive of the paper's parent company, Hollinger International Inc. Fitzgerald would later be called upon as an independent prosecutor in Washington to investigate the leak of a CIA operative's name, a case that led to the jailing of *New York Times* reporter Judith Miller and the indictment of the Vice President Richard Cheney's chief of staff, I. Lewis "Scooter" Libby. Fitzgerald, it seemed, never rested. That his name would become entwined with the Oliver case was something no one could have ever expected.

On January 27, 2005, Fitzgerald called a press conference to announce the results of an investigation that would create the link to Aloysius. His office had uncovered evidence of corruption within the ranks of the Chicago Police Department. Officers Broderick Jones and Corey Flagg, who had asked Eric Lee to help them on a drug raid on the night he was shot to death, were indicted on charges of being part of a ring of crooked cops. Flagg and Jones were accused of stealing guns and narcotics from drug dealers while on the job. Four officers in all were arrested in the sting, and all of them at some point had been assigned to the Englewood district where Eric had worked. Federal investigators alleged that the officers teamed up with complicit drug dealers to stage traffic stops as well as break into the homes of their rival drug dealers to rob them.

Judge Moran repeatedly had prevented Marijane Placek and Ruth McBeth from exploring the backgrounds of Flagg and Jones and using their prior disciplinary records in the trial, saying it was irrelevant. The lawyers were always suspicious why prosecutors never called those officers as witnesses, even though they were there that night. Now Marijane was booming with excitement. She called me after hearing the news. "This is a real interesting twist," Marijane said. "Isn't it great? Oliver might get out! Okay, okay, sorry. One step at a time. See, this is what we've been saying all along. We've been trying to bring out the allegations about these guys for a long time. There were rumors about these cops and rumors that Lee found out what they were doing. I think Lee knew something. What if he was the one honest cop who needed to be silenced and he was lured there? Oliver was the perfect fall guy. What if, you know, they decided to frame Oliver? I don't know if it happened that way. But the jury should have been able to hear that theory."

Marijane and Ruth decided they immediately had to file a motion to vacate Aloysius's conviction based on this development. They would ask Judge Moran to reopen the case and allow the defense to investigate the newly uncovered information. They also wanted the court to appoint a special prosecutor to look into the matter. But everything did not fit neatly. The alleged incidents for which Flagg and Jones were indicted occurred three years after Eric was shot. Still, Marijane believed the recent arrests represented a fraction of the corruption, that the officers were involved in a pattern of misconduct long before their arrests. She had evidence that six months before Eric Lee was killed, Jones broke into a house without a warrant and took marijuana from the house without reporting it to his supervisors, earning a thirty-day suspension from the department.

According to the U.S. Attorney's Office, the allegedly corrupt officers were discovered by accident when they tried to rob four drug dealers who happened to be under surveillance by another group of undercover officers. Jones had drawn attention to himself when the undercover offers saw him driving a Cadillac Escalade with a Fraternal Order of Police sticker before attempting to rob the dealers. Fitzgerald singled out Jones as the main organizer of the group who recruited fellow officers. Jones should not have even been working the streets during these robberies. He had been stripped of his police powers a year earlier on charges that he helped a shooting suspect escape arrest. He was supposed to be on desk duty answering nonemergency phone calls, but prosecutors charged he was out leading the group of rogue cops. According to the federal complaint, the group of officers tried four times to rob dealers, but succeeded only once when they staged the phony arrest of a drug dealer behind a car wash and kept the man's money and marijuana. On another occasion, their plans failed. Jones got a tip from a drug dealer about a house where the dealer believed there was at least $20,000 and five kilos of cocaine. Jones gave Flagg the wrong address, and when Flagg broke into the house, there was nothing, according to the complaint. "There are other people involved and other officers involved," Fitzgerald said at his news conference. "We intend to get to the bottom of it."

News of the new federal indictments drew the attention of Chicago politicians, who seized the opportunity to call for further investigation. Alderman Isaac Carothers, the head of the city council's police and fire committee, insisted authorities reopen the Oliver case. "These two officers supposedly called Eric Lee for backup and now they're charged," he said. "They may well have been the ones who put Eric Lee in harm's way." A day later, Alderman Ed Smith joined in calling for further inquiry into Eric's death. Smith, who was the chairman of the city council's black caucus, said that if Chicago police won't reopen the case, then the federal government should. "If there's any chance of these people having anything to do with the death of Eric Lee, then we ought to know that," he said. "If it's found out that they are involved in any kind of way in his death, then they ought to be charged with murder." Smith went so far as to say that Aloysius might be sitting in prison for a murder he did not commit alone. Smith, as well as Carothers, did not believe Eric was a rogue cop, but rather an honest one who stumbled into the corruption and might have known too much.

The police superintendent, Phil Cline, dismissed it all as conjecture. He issued a statement saying he was confident that Aloysius was the sole shooter and only person responsible for Eric's death. Plus, Cline pointed out, the state's attorney said the indictments of Jones and Flagg were related to activities long after Eric was killed. Case closed. But the federal corruption investigation widened as FBI agents searched the lockers of officers in other districts during the next few weeks. The developments also brought out calls from activists in Englewood to examine the district more closely and look into all the arrests those officers made in that community, a place with a long history of distrust with the police, just as Lillian Oliver had said. She always complained about dirty cops in that neighborhood, and now her allegations may be proven correct to some degree. Ruth felt vindicated after learning of the indictments. "I suspect this has been going on long before 2004. I understand what Lillian Oliver was saying about bad cops," she said. "Not only are they not out there protecting people, they are out there committing crimes themselves. Isn't this cool? I'm very excited about this. I tried to call Oliver, but I couldn't get him. I want to see good things for him."

On February 3, 2005, Ruth and Marijane returned to Judge Moran's courtroom to file their motion for a new trial and asked for an independent prosecutor to handle an investigation. Marijane again raised the possibility that someone other than Aloysius wanted Officer Lee dead. "We're saying that this is, in fact, an alternative theory." Assistant State's Attorney David O'Connor implored the judge to dismiss their request. The case was solid, he said. Aloysius did it. Shawn Lee cried during the brief hearing during which Moran said he would take it under consideration and hear arguments at another time. There was much to absorb and to consider.

Downstairs in the lobby, Marijane stood before reporters and cameras. "What we want to do is put together all the pieces of this puzzle to see what happened that night. I am not criticizing the victim," she said. "We believe Officer Lee was as much a victim as Mr. Oliver was a victim. We are looking for justice not only for Mr. Oliver, but for Officer Lee." As she said this, Shawn Lee hustled by the cameras and left the courthouse with Eric's parents.

Later that afternoon, down on the South Side just blocks from where Officer Lee was killed, community activists gathered at St. Stephen's Evangelical Lutheran Church for a news conference. It was a small, ornate church with a wood relief carving of the Last Supper on one wall and organ pipes rising fifteen feet behind the altar. The afternoon winter light streamed into the sanctuary though stained glass. Marijane, Ruth and Northrop arrived about ten minutes late, a minority of white faces in a room filled mostly with blacks. Julie Norman and her husband, John, joined the group behind a podium at the altar. The Reverend Anthony Williams stepped forward and spoke in a sermonlike oratory, his deep voice resonant and powerful. His message was intended to draw outside attention to his community, and he urged officials to provide greater scrutiny to the officers who worked in their district. "When we heard and discovered there were rogue cops we had major concerns. The Seventh district must be investigated. Was Eric Lee a Serpico?" he said, referring to the famous New York City cop who went undercover to expose corruption. "There is some mystery surrounding Officer Lee's life."

Marijane stepped up to the podium and looked out among the few who had gathered in the church. Her speech was really more for the media than anyone else, sound bites for the six o' clock news. "This is what the good reverend is fighting for," she said. "Even when we were investigating the Oliver case, we saw people who were terrified that the criminals were being protected by the police.

Over $100 million has been paid out to those who have been wrongly convicted. What we're seeking now is to stop the corrupt system. We believe Aloysius Oliver was wrongly convicted. We believe someone else shot Eric Lee." Reverend Williams squeezed in. He added that he did not want to cause greater animosity between the police and residents because of a few bad cops. "In communities like Englewood, a lot of young people know this goes on," he said. "But we don't want to demonize police. We're not antipolice. We've tried to put our community in a positive light, and when we hear things like rogue cops, it doesn't help."

"I've been in the criminal justice system a long time," Marijane added. "I don't live in this community, but it's not a surprise to me. I know about rogue cops. My clients constantly say it over and over again."

A neighborhood resident named Hal Baskin had been standing at the altar patiently waiting to speak. He was heated up. "The community is outraged," said Baskin, cofounder of an organization called the People Educated Against Crime in Englewood (PEACE). "You've got senior citizens afraid to call the police because they are afraid the police will tell the drug dealers." His voice was booming, filling the emptiness of the church. He was skeptical, too, of the police version of how Eric Lee was killed. "This could be a fabricated story," he said. "I think ninety percent of the people here are hardworking people. Five percent are great and five percent are rotten to the core."

The speech making ended after about half an hour and everyone filed out of the church into the frigid air. Could Officer Lee really have been a Serpico who was silenced, or was all this just rhetoric and hyperbole? There was no telling how far Marijane and Ruth would be able to go. In the meantime, the state's attorney's office began to see the fallout from the federal probe. By May 2005, prosecutors had to dismiss at least ten pending felony cases in which one of the indicted officers had made the arrest or was somehow involved. The state's attorney began reviewing more cases as defendants sought to have their convictions overturned. One man who was serving a ten-year sentence for dealing drugs was freed from prison because the prosecution's only witness was Officer Jones, whose credibility was now in question. In an interview after Marijane's press conference, David O'Connor said he was still convinced of Aloysius's guilt and that all this speculation was unfounded. "There was never any doubt he was guilty," he told me when I asked about these developments. "Certainly the defense has tried to weave some theories."

Judge Moran was in no hurry to rule on the defense request for a new trial. He let months pass, leaving Marijane and Ruth to assume that the long delay was a sign that he was pondering the legal issues with great care and deliberation. Moran twice scheduled hearings only to later postpone them. Marijane guessed that the judge wanted to see whether the federal investigation into police corruption was going deeper and what it might uncover. She and Ruth also heard a rumor that another officer from Eric's district was assigned to desk duty because he was under investigation, as well. "Now it looks like anything is possible. It could be explosive," Ruth told me one afternoon in her office. "For me this all explains a lot of the things that Mr. Oliver was talking about. I think a lot of traumatic things happened that night at the police station. I have no doubt he was roughed up. Can he go back and remember that sequence? Does he know more than we do? Was there something else going on out there? I still don't know if there was another shooter out there. I still have a question about it in my mind."

Spring and summer went by without a word from the judge. Marijane and Ruth had since moved their attention to other cases. Aloysius was marking his days in Stateville prison, about three hours by car south of Chicago. His mother visited when she could. "He's keeping his head up," she told me. "It's a matter of time, but the truth will come to light. I know the lawyers are doing what they can, but they're getting stonewalled. We're just going to take it one day at a time." Officer Lee's parents grew increasingly impatient, feeling that the delay was insulting and discourteous. "I am surprised it has taken this long," Bobby Lee said when I asked what he thought about the legal wrangling. "We wanted to start healing with this. We thought we could get some type of healing going. This goes on and on and on. What about consideration for our family?" Eric's parents were offended that Marijane proclaimed she wanted justice for both Aloysius and for Eric Lee in the same breath. They did not believe the theories, that there was a longstanding pattern of corruption, that Eric was killed because he was about to expose scandal in the police department. "When she said she was doing this as much for Eric as for Oliver, that was just arrogant," Anna Lee said angrily. "This just reopens the wounds. It seems like they keep reopening the wounds over and over again. It's been so frustrating. You wonder if anything happened to their families how they'd feel. I bet it would be a different story."

At the courthouse, Marijane and Ruth tried more murder cases. The clients kept coming, one after another, supplied from the streets of a city where people kept killing one another with guns, knives and their own hands. Twice they saved clients from first-degree murder convictions, persuading juries to instead convict them of second-degree murder. They won an acquittal for a gang member charged with gunning down a rival. Marijane saved another client from the death penalty after he was convicted of killing two men and wounding another, arguing that his death would bring no good to society, and do nothing more than satisfy a bloodthirsty call for justice.

On November 22, 2005, two days before Thanksgiving and nearly ten months after the defense team filed its motions, Judge Moran finally was ready to make his ruling. The fall sky was bright and clear that morning, and the wind whipped in chilly gusts across the city, tearing the remaining brittle leaves from their trees and making the 30-degree temperature feel as if it were in the teens. The courthouse was not as busy as usual. Many of the lawyers and employees already had taken time off to begin the holiday week, and judges tended to avoid scheduling jury trials then. Marijane, Ruth and attorney Andrew Northrup arrived together in Moran's courtroom around 9:30 a.m., and took their seats at the defense table. Aloysius, who remained downstate in prison, would have to learn of the outcome by telephone. Neither Aloysius's mother nor his sisters came to court since he wasn't going to be there. As the lawyers waited for the judge to come in, Marijane worked on one of her newspaper crossword puzzles. Officer Lee's parents Anna and Bobby, along with his widow, Shawn, and her mother filed in and sat down in their usual places on the judge's right side. Prosecutors James McKay, David O'Connor, and Joe Magats sat at the front table, facing the judge. There was no media here today. The usual courthouse reporters were elsewhere in the building working on other stories. Most of the benches were empty, save for a few other lawyers and defendants who had pending business with the judge that morning. For most, it was just another day in court.

A bailiff instructed everyone in the room to rise, and Moran came in. The judge called the attorneys up to the bench and without preamble and without explanation, quickly read the defense motion aloud. And then he said simply, "Motion denied." That was it. Moran offered no reasoning, no speech, no written opinion to elaborate. The evidence simply did not merit a new trial. The entire event took less than two minutes, and seemed so understated, the brevity so out of proportion to everything that preceded it—the press conferences and news stories, the federal investigation and the speculation, the incendiary remarks from Marijane and the angry speeches from the politicians.

"Thank you, judge," Marijane said, nodding to Moran. She, Ruth and Northrup walked back to the defense table to gather their things, saying nothing more. Out in the hallway, Eric's family thanked the prosecutors, relieved that they could face the holidays without the stress of another hearing, another court date, another reason to prolong their pain. Ruth had to meet a client in the jail, and went on her way. Downstairs near the elevators, Marijane ran into Matt Vandenbroek, the reporter for City News Service, and told him about the ruling. He took out his notebook and asked for a comment. Never one to capitulate easily, Marijane said that this was not the end, that she would file a motion asking the judge to reconsider, and then she would seek some type of legal redress or intervention in federal court. She could not have said anything else. She would not have said anything else, for her nature was to never say die. Marijane delayed conceding defeat yet another day by announcing her intention to pursue the case further, to take it as far as it could go. Clients like Aloysius survived by clinging to the hope that courts of appeal would overturn their convictions, that judges would find the legal process had been somehow perverted. And indigent clients like Aloysius were entitled to more free legal help in that pursuit. The taxpayers who funded his public defenders also paid for appellate defenders who could continue his cause until he won or could appeal no more.

Marijane's legal arguments and theories about the Oliver case may have been deflated on this day, but she told me that she felt far from defeated. "Look, we won," she said later. "He got life." And so it was. The client got life. That was indeed considered a victory by the Public Defender's Office. Marijane was in a jolly mood for the rest of the day. A month of holiday parties were coming up, including her combination Christmas and birthday bash at the racetrack, as well as gatherings with friends at her home on Thanksgiving and Christmas Eve. Then, right after New Year's, she had a new trial to look forward to. "It's going to be *wonderful*. I can't wait," she said. The defendant was Keon Lipscomb, and he earned the spot as Marijane's new all-time worst client, a distinction that hadn't seemed possible among the thousands of rogues she represented during the past two decades. Lipscomb was facing trial on charges of raping and beating to death his girlfriend's two-year-old daughter, Unique Thomas, and disposing of the body in a garbage can. Lipscomb confessed, explaining how he raped and beat the toddler while his girlfriend was in the hospital giving birth to a child that he fathered. While in jail awaiting trial, Lipscomb smacked a doctor with a stool, set mattresses on fire and hurled cups of urine at guards. He threatened and insulted Marijane when she visited him to discuss the case and fired her thinking he could do a better job being his own lawyer, an experiment that did not last long. "I can't *wait* to go to trial," Marijane said once more. "It's going to be the most wonderful thing."

CHAPTER TWENTY-TWO

Walking Away

MARIJANE PLACEK'S UNDIMINISHED ENTHUSIASM for the job was not always matched by her colleagues in the Murder Task Force. Years on the job took a toll, and eventually became too much for some lawyers to bear. The strain on their families, marriages and mental health became too high a price and forced them to leave the office altogether. It stopped being fun. I asked some of the original task force members to talk about what made them walk away from a job they once described as the most exhilarating experience of their lives.

William Murphy, founding father of the Murder Task Force, told me that after several years running the unit, he felt himself crawl deeper and deeper into a dark place that haunted him with fear, stress and despair. He suffered maddening headaches, had trouble sleeping and dulled his pain with drink. He kept a journal at the time, which he shared with me. "The stress around here is unbeliev-able," he wrote in 1979. "One lawyer informed me he can't go into court on another death penalty case, another has been grounded for the last two weeks with stress-related headaches that were described as a thousand times worse than migraines, and everyone else is slowly going nuts." Researchers doing a study of high-pressure ca-reers interviewed Murphy's team of lawyers. After completing the study, one researcher told Murphy that his staff was in trouble. "He told me we were under more stress than any other group," Murphy recalled. "That study stressed *me* out. People on the Murder Task Force were under more stress than air traffic controllers."

Murphy wasn't surprised. He felt nervous every time he walked into court. Before a trial, he often vomited because he was so frightened. While representing a man accused of abusing and killing his young son, Murphy got forty pieces of hate mail, one of which appeared to be written in blood. He had three ulcer attacks while representing another client, and nearly lost his mind after a seventeen-year-old, whom he truly believed was innocent, was found guilty of murdering four children. Murphy went home after that trial, threw a chair through a window, got drunk, jogged for five miles and collapsed from exhaustion. "It was like the worst day of my life." He got further depressed watching his lawyers lose death penalty cases. "I don't see how I can keep sending attorneys to continually beat their heads against the wall—it's like one suicide mission after another," he wrote in one journal entry. Murphy knew he had to do something to help keep his staff sane. He hired mental health counselors to come to the office for a special session on dealing with the stress. "I was moved to tears listening to their feelings," he said. "They spoke of the awesome responsibility they felt and the lack of respect they got for what they did."

Eventually, Murphy got tired of battling the stress, the office politics and low salary. He had a family now and needed more money to support them. In August 1980, six years after he created the Murder Task Force, Murphy decided to leave the public defender's office altogether. Before his last day Murphy went to court to watch one of his lawyers try to save a man's life at a sentencing hearing. When Murphy walked away he cried once more; not so much for the defendant, but for what he believed were the impassioned but ultimately fruitless efforts of his colleague.

Murphy was recalling those long ago days during an interview in his office on the seventeenth floor of a downtown Chicago office building. He was now in private practice. He still had a thick head of hair, though it was more white than black, and he continued to take on criminal cases from clients who had the money to pay him. "In private practice, you get easier cases," Murphy told me. "I needed that because I had to put two daughters through college." His first case as a private lawyer was for a client charged with drug possession. His fee was $500. "It was easy," said the lawyer who once saved a woman from being convicted of twenty-three counts of murder.

Two weeks after going into private practice, Murphy said he was bored.

Bob Queeney remembered the moment he decided to quit. He had come home after the jury voted to execute his client, George Del Vecchio. The case had consumed him for the past several months, separating him physically and psychologically from his family. During the trial, he came home late every night and left early for the courthouse each morning. The day he lost, Queeney arrived home trying to absorb the fact that his client was going to be executed. He parked his car and began walking up the stairs to the front door of his old Victorian house. His wife and two children, ages one and three, were sitting on a bench in the entranceway and greeted him at the door as he walked in. He was hoping for hugs. "My son said to me, 'Get out of here. You don't live here anymore!' And I started to cry. That's when I decided to write my résumé. I can't tell you how hard that was." Queeney's voice quavered and his eyes watered as he recounted the story.

His son's remark had unleashed the emotion that had accumulated from years of overwork and not enough time at home, the blinding preoccupation with his occupation. Queeney's wife once complained that he talked about murder as if he were describing a trip to the grocery store. "I had been doing it for eight years. I was getting my share of bad cases. I mean, I had a case in which my client made a shoeshine boy give him a blowjob and then blew his head off. They found the body with come in his mouth," Queeney said, underscoring the grotesqueness of it all.

So he left. "I found work at a somnolent civil law firm, and I was able to go home every night," he said as we sat in a conference room of his law firm talking about the old days. "I needed to go home every night."

Months before he would make his final argument pleading for the life of Hernando Williams, Todd Musburger had thought of walking away. "I was really struggling with whether I should leave the public defender's office," he recalled. "I felt that everything was crashing in on me." Musburger hovered near a nervous breakdown during the final weeks of the Williams sentencing hearing. His conscience was troubled enough by feeling responsible for his client's life, but the assault on his character outside the courtroom came as an unexpected blow. At a synagogue service, members cornered Musburger's wife to ask how her husband could represent the man who killed Linda Goldstone, a Jewish woman. People who came to watch the trial made disparaging remarks to Musburger when he walked into court. "There was never any greater pressure on me or my family," he said. He spent so much time away from home, he worried about the disconnection he had created with his son and decided to bring the eight-year-old boy to court to show him what his father was doing. During a break, Musburger told me that Goldstone's mother came up to him and asked, "What kind of a father are you?"

"The Hernando Williams case changed my life. It made me realize I couldn't continue in that environment. I don't know how others do it, because I had only one death penalty case. It was a brutal experience. It took some time to even come to grips with that. I had to be away from it."

Musburger went on to become one of Chicago's best-known entertainment lawyers, representing television, film and radio talent along with former Chicago Bulls Coach Phil Jackson. But he told me that what he experienced as a public defender, especially during the Williams trial, made much of his modern-day work seem unimportant by comparison. A bankruptcy lawyer once hired Musburger to handle a case because of his trial experience. "He said to me, 'I'm really glad to have you because you seem to be able to handle the pressure of this.' And I remember thinking, This is only money. The only thing that can happen to us is that our client will lose money. Until you sit next to someone who can lose his life, you don't know what pressure in a courtroom is all about."

Hernando Williams, after exhausting sixteen years of appeals, was executed by lethal injection in 1995. There was not a day that went by when Musburger didn't think about that trial and how it changed his life. "It was a haunting case. And it continues to haunt all of us."

* * *

Stuart Nudelman left the task force to become Judge Nudelman, and now had a beautiful corner office on the twentieth floor of the Daley Center with a stunning view of downtown Chicago. He presided over civil cases. "It's really boring," he told me when I went to visit him there after court one evening. On one wall of his office he kept a reminder of the more exciting days, courtroom sketches from the Williams trial. Like Musburger, Nudelman was taken to his limits during that trial. He dropped weight, couldn't sleep and dared not talk about what he was doing with family or friends. He worked on Thanksgiving and was afraid to join his family later for fear of ruining their good spirits by talking about the case. "We could not be with human company," Nudelman recalled. "I missed my wife's birthday that year. I'd never done that before. I would stay away from my children for fear of spanking them. There are a lot of things you can't take home. The only people I could share it with were my public defender family. I loved being a public defender, but death penalty cases were a terrible drain on everybody. It destroyed people. It wreaked havoc on you."

Like Musburger, Nudelman felt a personal responsibility for Williams's life, a responsibility that seemed an unfair burden and the kind of pressure he was not willing to take on for the rest of his legal career. "You build up a relationship with this person and you find yourself starting to realize that you could be sitting next to a dead man. As heinous as their crimes may be, it's still very difficult. As the stakes got higher and higher, it got very emotional for me, and I kind of ran out of steam." He left the public defender's office in 1985 after a thirteen-year career. "How they do it day in and day out, I don't know," he said. "They do something few are able to do."

Shelton Green supervised the Murder Task Force for eight years before calling it quits. He left in April 2003, nine months before the Oliver case got to trial. Shelton hadn't really planned on walking away, "but I got an offer I couldn't refuse," he told me. The county was offering long-term employees early retirement packages, and Shelton qualified with twenty-two years on the job. He struggled with the decision but ultimately took the deal with the intention of getting back in the game elsewhere. On his last day of work, Shelton did what he loved doing best. He went to court and argued to save one more client from the death penalty, asking the jury to show the kind of mercy that his client, who killed and eviscerated a teenage girl, did not. The judge was moved enough by Shelton's final argument to give Ralph Andrews life in prison for raping and killing Susan Clarke, sixteen.

Shelton didn't remain in retirement long. Within a year he took a job with the Winnebago County Public Defender's Office in Rockford, Illinois, a city of about 152,000 about ninety miles northwest of Chicago. Shelton had to start at the bottom, but he felt on top of the world because he got to spend the majority of his time in court once again. I drove up to Rockford to visit him on a brilliant fall day in late September 2004 to see how he was doing. We sat at an outdoor café in the downtown business district. Shelton was still smoking Winstons and drinking coffee. He was tanned, fit and looked relaxed. "They do things a little slower around here," he said. "They're very easygoing. The judges are nice, and the state's attorneys don't like a fight." Shelton told me he felt out of place at times. "I had a murder trial out here and during the trial the state attorney said we never had someone as direct as you around here," he said. "I do feel like I have an advantage sometimes." He doesn't get nearly as many murder cases as he once did, and the slow pace was frustrating. Shelton grabbed another Winston and told me he'd rather be doing nothing else. "For me, it still is fun."

The veteran lawyers who remained in the task force in Chicago were aware of the personal and psychological risks of being on the job for so long and struggled to balance their lives inside and outside the courthouse. "I can shut off the misery I see here on a daily basis by looking at this job as an athletic competition and shut out the hell and the havoc," Bob Strunck told me. "This is like the Notre Dame Fighting Irish versus the USC Trojans. It's a game." Sports was Strunck's refuge and his own perfect metaphor what he did for a living. The spirit of competition helped drive him in the courtroom and gave him pleasure outside it. He was a season ticket holder to the Chicago White Sox, and every fall was glued to the television during college football season. He went to the Indy 500 every year with a buddy. Yet these diversions never completely released his mind from the madness he encountered at Twenty-sixth and California, the appalling cases he continued to see every day. "It never fucking ends. I've got a naked guy who was running through Uptown, wearing nothing but a sock and stabs a guy to death. He just drank a half bottle of Kettle One and then stabbed this guy on the street," Strunck said. "Here's another one: This guy was having sex with his daughter and then he found out she was pregnant. He took her down to some building, chained her to a fence and beat her to death. I mean, this was fucking awful."

Awful, yes, but in many ways not shocking anymore. Strunck had been a public defender now for twenty-one years, fifteen of them on the task force. "I've had a lot of bad cases. When you first start this job and get your first murder cases, a lot of these cases will scare the hell out of you," he told me. "And then you've seen them all and get used to it. The drug dealers and gangbanger murders are a dime a dozen. But doing your natural daughter and then murdering her? That ain't pretty. When you're young these cases scare you and you later get used to it, but that one still scares me." He could not divorce himself from the suffering that he saw every day, the victims and the families who came to court and watched as he, a father, defended the man who killed his own daughter. "We would not be human beings if we didn't know what was going on in there and feel it," he said. "You see these families of victims. Their lives are destroyed and you see the defendants' families and their lives are destroyed."

Strunck hated his job and he loved it. "It's kind of like a car wreck. I don't want to be part of it, but it's invigorating. It's as rough as being a steelworker or an autoworker but their job is done at the end of the day. They don't take it home with them. In your head, this job is always there. It's there at the Rolling Stones concert. It's there at my daughter's gymnastics recital." He still had an uneasy time talking about his work with his wife, who sold medical benefits for an insurance company, and could not even begin to relate his day at the office to his daughter, Anastasia, eleven, young and sweet and far removed from his world. "It's frustrating when they don't understand what you're going through," he said. Sometimes his victories were too awful to even share with his family. How do you come home and explain that you just saved the life of a serial killer who smoked crack and murdered three women?

While Marijane and Ruth McBeth were defending Oliver, Strunck did just that. He represented Ronald Macon Jr., who police said terrorized women on the city's South Side. Macon owned up to his crimes and didn't bother with a trial. He decided his best shot at life would be to plead guilty and admit that he murdered the three women after drinking, smoking crack and having sex with them. Prosecutors wanted the death penalty and offered no deals even after Macon pled guilty. During Macon's sentencing hearing, Strunck argued to save Macon from execution and, just as he did in dozens of death cases before this, told the judge of his client's abused childhood. Strunck explained to the judge that Macon's father beat the boy and shot his wife during an argument as the terrified boy watched. Strunck pulled out something else: Macon, a drug addict, was HIV positive. He was already sentenced to death. There seemed little point in hastening his death in the so-called name of justice. "Having HIV does not excuse any of this conduct," Strunck told Judge James Schrier. "However, it does explain some of the rage." Schrier sentenced Macon to life, whatever life he had remaining. He didn't save the world that day, but to Struck it was an important victory, for his client and for himself. "I felt an immense sense of relief," Strunck said. "He's alive. To me, that matters. I saved his life, and now it's up to him to make something of it. What I've done is give him a chance. That makes me feel good." Strunck could go home, satisfied he did something worthwhile, and adding to his list of victories. "I know that I've literally saved a lot of lives. And I would hope that I've affected some clients' life in a positive way. Maybe I helped straighten out someone's life. I don't know."

"I'm on my third marriage," Woody Jordan said when I asked whether the job had taken a toll on him. "What does that tell you?"

That was part of the price for the life he chose. Woody had been on the task force for fifteen years, a public defender for more than twenty. The world that Woody lived in, a world populated with killers and gang members, junkies and thieves, was not easy to share. At times, he was so immersed, so sealed off from others that he didn't even know it. Woody realized one day just how far removed he had become. He was walking around downtown Chicago on a busy afternoon: men and women in business suits, shoppers carrying bags from department stores, tourists strolling along Michigan Avenue. Woody remembered feeling strangely out of place. "Then it struck me," he said. "I'm around normal human beings. They're dressed appropriately. They're polite. I thought, What am I doing here?"

Woody told me that he was planning to leave the job soon, most likely after he finished defending suspected serial killer Paul Runge. He was building a home in his native Tennessee where he planned to retire and live on a big compound with his family. "I only have one of these death cases left in me," Woody said. "I won't have anything left in me after that." He had pictures of the property and drawings of the home on his desk. He showed me the property and partially constructed homes. "It's only a block and a half from the Tennessee River," he said. "I'm gonna hunt, I'm gonna fish, I'm gonna drink."

Ruth McBeth felt the isolation just as Woody had. "We can't even explain to people what this is like. We've been to battle and we come home, and other people just can't understand," she told me. "You have nice middle-class people asking you about your job and they say, 'You must have some stories.' And you tell them something like, 'Oh, I had this client and she cut up her baby in pieces and fried it up like chicken,' and that usually stops people at parties and barbecues. I mean, there are people suffering. These are people at the lowest points in their lives. What are they expecting to hear? Nice stories? This is a sad story." Ruth's husband, Jeff, also was an attorney, though he practiced civil law with an insurance company in a much more civil world. She didn't talk much about her work with him at home. "He's a very sensitive soul and sometimes it's too much for him. He can't stomach that much," she said. "I think over time this job is coarsening. It's not just about being vulgar, but being cynical about things. By being coarse I mean riding roughshod over people to get what you want. I think in some ways, this job also has helped me see more of a reality and made me more compassionate."

Her son, Andrew, was eleven when the Oliver case concluded and was old enough to start asking more specific questions about what his mom did. During one murder case, he asked his mom about her client, wanting to know why he would want to kill someone. Ruth explained that the defendant was once a little boy like Andrew, and when he was young someone he trusted and thought loved him threw the boy out of a second-story window. He had the kind of childhood that Andrew never could have imagined, and would never have. Ruth tried to explain to her boy that what we saw and experienced as children shaped us into the adults we would become. "I told him that some of these people have been hurt for a long time. He asked me 'Why would someone do that?' Some things are hard to explain."

When Marijane returned from the courthouse at the end of the day, she was greeted by two gregarious, drooling, excitable dogs, Gus and Spartacus who, on lucky nights, would get big hunks of leftover steak from her lunch or dinner at Bacchanalia. She lived in a classic one-story brick bungalow in a suburb just west of the city. It had been re-habbed since the kitchen fire, though she still had many possessions in boxes. The books that survived the fire were back on the shelves. In the living room was a leather sofa and leather reading chair. Fabric was out of the question with the dogs, who were permitted to make themselves at home on the scratch-marked but durably covered furniture. This was their home, too. Marijane was an insomniac and stayed up past midnight every night. She always had the television on for company, even if she wasn't watching. Her favorite shows included *South Park* and *Deadwood*. She recently invested in a fifty-two-inch projection set, which took up nearly an entire wall.

"I was engaged several times," Marijane told me as she settled back into the sofa late one afternoon. The engagements never went further because her beaus never measured up. They did not share her passions for theater, for classic literature, for the law, and she knew she was a difficult and sometimes volatile person who probably would not have settled comfortably into family or domestic life. She thought she would have made a lousy mother because of her temper and controlling nature. Marijane had a wide circle of friends and companions who joined her at the theater, at the racetrack, the museums, the Humane Society events and annual pet parades. She didn't believe that her job ate away at anything. When she walked away, she walked away.

Marijane was among the longest-serving members of the Murder Task Force after sixteen years (twenty-four years in all with the public defender's office) and remained excited about coming to work each day. It was her life. Her motives for staying were not like the others'. She never gave stock answers about why she was a public defender, how everyone deserved a defense or how much she cared for the poor and the helpless. She found such explanations trite. Instead, she offered a story from her childhood. When Marijane was about eight years old, her father took her to the old Michael Todd Theatre in downtown Chicago to see the film *Judgment at Nuremberg*, which tells the story of how German Ministry of Justice officials were tried for their complicity in the Holocaust. The film contained documentary footage from the concentration camps, the skeletal figures wandering near death, the piles of bodies, the children and the survivors. Those were scary images for a little girl. Marijane was terrified, and cried.

"Why did you do this to me, Daddy?" she asked.

"Because you need to see this and never forget. We can't let people do this. We can't sit by and let things like this happen."

Thinking back on that day, Marijane said the film exposed her to the frightening notion that people with whom we place our trust—our government, our police, our highest authorities—were capable of lying and of committing unspeakable acts despite the laws created to safeguard society. Those entrusted to uphold the law do not necessarily follow it. "You just can't trust government. There is a higher law. You have to stand in to protect it. Because, like my father said, this is what happens when good people shut their eyes," Marijane said. Yet she was careful to explain that she was not a do-gooder, even though the consequences of her actions might do good for others. She saw herself as a serving the law, and it mattered not that she did it as a public defender because she could have done it as a prosecutor had she made that choice early in her career. She didn't care about the little guy as much as she cared about fighting for reverence of the law, to bring order to the world by honoring the law and seeking respect for her efforts, win or lose. "When you see a perfect trial, an absolutely perfect trial, it's a beautiful thing no matter who wins. When it's clicking right, all of the sudden, it's like the melding of what I was born to do. Here you are standing alone, and you can move the world. If you can imagine, all of the sudden, looking in the face of paradise where you don't want to be anywhere else in the world, you want that moment to freeze. This is like the face of God. This is nirvana. This is heaven."

When Marijane spoke about her passion to be a worthy lawyer, she often made reference and paid reverence to Shakespeare's *Henry V,* just as she had during the night of celebration after Aloysius Oliver got life instead of death. Marijane had read it, seen it on stage and on film perhaps a hundred times or more since she was a girl. The scene that so moved her was King Henry's speech on the eve of battle with the French at Agincourt, act IV, scene III. The king's words explained her view of what it meant to fight against impossible odds. In the play, King Henry's troops were weakened by casualties, disease and the lack of reinforcements because of their distance from England, yet they were on the brink of a monumental fight. Morale was low among the English soldiers, and King Henry rose to rally them with what became known as the St. Crispian's Day Speech before they charged into battle. Sometimes before she left home for a trial, Marijane got up early and watched a videotape of the film version of *Henry V* starring Kenneth Branagh in the title role, and listened to that speech before going to court, inspired by its message of fearlessness and honor of battle. Once again, she launched into the speech.

"If we are marked to die," Marijane began, reciting from memory, and delivering her lines in a deep, resonant voice, projecting as if she were onstage. "That's what we're here for. If we win, so much more the glory." She continued, her voice rising. "This day is called the feast of St. Crispian. He that outlives this day, and comes safe home, will stand a tiptoe when this day is named, and rouse him at the name of Crispian. He that shall live this day, and see old age, will yearly on the vigil feast his neighbors and say, 'Tomorrow is St. Crispian' Then he will strip his sleeve and show his scars . . ."

Marijane held out her forearms turned upward, her eyes teary, her voice shaking. "And say, 'These wounds I had on St. Crispian's Day.' " She stopped for a moment. "We in it shall be remembered, we few, we happy few, we band of brothers," she continued, struggling to remember. "For he today that sheds his blood with me, shall be my brother . . . And gentlemen in England now abed, shall think themselves accursed they were not here and hold their manhoods cheap whiles any speaks that fought with us on St. Crispian's Day!" She shook her right fist in the air and then was silent.

"That's it," Marijane said, her eyes glistening, cheeks streaked. "Maybe I didn't do it that well. If you ever saw real heroes, you'd understand. I was brought up with people who did unbelievable things. My father did unbelievable things. People he introduced me to did unbelievable things. They didn't brag about it. They commanded respect. This is what I've been striving for all my life. This is what I tasted and want to feel. I want to feel that. I'm not worthy of it yet. And I'll tell you why I'm not worthy of it yet. Because I want it. To be truly worthy of it, it's just given and you don't pay attention to it. I'm not that good of a person. I know that sounds silly. But that's what I've learned from plays. You realize why people fight and why they do battle."

The next morning, Marijane would go back to the courthouse bearing the scars from battles past to do battle once more.

Acknowledgments

This book came to life thanks to a group of public defenders willing to expose themselves professionally and personally without fear and without restraint. They generously gave their time, answered my questions and let me tail them around the courthouse as they tried to do their jobs. Shelton Green, former chief of the Murder Task Force, opened the doors that made it possible. I will always be indebted and grateful to him. Shelton introduced me to Marijane Placek, who became my main guide around the courthouse and was extraordinarily helpful in and out of court. She spoke with a candor I have rarely seen. Marijane began as a source and wound up a friend. I am also grateful to Ruth McBeth, a talented and humble lawyer who usually shied away from publicity but took a chance and opened herself up for this book. Julie Norman sat with me for hours and explained what it meant to be a mitigator, opening my eyes to the seemingly impossible task of trying to find good in some very bad people. Julie is a woman of great compassion and commitment to a cause for which she strongly believes. The rest of the legal team in the Aloysius Oliver case also gave me their time and expertise, and without them I could not have filled in many of the blanks. Thanks to Rich English, Andrew Northrup, Chris Andersen, and John Peterson. John Nixon taught me more about guns in one afternoon than I had learned in a lifetime, and showed me just how hard it really is to shoot a .357 Magnum accurately. Aloysius Oliver permitted me to speak to his lawyers about his case, and without that cooperation I would not have been able to tell the full story of his legal defense. Aloysius also took the time to speak with me on his own without his lawyers present, and I am grateful for his willingness to talk. His mother, Lillian Oliver, let me into her home on several occasions to talk about a difficult subject. I am thankful to her, and to her daughter Angela, who also contributed to this book.

Shawn Lee, the widow of Officer Eric Lee, was gracious by agreeing to be interviewed and understanding that this project was about the people who defended the man who killed her husband. Bobby and Anna Lee, the late officer's parents, allowed me into their home to share stories about their son and relive the most awful moments of their lives. I thank them all for taking the time to reminisce about Eric for this book. From the Cook County State's Attorney's Office I must thank James McKay and David O'Connor, who also sat down for interviews after the Oliver trial. Sandy Chavez of the victim witness assistance program was invaluable in helping me see the other side. Marcy Jensen helped make the right introductions, and I am thankful to her as a friend and colleague. From the Chicago Police Department, my thanks to Officer Andre Green, who told me about life after losing his partner, and Dave Bayless, the police spokesman, who helped set up interviews and answered my many questions.

In the Murder Task Force office, there were a number of lawyers I visited regularly who were always game for a conversation if they weren't busy in court. Woody Jordan let me plop on a seat in front of his desk and told me stories. When he wasn't talking about last night's White Sox games or the Final Four, Bob Strunck talked murder with me and how he tried to stay sane. Other lawyers in the office also spoke with me to help me understand their work. I couldn't use everyone's stories or comments in this book, or may have used only fractions of what they said, but nonetheless found them all invaluable in getting the big picture. My appreciation to Bob Galhotra, Susan Smith, Mike Mayfield and Crystal Marchigiani, who took over the task force after I began researching this book. Also thanks to Jose Hernandez and Aurora Rodriguez for taking my calls, getting documents and looking up cases. The late Robert Cavanaugh, a great lawyer who died before we got to know one another better, was among the first people I met in the task force. Former members of the Murder Task Force provided me with stories about the old days and gave me perspective on how the office developed. My deepest thanks to Bill Murphy, Bob Queeney, Todd Musburger and Stuart Nudelman, who helped paint a picture of the early days. Also thanks to Richard Kling, Andrea Lyon, Jamie Carey and Rita Fry.

Stephen Richards, who left the task force to join the State Appellate Defender's Office after I began this book, was among the first lawyers I interviewed and inspired me to pursue this project further. Allan Sincox, also with the State Appellate Defender's Office, told me the story of Betsy Elhert and what it means to stick with a case you believe in.

Others inside and outside the courthouse assisted me with this book in different ways. Reporters Jeff Coen from the *Chicago Tribune*, Stefano Esposito of the *Chicago Sun-Times* and Matt Vandenbroek of the City News Service of Chicago were always willing to help me with background, tracking cases and filling me in if I missed a quote or needed the spelling of someone's name. They were great companions throughout the Oliver trial and beyond and allowed me to hang out in the press room as if I were one of their own. Sketch artist Lou Chukman helped pass the down time during the trial by engaging me in discussions of great books and literature. Others I must thank include Peg Solomon, Francis Wolfe, David Bow, Michael Huskey, Paul Dorcic, Fred Cohn, Barry Levenstam, Crystal Carballos, Beth Murphy and Larry Heinrich. At the Cook County Department of Corrections, I must thank my friends Eric Dean Spruth and Denise Colletti, art therapists who work with mentally ill detainees. They showed me a human and compassionate side of those accused of crimes.

A writer is fortunate to have family, friends and colleagues who make themselves available to advise and inspire, day or night. Miles Harvey was with me every step of the way, urging me to stay with the project when I feared it was faltering and pushing me to think harder and write smarter. I am lucky to have such a great friend and to know such a talented writer. Dave Wieczorek, a mentor, editor and friend, supplied me with examples of wonderful work from other writers to stimulate and inspire me. Dave also challenged me, as always, to push myself. Marc Davis, my father, the writer, journalist, novelist and artist, helped regenerate my enthusiasm when I was down, helped me find the answers when I was stuck and instilled the confidence that I could write a book. How blessed I am to have a father as a best friend and fellow writer. My mother, Judy Davis, read early chapters of the manuscript and offered the kind of comments and advice that only a mother could. Others who advised, encouraged and listened were my sister, Laura, and my dear friends Zack Nauth, Rich Cohen, Paul Budin, Kenny Golub and Matt Brandabur who make up the *grupo del hombres*. My gratitude goes also to the entire Sanders family, which has embraced me as one of its own. I am grateful to Michael Connelly, a friend, colleague and former fellow crime reporter who inspired me as a writer and showed me it's possible to break free from the bonds of daily journalism. Renee Krause, my first mentor on the crime beat at the South Florida *Sun-Sentinel*, taught me about bringing compassion and heart to an often dark job. My thanks to Anne Ryan and John Zich, extraordinary photographers, colleagues and friends, who are a joy to work with and represent the very best of their profession.

My editor, Wendy Walker, saw the potential in this book and encouraged me to let it take flight. Her careful reading, sharp editing and insightful suggestions helped make it richer and stronger. I'm fortunate to have had such a wise counselor and strong advocate. A heartfelt thanks to my agent, Philip Spitzer, who never gives up on a writer or a manuscript he believes in, and is among the most generous and classy people in the business.

Finally, to my wife Martha, whose creative spirit, boundless energy and unwavering encouragement kept me going: Thanks for coming along on this bumpy ride and for giving me your counsel, support and love. You are my heart.

A Note on Sources

This book is a work of nonfiction. The stories and narrative were drawn from interviews I conducted with the principal characters, as well as from my own observations. Those events which I did not directly observe, and quotes from conversations in which I was not present, were based on accounts from at least one, and preferably two of the participants or were taken directly from court documents, transcripts, depositions and police reports. In addition, I pieced together accounts of past events from newspaper stories that appeared in the *Chicago Tribune*, *Chicago Sun-Times*, *The Daily Herald* of Arlington Heights, the *Daily Southtown* and the *Chicago Daily Law Bulletin*.

Several books also informed my writing. Two books proved invaluable in chapter 8 on the history of the Cook County Public Defender's Office: *The Public Defender*, by Lisa J. McIntyre (University of Chicago Press, 1987), and *Public Defender*, by Gerald Getty and James Presley (Grosset & Dunlap, 1974). Books by Chicago authors also were helpful in piecing together the history and the contemporary workings of the courthouse. *Unspeakable Acts, Ordinary People* (University of California Press, 2000), by John Conroy, details the allegations of brutality of former police commander Jon Burge, and *Courtroom 302* (Alfred A. Knopf, 2005), by Steve Bogira, is a masterful account of life at Twenty-sixth and California during a year inside a single courtroom. I consulted other books as well. *The Prosecutors* (Dutton, 2003), by Gary Delsohn, showed me how the other side works. Scott Turow's *Ultimate Punishment* (Picador, 2003) offered a thoughtful and insightful examination of the death penalty. Finally, the writings of Clarence Darrow showed me how a master lawyer argued for human life. A collection of his oratory can be found in an excellent volume edited by Arthur Weinberg called *Attorney for the Damned* (University of Chicago Press, 1989), which inspired the title for this book.

Index

Redd, Frank, 49, 223
reversed convictions, 95, 102–4,
   186, 191–92, 223
   see also wrongful convictions
Riley, Jim, 72
Ringling Bros. and Barnum &
   Bailey Circus, 28–29
Robert Taylor Homes, 117, 237
Robinson, Willie, 53
Rogers, Damon, 11–13, 62–63,
   176, 257
   courtroom testimony of, 150–52
Rosary College, 27
Rosenblum, Steve, 121
Runge, Paul, 50–52, 283
Runnion, Joseph, 6, 75–76, 229,
   232
Rush, Raphael, 184–85
Rush, Reginald, 185–86
Ryan, George, Governor of Illinois,
   corruption charges against, 96,
   265
   death penalty reform and, 96,
   98–99
   suspension of death penalty by,
   104–5

Sacco, Nicola, 90–91
St. Stephen's Evangelical Lutheran
   Church, 269
Salem Baptist Church, 18, 235
Santos, Edar Duarte, 103–4
Scanlan, Kickham, 81
Schanmier, Joan, 189, 190
Scholz, Richard, 53
Schrier, James, 282
Schultz, Lon William, 58
Scott, James, 125
Sedlek, Frank, 243
Sellier & Bellot, 109, 113

sentencing hearings, 207–8
   in Del Vecchio case, 221–22
   in Melka case, 217–19
   in Oliver case, 196–97, 203, 206,
      224, 225, 233, 240–52, 262
   in Williams case, 210–15
Service, Robert, 25
7th Calvary, *see* Englewood
   Rangers
Sexton, Brian, 125
Shakespeare, William, 25, 253,
   286–87
"Shooting of Dan McGrew, The"
   (Service), 25
Simmons, Henry, 121, 126
Sincox, Allan, 55, 131
   Ehlert case and, 186, 189–90,
      191, 192–93, 194
Sixth Amendment, 80, 83
Smith, Ed, 267–68
Snow, LuAnn Rodi, 17
Solomon, Peg, 177, 181, 182–83,
   229, 230, 231, 252
Speck, Richard, 84–85
State Appellate Defender's Office,
   186
State Attorney's Office, 4, 8, 15, 60,
   65, 142, 200, 205
state's attorneys, 46
"stealing the flag," 116–17, 120–21
Steinken, Richard, 117
Stone, Randolph, 88
Strouse, Brian, 16, 123, 124, 125
Strouse, Kathy, 125
Strunck, Anastasia, 281–82
Strunck, Bob, 44–46, 97, 98,
   280–82
Strunck, James E., 45, 210
Summer, Thomas, 124
Supreme Court, U.S., 83, 94